Avant-Garde Art in Ukraine

1910–1930

Contested Memory

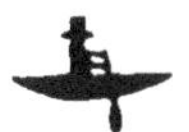

Avant-Garde Art in Ukraine 1910–1930

Contested Memory

MYROSLAV SHKANDRIJ

BOSTON
2019

Library of Congress Cataloging-in-Publication Data

Names: Shkandrij, Myroslav, 1950- author.
Title: Avant-garde art in Ukraine, 1910-1930 : contested memory / Myroslav Shkandrij.
Description: Boston : Academic Studies Press, 2019. | Includes bibliographical references.
Identifiers: LCCN 2018058734 (print) | LCCN 2018061401 (ebook) |
ISBN 9781618119766 (ebook) | ISBN 9781618119759 (hardcover)
Subjects: LCSH: Art, Ukrainian–20th century. | Avant-garde (Aesthetics)–Ukraine–History–20th century.
Classification: LCC N7255.U47 (ebook) | LCC N7255.U47 S55 2019 (print) |
DDC 700.9477/09041–dc23
LC record available at https://lccn.loc.gov/2018058734

ISBN 978-1-64469-627-9
ISBN 978-1-61811-976-6 (ebook)

Book design by Lapiz Digital Services.

Cover design by Ivan Grave.
On the cover Mykhailo Boichuk (attributed). *Shevchenko Day*, 1920.

Published by Academic Studies Press.
1577 Beacon Street
Brookline, MA 02446, USA
press@academicstudiespress.com
www.academicstdiespress.com

Acknowledgments

The author gratefully acknowledges the following:

Zorya Fine Art Gallery for permission to reproduce a modified version of "Kyiv to Paris: Ukrainian Art in the European Avant-Garde, 1910–30," which appeared in 2005 on the Zorya Fine Art website at http://www.zoryafineart.com/publications/view/11.

The Ukrainian Museum in New York for permission to reproduce material from *Propaganda and Slogans: The Political Poster in Soviet Ukraine, 1919–1921* (2013). The posters in the above publication were donated to the Museum by D. Jurij Rybak and Anna Ortynsky: *Drive Off the Kulaks* (page 32), *Ivan Franko* (42), *Shevchenko Day* (44), *Peasant, the Worker Has Joined the Red Army* (46), *First Aid for the Wounded* (50), *Comrade Peasants! Hand in Your Grain Tax* (60), and *The Hungry Await Help* (64).

The Jewish Heritage Centre of Western Canada for permission to reprint with modifications "Jews in the Artistic and Cultural Life of Ukraine in the 1920s," which appeared in *Jewish Life and Times: A Collection of Essays*, Vol. 9, edited by Dan Stone and Annalee Greenberg, 85–99 (Winnipeg: Jewish Heritage Centre of Western Canada, 2009).

The University of Toronto Press for allowing me to reprint a shortened and modified form of "Politics and the Ukrainian Avant-Garde," which appeared in *Modernism in Kyiv: Jubilant Experimentation*, edited by Irena R. Makaryk and Virlana Tkacz, 219–97 (Toronto: University of Toronto Press, 2010).

East/West: Journal of Ukrainian Studies for permission to reproduce material from "The Steppe as Inspiration in David Burliuk's Art," *Journal of Ukrainian Studies* 30.2 (2005): 51–67.

Indiana University Press for permission to reprint parts of the article "National Modernism in Post-Revolutionary Society: The Ukrainian Renaissance and Jewish Revival, 1917–1930," which first appeared in *Shatterzones of Empire: Coexistence and Violence in the German, Habsburg,*

Russian, and Ottoman Borderlands, 238–48, edited by Omer Bartov and Eric D. Weitz, 2013.

Mary Holt Burliuk and the Winnipeg Art Gallery for permission to reproduce David Burliuk's works and photographs from her family collection.

Brigitta Vadimovna Vetrova for permission to reproduce photographs and works by Nina Henke and Vadym Meller from her family collection, and Nina Vetrova-Robinson for permission to reproduce *Carnival* from her family collection.

The National Art Museum of Ukraine in Kyiv and the Lviv National Art Gallery for permission to reproduce Mykhailo Boichuk's photograph and works.

Contents

List of Illustrations

Introduction: The "Historic" Avant-Garde of 1910–30

In the second and third decades of the twentieth century the avant-garde generated a prodigious cultural ferment among artists from Ukraine. One of the first avant-garde art exhibitions in the Russian Empire, the Link Exhibition of 1908, took place in Kyiv, and Ukrainians participated heavily in all the early displays in Moscow and St. Petersburg. In the pre-war years they worked among avant-gardists in Paris, Munich, St. Petersburg, and Moscow. Early in their careers some of the great innovators of Ukrainian art, such as Volodymyr (Vladimir) Tatlin, Alexander Archipenko, Alexandra Exter, David Burliuk, Ivan Kavaleridze, Vadym Meller, and Mykhailo Boichuk, spent time in Paris, Munich, or Berlin. Burliuk and Meller exhibited with Der Blaue Reiter (The Blue Rider) group in Munich in 1912. Influences traveled from East to West, as well as West to East. Exter, for example, participated in the Link Exhibition, then in Paris, where she met Picasso, Braque, Léger, and Apollinaire, along with other artists from Ukraine, such as Archipenko, Nathan Altman, David Shterenberg, and Wladimir (Volodymyr) Baranoff-Rossiné (Baranov) living in the city. Up to the time she finally emigrated to the French capital in 1924, she divided her time between Paris, Moscow and Kyiv.

Ukrainian artists made major contributions to the international avant-garde. Kazimir Malevich's suprematism, Tatlin's constructivism, Burliuk's futurism, Archipenko's cubist sculptures, Exter's theater art, and Boichuk's monumentalism or neo-Byzantinism represent only a few examples of their experimentation. Yet, as part of a specifically Ukrainian avant-garde they have been understudied. Even the connections between them have frequently gone unrecognized. This has obscured their contribution as a group to the international movement.

The present volume brings together exploratory essays with the aim of introducing readers to this avant-garde and tracing what in fact was a generational experience that stretched from the pre-war years in Paris and Western European capitals, through the turmoil of 1917–22, to the end of the Soviet 1920s.

Throughout the twentieth century the goal of international recognition remained something of an idée fixe for Ukrainians, who often made conscious efforts to bring the country's unique traditions, sensibility, and worldview to the European cultural high table. Ironically, this goal was perhaps most successfully accomplished by the century's first and, one might argue, least self-conscious generation, the avant-garde. It was in many respects the most closely integrated into Western European culture. Today the achievements of individual artists have been recognized in many cases, but the Ukrainian dimension to their legacy has not. Somewhat paradoxically, celebrated artists from Ukraine seldom have their roots and sense of identity acknowledged. This aspect of the interpretative matrix is not applied to them—neither, for example, to Burliuk and Malevich, who identified themselves as Ukrainians, nor to Sonia Delauney, Exter, Archipenko, and Tatlin, who linked their work to a Ukrainian inspiration. The essays that follow explore the meaning of such self-identification in specific cases and the distinct accent these artists brought to international art. Five of the essays have been modified and updated from earlier publications.

The first half of the book records the emergence of artistic schools and styles, and the attempt by artists to deal with urgent political and cultural issues. Several essays deal with the cultural and political background in the 1920s. They indicate that the experience of the avant-garde in Ukraine was not the same as in Russia, a fact deliberately ignored in Soviet times and one that has so far attracted insufficient attention among Western researchers. The "Cultural Renaissance" of the 1920s in Soviet Ukraine, the Jewish artistic revival in the country during this decade, the final hurrah of the avant-garde in Kharkiv in the years 1928 to 1930, when experimentation had already been closed down in Moscow and Leningrad—all of this created a situation different from the one that existed in Russia. After contact with the West was broken off at the end of the twenties, Ukrainians were only allowed to participate in "all-Soviet" exhibitions and any attribution of particularism to their work was most commonly defined as "bourgeois nationalism." Research into the avant-garde and a fuller understanding of this period only became possible when in the 1990s exhibitions were mounted and new materials became available following the opening of Ukrainian archives.

The second half of the book focuses on five individuals: David Burliuk, Kazimir Malevich, Vadym Meller, Ivan Kavaleridze, and Dziga Vertov. These essays challenge some long-established views, arguing, for example, that the Ukrainian context throws light on crucial aspects in the lives and work of these figures. Each individual artist presents particular problems of interpretation, but by situating their work within an analysis of personal biography and cultural context, the essays aim to provide a better understanding of artistic achievement. The focus is mainly on the development of visual arts: painting (Burliuk, Malevich), propaganda posters (Boichuk), theater art (Meller), sculpture (Kavaleridze), and film (Vertov) are examined. Most of these artists experimented with different media. Some, such as Burliuk and Kavaleridze, were also writers, a fact only tangentially discussed in this volume.

The achievements of this generation were remarkable—all the more so, it could be argued, because they were accomplished in a time of rapid cultural transformation and political upheaval. Today this legacy resonates with many contemporaries, particularly in Ukraine, where the avant-garde plays a prominent role in debates around cultural memory. The tensions that have surfaced in these debates indicate the importance of understanding the experience of the great innovators who worked in the early twentieth century. This book examines both the nexus between art and politics and the lives and works of some brilliant and still controversial figures. The search of these avant-gardists for self-awareness and a new modern identity still provides many valuable lessons for contemporaries.

Forging the European Connection

Kyiv to Paris: Ukrainian Art in the European Avant-Garde, 1910–30[1]

Modernism emerged at the end of the nineteenth century as an international movement in the arts that emphasized the idea of a radical break with the past and the possibility of a transformed world. Rejecting realism and naturalism, it searched for new literary and artistic forms, often under the influence of photography, cinema, new technologies, and recent discoveries in the sciences. Pre-1914 European modernism is today often associated with the movements of impressionism, symbolism, cubism, and abstractionism. The second wave of modernism, which spanned the years 1914 to 1930, is linked with futurism, constructivism, expressionism, and surrealism, and is also commonly identified with the avant-garde, largely because many of its members were strongly influenced by the rise of radical politics, and sometimes saw themselves as a culturally advanced party preparing the way for revolutionary change.

Boris Groys has argued that the Russian avant-garde was implicated in the totalitarian politics of the twenties and thirties by virtue of its desire to restructure the world "according to a unitary artistic plan" (Groys 1992, 21). However, radical ways of seeing were as often as not rejected by the Bolshevik Party and its acolytes, particularly after they achieved power. The Ukrainian avant-garde in particular cannot be unambiguously identified with the Bolshevik Revolution. It preceded this revolution, frequently challenged it, and was ultimately destroyed by it.

The propagandistic aspects of the Soviet avant-garde, which became dominant, even overwhelmingly so, in the late twenties, have attracted

1 This chapter is adapted from an article that appeared on the Zorya Fine Art website in 2005: http://www.zoryafineart.com/publications/view/11.

disproportionate attention among many scholars, who frequently allowed this political and ideological focus to overshadow other innovations. When the West rediscovered the "Eastern" avant-garde in the last decades of the twentieth century, the primary focus was often on its visionary politics and achievements in abstract art. But this movement in the arts was always a complex phenomenon, full of competing crosscurrents. In the 1990s, as new information long suppressed under Soviet rule surfaced, it became clear that the "Eastern" avant-garde not only differed significantly from the "Western," but was more differentiated internally than had been assumed. Numerous exhibitions at this time explored the different national backgrounds of avant-gardists.[2]

Pre-war Paris was visited by numerous artists from Ukraine. Among them were Alexander Archipenko, Alexandra Exter, Mykhailo Boichuk, David Burliuk, Wladimir Baranoff-Rossiné (Baranov), Sofiia Levytska (Sonia Lewitska), Abram Manevych, Yosyp Chaikov (Joseph Tchaikov), Vladimir (Volodymyr) Tatlin, and Vadym Meller. They joined prominent older modernists already living there, such as Oleksandr Murashko, Lev Kramarenko, Mykola Burachek, and Ivan Trush.[3] It was common at the time for students from Ukraine to be sent to France and Germany as part of their education. In fact, from 1908 to 1914 there were so many Ukrainian artists in the city that they had their own club called the "Cercle des Ukrainiens à Paris" situated in the Latin Quarter at rue Thouin 14, which housed a library with periodicals from Ukraine. Archipenko was an active member, sang in the choir and conducted tours of Paris salons (Popovych 1977, 14).[4] Travel appears to have been relatively easy. Ivan Kavaleridze has recalled how simple it was to obtain a visa in Kyiv. After producing his passport and ten roubles, he picked up his visa the following day, purchased a train ticket for thirty-two roubles and sixty kopecks and caught the train (Kavaleridze 2017a, 102–3). From Western Ukraine, then part of the Austro-Hungarian Empire, travel was even more straightforward. Although the First World War and the 1917 Revolution in the Russian Empire sealed borders and restricted movement, some artists, such as Oleksander Hryshchenko

2 These exhibitions are mentioned in chapter 11. For post-Soviet reassessments of the avant-garde by Russian scholars see Krusanov 1996, 2003, Petrova 2001. For fresh approaches by Western scholars see Antonova and Merkert 1996, Rowell and Wye 2002. For the best recent volume on Ukrainian artists in Paris see Susak 2010.

3 For a list of 250 Ukrainian artists in Paris see Susak 2010, 361–90. She writes that in 1910, there were 120 members in the Hromada, the colony of émigré Ukrainian artists in Paris (48).

4 On Archipenko's years in Paris see Susak 2010, 67–73.

(Alexis Gritchenko, Grischenko) and Mykhailo Andriienko-Nechytailo (Michel Andreenko), still found their way to Paris.[5]

Some figures were only briefly in the West, but still made a large impact on the international avant-garde. Tatlin visited Berlin and Paris. His mother was Ukrainian and he was known for wearing an embroidered Ukrainian shirt, singing *dumas* and other ancient songs, and even constructing banduras. In 1913 he found himself in Germany with an orchestra of Ukrainian bandura players, pretending to be a blind musician.[6] Apparently the Kaiser himself expressed an interest in his playing and singing. Later in France, Picasso was reportedly thrilled by his performance and invited the player to his studio. Here the blind man opened his eyes in enthusiastic appreciation of Picasso's art. In spite of Tatlin's offer to be an assistant (washing brushes, preparing canvases), Picasso is said to have shown him the door (Bazhan 2004, 77). Since Archipenko was creating his early constructivist forms in Paris at the time, it is likely that Tatlin saw them. After returning from Paris, he began to make his own, now famous counter-reliefs in 1914 and 1915.

Other cities, such as Munich, Berlin and Geneva, also attracted artists, among them Meller, Burliuk and Archipenko. After 1922, the work of Tatlin, Malevich and Exter became known in Germany, where it had a strong resonance. Malevich was in Berlin in 1927, and Boichuk visited the Bauhaus in 1926 and 1927. The latter's Mezhyhiria Art and Ceramics Institute, created in 1928, was partly modeled after the German art school.[7] Numerous artists from Lviv in Western Ukraine also worked in Archipenko's Berlin studio in the early twenties before moving on to Paris, although the strongest contingent of artists was always in the French capital.

Conceptualization of the Ukrainian avant-garde has been hampered by the fact that it has often been subsumed under the term "Russian." For some artists this might be an adequate characterization, especially for those who were originally from Ukraine, spent time in Western Europe before the First World War, but then lived most of their creative lives in Moscow or St. Petersburg (Petrograd/Leningrad). Among them one might count Aleksandr (Oleksandr) Shevchenko, who was born in Kharkiv,

5 On the Parisian life of Hryshchenko and Andriienko see Susak 2016, 98–105, 112–19.

6 The bandura is Ukraine's national instrument. It became popular in the sixteenth century, when wandering minstrels used it to accompany the singing of epic ballads. The instrument has between thirty-two and fifty-five strings and combines features of the lute and harp.

7 The Mezhyhiria Art and Ceramics School was founded in 1921 and 1922. It was renamed the Mezhyhiria Art and Ceramics Technicum in 1923, the Mezhyhiria Art and Ceramics Institute in 1928, and the Ukrainian Technological Institute of Ceramics and Glass in 1931.

and then worked at Eugene Carrière's studio and the Académie Julian in Paris (1905–6); Nathan Altman, who was born in Vinnytsia, studied under Kiriak Kostandi at the Odesa School of Art, and was in Paris on two occasions (1911–12 and 1928–35); and David Shterenberg, who was born in Zhytomyr, studied in a private studio in Odesa (1905) and then in the École des Beaux-Arts, the Vitty studio in Paris (1906–12) and Fernand Léger's studio, exhibiting in various Paris salons before moving to Russia. However, the identity issue is a complex one. Interaction among Ukrainian artists, even when they lived in one of the two Russian capitals, was often intense, and their links with colleagues in Ukraine frequently remained strong. Shevchenko's close collaboration with Hryshchenko (Gritchenko) in Moscow is one such case. Aware of these difficulties, art historians have sometimes identified these artists as members of both the Russian and Ukrainian avant-gardes. Another complication is the fact that many artists from Ukraine were of Jewish origin. Often their careers began in Kyiv and then moved, sometimes via Paris or German cities, to Moscow.[8] They, of course, brought their own perspective to the rich interaction that produced avant-garde experimentation. As a result, many figures simultaneously belonged to, and are claimed by, the Ukrainian, Russian, Jewish, and Western European avant-gardes.

Nonetheless, it is clear that a number of the most prominent figures in this European avant-garde not only came from Ukraine but drew attention to this fact. Such a self-identification was made by Burliuk and Malevich. The work of a number of others, among them Sonia Delauney, Archipenko, Exter and Tatlin, can be linked to a Ukrainian inspiration. This raises some rarely examined questions. How was their work in Europe and interaction with Western artists influenced by their origins? Are there common features among avant-garde artists who came from Ukraine? As members of Western European, Russian or other avant-garde circles, to what extent were these artists also part of the Ukrainian avant-garde movement, one with its own distinct traits and sensibility?

Even a cursory examination of the artists' biographies reveals a startling amount of travel, which, of course, facilitated the exchange of creative ideas. Discussions of the "Eastern" avant-garde have usually conceptualized influences as flowing from West (Paris, Munich, Berlin, Vienna) to East, although this view has always been challenged.[9] It is now more widely

8 On Jewish artists from Ukraine who worked in Paris see Susak 2010, 122–53.

9 During the third trip of his Kamernyi Teatr to Germany in 1930, the Moscow theater director Aleksandr (Oleksandr) Tairov, who was born in Ukraine, declared that the "influence is from East to West and not the opposite" (quoted in Koliazin 1996, 174).

accepted that influences in the pre- and post-war years also ran from East to West. However, artists from Ukraine also traveled in large numbers north, to the two Russian capitals. Since the focus of art historians and critics has generally been on events in these cities, they have invariably conceptualized the flow of influences as traveling exclusively from North (St. Petersburg and Moscow) to South.[10] The reality here is also more complex. A pioneering, democratizing, anti-establishment impetus originated in the "South" in part as the expression of a marginalized identity. This suggests that a better conceptualization of "traffic patterns" is required, one that would allow developments in Kyiv, Odesa, Kharkiv, Chornianka (Chernianka), and other nodal points to be seen in a context that accounts for the Ukrainian dimension. A brief look at the career of Exter, for example, demonstrates the important role played by the creative ferment in Kyiv.

Exter

Exter appeared regularly in Paris after completing the Kyiv Art School in 1906. She studied in Carlo Delvall's studio in the Académie de la Grande-Chaumière in Paris (1909), and contributed to the earliest avant-garde exhibitions in the Russian Empire, including the Link (Zveno or Lanka) Exhibition in Kyiv (1908). Through Serhii Yastrebtsov, with whom she had entered the Kyiv Art School and who wrote French poetry under the pseudonym Serge Ferat, she was introduced to Guillaume Apollinaire's circle. Joining forces with Picasso, Braque and Léger, she began exploring cubism. In 1911 she met Sonia Delauney and was affected by the latter's chromatic futurism. From Paris Exter then brought back to Kyiv works for Oleksandr Bohomazov, the Burliuk brothers, and others to see. In 1914 she produced the first monograph on Picasso.

The interaction of the Kyiv futurists (especially of Exter, Bohomazov and Burliuk) generated some of the first avant-garde activities within the

10 Krusanov speaks of the "advance of the left into the provinces" but also admits that between January 1915 and February 1917 there were over ninety various futurist events outside Moscow and Petersburg and about sixty in the two cities (Krusanov 2003, book 2, 9). His book is constructed as a study of the dissemination of futurist ideas from the two capitals to the provinces and shows no interest in local or indigenous agency, even though he admits that from October 1917 until the Spring of 1922 Ukraine, Crimea and Southern Russia were cut off from "the center of the country" (Krusanov, 75). When he does turn to Ukraine, he focuses heavily on the activities of Russians and Russian-language publications, even though their activities in the twenties were marginal as compared to those of the Ukrainians.

Russian Empire. All three were influential in teaching and publicizing the new art. They first presented themselves in the November 1908 Link Exhibition in Kyiv, where the main contributors were David and Vladimir (Volodymyr) Burliuk, Bohomazov, Exter, and Baranoff-Rossiné (Baranov). They again exhibited together in Kyiv in 1914 at the Ring (Russian: Koltso, Ukrainian: Kiltse) Exhibition. Artists from Russia also participated in these exhibitions and the Kyivans exhibited in Moscow and St. Petersburg, but during the years of war and revolutionary upheaval (1914–22), when Kyiv was cut off from both Western Europe and Russia, a strong indigenous avant-garde appeared. During these years an intimate awareness of Western artistic developments allowed Exter to create a unique style in both painting and set design. Beginning in 1918 Exter and Vadym Meller designed costumes for Bronislava Nijinska's dance studio and a number of theaters in Kyiv and Moscow. Exter taught at her own studio in Kyiv (1918–20), then at the Higher Art and Technical Studios in Moscow (1921–22) before emigrating to Paris in 1924, where she opened another personal studio. She also exhibited at the Exposition Internationale des Arts Décoratifs et Industriels Modernes and taught at Fernand Léger's Académie d'Art Moderne. Her influence was also exerted indirectly through the work of numerous outstanding painters and stage designers whom she trained. They included numerous Jewish artists: Nisson Shifrin, Isaak Rabinovich, Isaak Rabichev, Boris (Borys) Aronson, Solomon Nikritin, and Aleksandr (Oleksandr) Tyshler.

Exter's international reputation was secured by her permanent move to Paris, where she was able to spread an "Eastern" influence. She blended cubism, constructivism, and primitivism in her theater designs, costumes, and art. It is less well known that in Kyiv she supported "naïve" artists, usually women artisans from villages who produced embroidered scarves and towels or woven rugs. Her interest in brightly colored folk murals, embroideries, and Easter eggs was stimulated in Kyiv, where she prepared posters for an exhibition entitled "The Folk Art of Bukovyna and Galicia," which opened on April 16, 1917, and where on March 31, 1918, at the opening of an exhibition devoted to the decorative works of Yevheniia Prybylska and Hanna Sobachko, she gave a talk describing the colors and rhythms of decorative folk art, linking the popular love of color in "young" Slavic nations to ancient icons (Exter 1990, 18).

In post-war years the Ukrainian influence in Paris was strengthened by the arrival of immigrants, who brought an awareness of the distinctive work produced in Kyiv by Exter, Meller, Bohomazov, Issakhar-Ber Rybak, and their circle.

Generalizing, one could say that Ukrainian artists in both Kyiv and Paris made important contributions to the international avant-garde in two areas. Firstly, they rekindled the already existing interest in primitivism, filtering it through an awareness of their own folk art and icon. Secondly, they infused the avant-garde with a love of color, texture and movement. Exter and Sonia Delauney (who was originally from Ukraine) are credited with transforming the muted grays and browns of Western cubism by introducing bright colors into modern design.[11] Although initially criticized by Léger for her exuberant use of color, Exter insisted that this was the "Eastern" contribution to cubism. Archipenko was one of the first artists to color sculptures. After the war, Hryshchenko (Gritchenko), Baranoff-Rossiné and Andriienko-Nechytailo (Andreenko) augmented the influence of these "Eastern" colorists.

Archipenko

Primitivism stimulated interest in ancient art and monumental forms, the study of which enabled Archipenko to make an international reputation as a sculptor. His paternal grandfather had been an icon painter, and his father was an inventor and professor of engineering at the University of Kyiv. At an early age the artist became interested in the relationship between mathematics and art, as well as in Byzantine art. He studied at the Kyiv Art School from 1902 to 1905 until he was expelled, according to one account, for criticizing teachers as "too old-fashioned and academic," and, according to another, for participating in a strike. In 1906 he held his first solo exhibition in Ukraine, then went to Moscow and in 1908 at the age of twenty moved to Paris. He quit the École des Beaux-Arts after two weeks because he found the academic system confining and tedious, and then studied independently. The Parisian years (1908–21) were his most productive. In 1909 he began making revolutionary sculptures, which he exhibited in the

11 Sonia Delauney (Terk-Delauney) was born in the Ukrainian town of Hradyzhsk near Poltava, but from age five she was raised by an uncle in St. Petersburg. Her memoirs, written late in life, begin by recognizing the profound effect on her work of her childhood in Ukraine. They provide a rhapsodic account of these early years. She studied in the Academy of Fine Arts in Karlsruhe before moving to Paris in 1905, where she married the French artist Robert Delauney in 1910. She imitated the patchwork quilt styles of peasant women and was best known for her instinctive color sense and her refusal to accept facile distinctions between the fine arts and applied or decorative arts. She was known for her robust primary colors, her work with fabric, fashion, textile, and costume design, and her color rhythms, dubbed "orphism" by Apollinaire.

Salon des Indépendants each year from 1910 to 1914, and the Salon d'Automne in 1911, 1912, 1913, and 1919. In 1912 he opened his own art studio in Montparnasse, working alongside Modigliani and Gaudier-Brzeska. Abstract, transparent, and painted sculptures were among his many innovations. He made *Medrano 1* (1912), the first sculpture in various painted materials (wood, glass, metal sheet, wire), created reliefs named "sculpto-peintures," which were generally made of painted plaster, and produced the first modern sculptures formed with negative space (concaves and voids that created implied volumes). He called for a renewal of "ancient polychromy which is far richer than the contemporary non-colored sculpture" (Archipenko 1969, 23) and in 1913 exhibited the highly colored sculpture *Pierrot* at Der Sturm Gallery in Berlin. *Boxing* (1914) was one of the most abstract modern sculptures done to that date. From 1919 to 1921 he exhibited in various European cities: Geneva, Zurich, Paris, London, Brussels, Athens, Berlin, and Munich. His solo exhibition in the Venice Biennale was ridiculed in the June 11, 1920 edition of *Il Telegrafo Livorno*, and Cardinal La Fontaine, Patriarch of Venice, advised the faithful not to attend. In 1921 he opened his own art school in Berlin, and then in 1923 moved to the United States.

Like other avant-garde artists of the time Archipenko tried not to copy forms in nature but to apprehend them spiritually and then capture their essence. The charm of his works, wrote Apollinaire, comes from an effortless sense of inward order (Apollinaire 1969; quoted in Karshan 1969, 12). It is a sense that comes from an awareness of ancient art: Egyptian, Assyrian, Greek, Scythian, Byzantine, and Greek. In his student days the artist had taken part in archaeological expeditions, and some critics maintain that early works such as his *Woman* and *Suzanna* (1909–10) recall the simple but powerful expressiveness of ancient stone idols that can be found in the steppe (Olenska-Petryshyn 1997, 490). The profound influence of these statues has been indicated by the artist himself, who recalled how as a small child he played on one of them, climbing over it. However, during dark evenings, he avoided passing it, because it struck terror into him. This same statue now stands in front of the National Art Museum in Kyiv. His interest in ancient art was probably linked to his fascination with cosmic dynamism, the sense of a unity between the highest and lowest forms, between solar systems and the cells of organisms. Art for him reflected the forces of the universe, and he felt that the best art crystallized intuitively sensed forms. Apollinaire was convinced that this aspect of his work reflected the presence of ancient belief-systems (see Karshan 1969, 12–14).

Burliuk

David Burliuk, another major figure in the avant-garde, attended the Royal Academy of Arts in Munich (1902–3) and the Académie Fernand Cormon in Paris (1904–5), participated in the Link Exhibition in Kyiv (1908) and was a driving force behind many of the early avant-garde exhibitions in the Russian Empire. His countless lectures on the new art included one in Exter's Kyiv studio, and he exhibited continually, both in the empire and at Western European venues, such as the Neue Kunstlervereinigung (New Artists' Association) exhibition in Munich (1910), the Paul Cassirer Gallery in Berlin (1911), and the famous Der Blaue Reiter exhibition in Munich (1912), whose almanac of the same name published his article "Die 'Wilden' Russlands." In 1912 he made a second trip to Western Europe traveling through Germany, France, Switzerland, and Italy. During the years of revolution he gave improvised lectures, performances, and exhibitions, eventually bringing his family across Siberia to Vladivostok and across the sea to Japan before emigrating to the United States in 1922.

Burliuk had an important early link to the Western avant-garde in Kandinsky, who had spent some of his childhood in Odesa. Partly as a result of this connection, the ground-breaking Izdebskii salons took place in Ukraine. The first, which exhibited many Westerners, was held in Odesa (December 4, 1909 to January 24, 1910) and Kyiv (February 12 to March 14 1910), before traveling to St. Petersburg and Riga. The second, which included scores of paintings by Exter, Burliuk, Konchalovskii, Lentulov, Tatlin, Larionov, Goncharova, and Kandinsky, began in Odesa (February 6 to April 3, 1911) and then traveled to Mykolaiv (Nikolaev) and Kherson (Krusanov 2003, Book 2, 6). It made an enormous impression, because it announced the presence of an indigenous avant-garde art within the borders of the Russian Empire.

Burliuk's links to Ukraine, as will be argued in a later essay, were stronger than is often admitted. David began by extolling a "wild, new beauty" that he associated with the forceful, simple and direct expression in folk creativity and ancient Scythian forms. In the course of a long creative life he would always return to this primary inspiration. Like Archipenko, he was fascinated by the powerful hidden energies within nature. The painterly expression of his intuitive apprehension of things can be found in his steppe landscapes.

Sophia Levytska (Sonia Lewitzka)

The Ukrainian expatriates in Paris were a varied group. Sophia Levytska was an early member. She completed the Paris Academy of Art in 1905.

Beginning as a cubist and fauvist, she moved into a post-impressionist style and became known for her illustrations of limited edition books, including Paul Valéry's *Ébauche d'un Serpent* (1922) and a French translation of Gogol's Ukrainian stories. Apollinaire followed her exhibitions and commented on the resemblance of her works to those of Sonia Delauney. Her Parisian contacts were many and her home was a frequent meeting place for Ukrainian artists. In 1931 she organized an exhibition that included Hryshchenko, Andriienko-Nechytailo, Vasyl Khmeliuk, Mykola Krychevskyi, Vasyl Perebyinis, and herself.[12]

Boichuk

In the years preceding the First World War, restoration work conducted on numerous icons had proven conclusively that they had originally been brightly colored. This came as a revelation to many. Since the late nineteenth century, excitement had also been generated by the restoration of frescoes in the most ancient Ukrainian churches, some of which like St. Sophia's Church and St. Michael's Church of the Golden Domes dated back to the eleventh century. In the years 1907 to 1909, Mykhailo Boichuk brought awareness of this art to Paris, where he organized a studio in which young Ukrainian and Polish artists experimented with a neo-Byzantine style, combining influences from the Ukrainian icon and folk arts, and the fresco art of the Italian quattrocento (the so-called "primitives").[13] The group's exhibition was reviewed by Apollinaire, who was himself of Polish background and had Ukrainian sympathies. He wrote favorably of the Zaporozhian Cossacks and produced his own French version of the famous, apocryphal "Letter of the Zaporozhians to the Sultan." It is possible that Archipenko provided him with a "copy" of the legendary letter and information about Ukrainian history.

Hryshchenko (Alexis Gritchenko)

Hryshchenko, who arrived in Paris after the revolution, also had a strong interest in the icon. He had specializing in biology in Kyiv and Moscow universities, but had also studied art in these cities and became involved in the modern art movement in Russia. During a brief earlier stay in Paris in 1911,

12 On Levytska see Susak 2010, 75–81.

13 On Boichuk in Paris see Susak 2016, 36–46.

he had met Andre Lhote, Archipenko, and Le Fauconnier, and developed an interest in cubism. He had also taken a trip to Italy to study the early Renaissance. In analyzing the Italian art of the thirteenth and fourteenth centuries and the icons of ancient Rus, he found that the old masters applied "cubist" solutions to problems of space and color. In this way Hryshchenko traced a link between the contemporary avant-garde, the so-called "primitives" of the early Renaissance and the icon. He was convinced that a full understanding of the icon had only become possible with the appearance of modern art. Like Andre Benois and Aleksandr (Oleksandr) Shevchenko, he found formal similarities between ancient icons and the work of Matisse and Picasso. Although the debate on the icon had been stimulated around 1910 by the final refutation of its darkness, the icon's formal, painterly qualities (as opposed to its religious importance or Christian symbolism) had never been investigated in the way Hryshchenko did in his two monographs, *O sviaziakh russkoi zhivopisi s Vizantiei i Zapadom* (On the Links of Russian Painting with Byzantium and the West, 1913) and *Russkaia ikona kak iskusstvo zhivopisi* (The Russian Icon as an Art of Painting, 1917). His own work blended a cosmopolitan worldview with formal features of Byzantine sacred art. In 1919, together with Shevchenko, he mounted an exhibition in Moscow called "Tsvetodinamos i tekhtonicheskii primitivism" (Colordynamos and Tekhtonic Primitivism), which was conceived as a counterbalance to production art. The two artists announced that only color, composition and "faktura" interested them. From 1919 to 1921 Hryshchenko lived in Istanbul, where he painted hundreds of watercolors. He then moved to France, where he became known for his exotic streams of oriental color.

In his Moscow years Hryshchenko played a prominent role in the avant-garde, both as a painter and theorist. He was able to reconcile the Western and Eastern avant-gardes and explain their common concerns and interests. Unfortunately, his importance was never recognized in the Soviet Union, partly because his avant-gardism was painterly and not political, and partly because the regime considered him a traitor for leaving the country. As a result, his canvases were cut up and given to students in Moscow's Higher Art and Technical Studios (Vkhutemas) to practice upon, and his name removed from art history. Later he exhibited in leading Parisian art galleries. He also displayed in Lviv in the 1930s at the Association of Independent Ukrainian Artists (ANUM, Asotsiiatsiia nezalezhnykh myshttsiv Ukrainy) and had personal shows in New York and Philadelphia. In 1963 he donated seventy works to the Ukrainian Institute of America in New York. These have now been transferred to Kyiv.

Andriienko-Nechytailo (Andreenko)

Mykhailo Andriienko-Nechytailo (Michel Andreenko) studied in Kherson before the war and placed his first cubist and abstract works in a Leipzig exhibition (1916–17). He worked in Petrograd, before returning via Kyiv to Kherson in 1918. In 1919 he studied in Odesa with Exter, and worked for the theater. The city was divided into zones and he had to cross the borders with a military escort of get to the theater and back. He then worked as a set designer in Bucharest and Prague, and finally settled in Paris in 1923. Influenced by de Chirico and the surrealists, his works in the 1930s expressed the loneliness and isolation of the individual, as well as the mysteriousness of things. In later decades he developed a naïve art that searched for harmonious forms and childlike innocence.

Baranoff-Rossiné (Baranov)

Wladimir Baranoff-Rossiné was also born near Kherson, and studied at the Odesa School of Art (1903–7) and the Imperial Academy of Arts in St. Petersburg (1908–9). He contributed to the Link (1908) and many early avant-garde exhibitions in the empire before moving to Paris in 1910, where he exhibited under the name of Daniel Rossiné from 1911 to 1914. In 1917 he returned to Russia, exhibiting in Petrograd and Moscow before emigrating to Paris in 1925. He exhibited at the Salon des Indépendents and other venues until 1942. In the 1910s he developed a style that represented a moderate futurism that was decorative, weightless, and full of light, spiral-shaped elements with silky textures. Like Andriienko's, his work was not politically engaged, but borrowed from the visual charm and spiritual harmony of the icon.

Redko

Klyment Redko studied icon painting in the Kyiv Monastery of the Caves from 1910 to 1914. Here he met Vasilii Chekrigin, with whom he discussed cubism, futurism, and other modern art movements, while examining reproductions of Picasso, Braque, Matisse, and other artists. He then studied at the Moscow Art School (1913), the Petrograd in the Society for the Advancement of Art (1914–18), and the Ukrainian Academy of Arts in Kyiv (1918–19). He was a friend of Nikritin and Boichuk. In 1920 he found himself in Kharkiv with Nikritin and Shterenberg, and then studied in the Moscow Vkhutemas (1920–22) where he associated with Nikritin, Tyshler, and other artists from Ukraine. In the eight years he spent in Paris (1927–35) before returning to the Soviet Union he participated in the Salon d'Automne (1927), had four personal exhibitions, and met Picasso and other leading figures. Boichuk, Sedliar and Taran spent time with him when they visited the city in 1927. Redko's early art is abstract and constructivist, but in the twenties he moved toward a realist style.

Avant-garde film

Ukrainians also made contribution to other, related art forms, notably the cinema. At the same time as Oleksandr Dovzhenko and Ivan Kavaleridze were producing avant-garde films in Ukraine, Yevhen Slavchenko (Eugene Deslaw) was making a reputation as an avant-garde film maker in Paris. He emigrated as part of the exodus that followed the defeat of the Ukrainian People's Republic (1917–20). Deslaw studied in Paris in the 1920s and at the École Technique Photo-Cinema in 1927. In that year he assisted Abel Gance in making the early French film epic, *Napoléon*. His abstract and experimental films include *Marche des Machines* (1928), *La Nuit Électrique* (1930), *Montparnasse* (1931), *Négatifs* (1932), and *Robots* (1932). He worked with Boris Kaufmann (a collaborator on *Marche des Machines*), Alfred Zinnemann (the photographer on *Marche des Machines*), Luis Bunuel, and Marcel Carné (his assistants on *Montparnasse*). Until 1930 he corresponded with the Ukrainian futurist journal *Nova generatsiia* (New Generation) and with Dovzhenko, whom he met in Paris in 1930. Deslaw is considered part of the so-called second wave of the French avant-garde, which included Fernand Léger, René Claire, Henri Chaumet, Man Ray, and Germaine Dulac.

Lviv

Even after the Soviet borders were closed to them, Ukrainians living in Paris could maintain contacts with Lviv, which during the inter-war years found itself within the Polish state. They worked closely with ANUM and a number of them, including Andriienko, Hryshchenko, Hlushchenko, Khmeliuk, and Perebyinis, sent works to Lviv for display in the 1930s. At the end of the 1920s a group of fourteen Jewish avant-garde artists from Lviv, many of whom had spent time in Paris, formed the organization ARTES (1929–35). They held thirteen exhibitions in Lviv, Ternopil, Stanislaviv (now Ivano-Frankivsk), Krakow, and also in Warsaw and Lodz in the years 1930–32 (Kotliar and Susak 2005, 323).

Kyiv milieu

It is clear from even such a short survey that a cohort of remarkably talented artists from Ukraine worked in Paris in the heyday of the avant-garde. The milieus that produced them (Kherson, Odesa, Kharkiv, Kyiv, Lviv) and the connections between them have seldom been investigated. It is impossible in an overview to examine these milieus, but a glance at one, Kyiv, is instructive. The city is particularly interesting and important, because it radiated a distinct influence and style throughout the years 1910 to 1930. Why was it such a powerful generator of avant-garde activity? Perhaps because radical transformations were already occurring there early in the twentieth century due to population migration and growth, industrialization, and modernization. It was reputedly the first city within the empire and the second in Europe to have an electric tramway (streetcar), whose image figures strongly in Bohomazov's futurist paintings, symbolizing movement and modernity's galvanizing impact on urban life. The shock of the new, combined with the discovery of a rich and vibrant indigenous folk culture, seem to have provided the initial creative spark for the Kyiv avant-garde.

Another factor was the Kyiv Art School, which from 1901 to 1920 produced many great talents, among them Exter, Meller, Kavaleridze, Archipenko, Bohomazov, Abram Manevych, Anton Pevzner (Antoine Pevsner), Aristarkh Lentulov, Isaak Rabinovich, Aleksandr (Oleksandr) Tyshler, Mark (Moisei) Epstein, Solomon Nikritin, Issakhar-Ber Rybak, and Anatolii Petrytskyi. It accepted Jewish students in substantial numbers, sometimes in opposition to the desires of government authorities. From 1901 to 1920, almost half the students in the School were of Jewish background. The resulting mix of talented and ambitious artists from different backgrounds had much to do with the generation of an innovative, creative atmosphere.

At least three other reasons were important in producing the artistic ferment in Kyiv, particularly during the revolutionary years and the twenties. One was the creation by the Ukrainian government (the UNR or Ukrainian People's Republic, 1917–20) of a Ukrainian Academy of Arts in 1917–18. It brought together some of the most talented professors, such as Vasyl Krychevskyi, Yurii Narbut, Abram Manevych, and Mykhailo Boichuk, and many gifted students. Although the institution went through two name changes under Soviet rule, it continued to exert a strong influence on artistic life in Ukraine throughout this period.[14]

A second was the creation of the Kultur-Lige by the same government. In pre-war years, Jewish students had graduated from a number of academic institutions such as the Kyiv Art School. Along with Jewish artists who were escaping revolutionary events in Russia, in 1918 they began participating in the work of the Kyiv Kultur-Lige, making the city into one of the world's most dynamic centers of Yiddish culture and the Jewish avant-garde. Although, after the organization's Sovietization in 1920, some prominent figures left, it continued its work until 1925, while its publishing house and art school survived into the thirties.

A third factor was the supportive atmosphere provided in the late twenties by the Kyiv Art Institute. In 1928, at a time when doors were closing to avant-gardists in Moscow and Leningrad, Malevich joined Tatlin, Bohomazov, Boichuk, and Palmov on the Institute's teaching faculty. Archipenko was also invited to teach there, although he declined the offer. The Institute was already the third largest post-secondary art school in the Soviet Union. Its able director Ivan Vrona dreamed of making it and the related Mezhyhiria Art and Ceramics Institute into a "Bauhaus of the East." The connections forged at the Institute between Malevich, Tatlin, Palmov, Bohomazov, and Boichuk have yet to be fully analyzed, but they obviously stimulated creative activity. As a result of all these factors, the late twenties produced a final blossoming of the avant-garde in the city. In these years the futurist journal *Nova generatsiia* (New Generation) published many innovative works, such as Malevich's history of art. In this way the Kyiv milieus nourished the avant-garde in its early years and provided it with a final refuge.

There may have been deeper historical reasons for the existence of supportive ground in Kyiv. It could be argued that the country had long been a meeting ground of cultural influences and was therefore prepared to confront and even welcome novelty. Already in the seventeenth century a distinct Western culture had arisen there, one that was baroque, Latin, and relatively cosmopolitan. Ukrainian Orthodox, Polish Catholic, Jewish rabbinical and later Hassidic cultures interacted or rubbed shoulders, and continued to do so for many generations. In the nineteenth century these

14 The Ukrainian State Academy of Arts was created in 1917. It was renamed the Kyiv Institute of Plastic Arts in 1922, then renamed the Kyiv Art Institute in 1924.

interactions were overlaid by a Russian imperial and bureaucratic culture. As a result, in the twentieth century, members of the avant-garde in Ukraine could, for example, be of Ukrainian, Polish, Russian, or Jewish origins, and might sometimes mix imperial and national or Christian and Jewish imagery in their art, much as occurred in the various literatures that were produced in Ukraine (among them Ukrainian, Russian and Yiddish). The coexistence of different viewpoints, and the possibility of shifting perspectives, is a feature of the avant-garde art from this period.

Moreover, it is too rarely noted that substantial contacts with Western art in the pre-war decades had prepared the ground for the Ukrainian avant-garde. The Viennese and Munich Secessions had a strong resonance in Ukraine. The different expressions of modernity in Paris, Munich, Berlin, and Vienna were accessible to Ukrainians directly from the sources. They developed their own versions of European movements, and were from the beginning prepared not only to witness but also to participate in the creation of a new art. As a result of their interaction with Europe the Kyivans already developed a new style in the pre-war years, one that was different from that of the Western and the Moscow fauvists and cubists. Exter's early works, such as *Genoa* (1913), *Constructivist Composition* (1916–18) and *City at Night* (1919), when compared with Bohomazov's *Bouquet of Flowers* (1914–15), Meller's *Composition* (1917–18) and *Urban Landscape* (1912–13), or Rybak's *City* (1917) indicate a close affinity.

Distinct character

In the years 1908 to 1930 Kyiv produced an avant-garde with a distinct character. At the risk of misrepresenting some aspects of a varied, evolving and dynamic milieu, generalizations about its uniqueness have been made. Its style, according to Nakov, was less aggressive formally, but structurally and compositionally more solid (Nakov 1991, 18). On the whole, the Kyiv milieu focused more on skill and knowledge of a craft. Bohomazov, for example, considered artists to be superior craft workers. What Nakov calls a "modestie artisanale" (Nakov, 21) differed from the constructivism that developed in the late twenties and aimed at complete mastery of technique, materials and conception. A similar concern with artisanal skills and proficiency in a craft can be seen in Boichuk, Archipenko and the Kharkiv artist Vasyl Yermilov. Nakov has also suggested that the work of the Ukrainian avant-garde as a whole is less haunted by a sense of metaphysical angst and more concerned with inner harmony. The Kyivans were less attracted to grand philosophical constructions or extravagant world-changing theories and more focused on researching color and rhythm or the energy of materials (Nakov, 21). The Boichuk School, perhaps as a result of the search for inner harmony, often preferred a subdued, delicately graded palette with quiet, "faded" colors. But a preference for "earth-like" colors was popular with a number of artists from around 1918 until the mid-twenties, including Anatolii Petrytskyi, Issakhar-Ber Rybak and artists associated with the Kultur-Lige.

Bohomazov in a number of ways typifies the Kyiv milieu. He studied in the Kyiv Art School (1902–5). After being expelled along with Archipenko in 1906, he worked with Hryshchenko in Crimea, painting in the open air, then studied in Moscow (1906–7) before returning to the Kyiv school (1908–11). He was co-organizer with Exter of the Link Exhibition (1908) and organizer of the Ring Exhibition (1914). He taught design in a commercial lycée, and in Kyiv's Jewish lycée, and in 1922 began lecturing in the Kyiv Art Institute. In 1914 he wrote "The Art of Painting," an unpublished text that became a manual of instruction at the Institute. It traced the evolution of the new painting through German expressionism, Kandinsky and Larionov, and offered the view that art was the distinct rhythm of its constitutive elements, of forms regulated by a complex inner logic. Like Archipenko and Burliuk, Bohomazov was fascinated with the hidden energy within matter. He saw the world as dynamic, constantly in movement and transformation. For him all forms changed as they impinged upon one another. Myroslava Mudrak has written that the artist instructed his students to "penetrate the pulsating features of their environment to draw out its qualitative and quantitative living movement" (Mudrak 1987, 138). She relates his idea of "internal agitation" to Archipenko's attempts in his "Archipentura" to capture real motion in painting (Mudrak, 138). Bohomazov's belief that sensation was "a physical, tactile and material sensibility" and should dictate an artist's method aligns him with other Ukrainian artists who tended to focus on the real world, the surrounding human and natural environment, and the artist's sensations (Mudrak, 139).

Ukrainians were often concerned with discoveries that were of local provenance or inspiration. They explored folk roots, painted local scenes, and found novelty in marginalized art forms, such as hand-painted sign boards, amateur carvings, embroideries, and popular icons. By celebrating local crafts, they implicitly challenged the division between high and low genres, or between applied art and easel painting. This democratic impulse often turned into a validation of national cultural traditions. It guided not only Kyivan artists who were of Ukrainian origin, but also those who were of Jewish origin.

Like the international avant-garde as a whole, the Ukrainian, in both its Kyivan and Parisian manifestations, had a visionary component. It aimed at a liberation of the imagination, brought important theoretical insights, and challenged accepted ways of perceiving the world by rejecting nineteenth-century forms. Stylistic integrity was more of a consideration for the Boichuk School and the Kultur-Lige, both of which aimed at the creation of an art with national roots, but most avant-gardists were more interested in personal moments of illumination and in breakthroughs to new ways of seeing and feeling. These kinds of inspired moments were sought primarily in primitivism, which for these artists usually meant folk art, ancient art or the icon. Gombrich has argued that throughout history the primitive has been extolled as a reaction to kitsch in art, to what was perceived as sugary and insipid. The primitive has been valued for providing the required antidote of a bracing, invigorating effect. The rediscovery of the icon played a similar role in overcoming established tastes. It challenged the idea, widespread in the late nineteenth century, that Western art had been making steady progress after the setback of the Middle Ages, and that this progress essentially meant moving away from the "clumsy and ugly manner of the Byzantines," through the "skillful, but still hard and angular style of the quattrocento," to the polish and sophistication of the Renaissance (Gombrich 2002, 8). The Ukrainian and Russian avant-gardists rejected this dismissive view of Byzantine art. They rediscovered the (often refined) beauty of the icon and the quattrocento, and confronted contemporary "realist" tastes with this revelation. The Boichuk School, in particular, made a cornerstone of these views and vigorously defended them in the 1920s. Boichuk's careful, balanced compositions and quiet color tones aimed at portraying characters in a state of grace. In this respect he differed from Burliuk and some Russian artists, whose reworking of the icon reveled in the "crude" and "grotesque." Their art was more reminiscent of popular *lubok* (broadsheet) prints and signboard art, with its strong colors and simple lines.

Theoretical concerns were sometimes animated by what Nakov has called a "euphorie coloriste" (Nakov 1991, 24). Considerable research and theorizing was devoted to color by a number of figures, among them Bohomazov, Palmov, Malevich, and Hryshchenko. Both the "Kyivan" and "Parisian" Ukrainians explored the possibilities of color in their artistic practice with great intensity. Much theorizing was also focused on the energy of materials. Ukrainians seem to have drawn inspiration from physical processes occurring in living organisms (the steppe, rural landscapes, the impact of city scenes on human perceptions). This focus on the rural or natural world made them different from Italian and, to a great extent,

Russian futurists, in whose works the urban often predominated, and who glorified the city and technology as forces capable of overcoming chaos and shaping nature. Malevich, as will be argued later, hesitated between the urban and rural, particularly when he fell under the influence of the Kyiv milieu in the late twenties. In fact, many Ukrainian artists, including Malevich, Burliuk, Palmov, Bohomazov, and Boichuk, seem to have rebelled against the tendency to glorify the urban, the mechanical, and the depersonalized. Instead, they presented the natural world as an alternative ideal. Although some constructivists and production artists were interested, at least for a time, in the mechanized collective, there was considerable resistance to this aesthetic among Ukrainians in both Kyiv and Paris.

Artists from Ukraine living in the West generally had little interest in extolling the machine age or political utopias, particularly in the late 1920s, when these trends became part of an almost mandatory, militantly political style in the Soviet Union. Their own negative experiences of the Bolshevik Revolution made them recoil from violence and treat impersonal mechanisms with suspicion. In general, they viewed the drive for political correctness as fundamentally destructive. This was true not only of the Parisian Ukrainians, but also of Burliuk. Even though he worked for *Russkii golos* (Russian Voice), a pro-communist newspaper in New York, and maintained a pro-Soviet line, he was profoundly ambivalent about the direction the regime and its art were taking. His return in the 1930s to a naïve art of innocent rural scenes aligns him with the anti-urban art favored by many of his compatriots. Ukrainians in particular were not prepared to see peasants and workers as dumb, passive raw material to be manipulated by a bolshevik vanguard. Their work, even in the Soviet Union, was usually an implicit, and sometimes an explicit, rejection of this approach. "Stalinist" constructivism, which came along in the late twenties and early thirties, and which exuded puritanical, humorless and conformist messages, led to a wrenching apart of the Kyivan avant-garde collectivity and a crushing of its creative inspiration.

Also important for this generation was what Nakov has called a "charge mystique" and "une élévation philosophique" (Nakov, 15). The interest in mysticism had been an important part of Russian modernism and its so-called Silver Age. However, in the case of many Ukrainian avant-gardists the search for the inexpressible and intuitive appears to have been rooted not in metaphysical or political abstraction but in the observation of nature. If the artist was to develop a new, universal consciousness, they seemed to be saying, it would have to be done through a greater awareness of physical processes. The steppe became for them a metaphor for nature writ large, and beyond this for the cosmos. For a number—Burliuk and Malevich among them—it represented animation, the interaction of numerous life forms, a life process sensed rather than understood. It also represented nature's vastness, abundance, and profusion. It was nature's power, rather than the machine's that fascinated them. This might also explain why the work of a number of artists, including Boichuk, Hryshchenko, Baranoff-Rossiné, and Bohomazov, has a softer, more organic appearance, as though dictated by natural growth, rather than by the superimposition of the observer's own dissecting analysis. The sculptures of Archipenko and Tatlin are also not inspired by the machine aesthetic but by an intuitively sensed inner harmony based on ancient forms, or by an artisan's awareness of the "natural" possibilities within materials and of the best work produced by craftsmen who work these materials. Tatlin's monument to the Third International has often been interpreted as the communist answer to the Tower of Babel, a propagandistic, militant, visionary political statement. It has rarely been suggested that its construction resembles the splayed wooden strips used to make the bandura, a gracefully constructed, elegant and functional instrument. Seen in this way, the tower's formal perfection is a tribute to human skill and ingenuity, both of which are rooted in a long artisanal tradition. In such an interpretation, Tatlin's work is not simply a call to an unattainable future. (The tower, after all, leads nowhere.) It can equally well represent harmonious design, artistry, and joy in human achievement.

Finally, it should be noted that, when seen in the broader European context, the importance of personal lyricism to the Kyivan and Parisian Ukrainians becomes apparent. Although initially attracted to analytical cubism, many quickly moved on to a gently intuitive, subjective expression of the visible.

The Ukrainian avant-garde's distinctiveness was therefore preconditioned by its emergence from a specific milieu (the Kyiv Art School, the Ukrainian Academy of Arts, the Kultur-Lige, the Kyiv Art Institute, and the national movement). Among its dominant traits were a passion for color; a romance with primitivism and kinetic energy; a focus on the local and national elements that were often rooted in the ancient past; a fascination with natural processes; and a concern with inner harmony and personal lyricism. Through these traits it brought its own distinct accent to the international avant-garde.

Politics and Painting

Politics and the Ukrainian Avant-Garde[1]

The twenty years in which the historical avant-garde burst upon the scene (1908–28) were a time of great political turmoil and intense ideological debate. Although primarily concerned with pursuing new forms of expression, many avant-gardists were both politically motivated and concerned with linking new ways of perceiving the world to the business of remaking it. Their aesthetico-cultural and political projects were often, therefore, coupled or fused. However, by the late twenties and early thirties, the era that Boris Groys dubbed "total art-politics" had taken over, and a radical simplification of form, a stridency of tone, and uniformity of expression came to dominate Soviet literature and art. Groys, Andrei Siniavsky and others have argued that the shift to this politicization of art had been psychologically prepared earlier and that the avant-garde played a significant role in the process. Most commentators, however, have viewed the two decades that preceded Stalin's "cultural revolution" of 1928–33 as fundamentally different from the years that followed. A more sympathetic view of the historical avant-garde has situated it in a tradition going back to Kant and the romantics, a tradition in which the intellectual tried to forge a new world by an act of will, often by retreating into the inner world of the spirit. In the 1908–28 period, such utopian world-construction produced visionary, ground-breaking works. It was only in the late twenties that these visionary artist-communards received the seductive proposal of managing a great cultural-political transformation, of becoming "engineers of human souls." Some accepted the invitation, but

1 This chapter is a shortened and modified version of my chapter "Politics and the Ukrainian Avant-Garde," in *Modernism in Kyiv: Jubilant Experimentation*, edited by Irena R. Makaryk and Virlana Tkacz, 219-97 (Toronto: University of Toronto Press, 2010).

Stalin's "cultural revolution" of 1928–33 and the ensuing purges and terror should be distinguished from the earlier period.

For one thing, the post-1928 period demanded a fundamental reinterpretation of the nature and function of literature and art. In literature, for instance, from the time of the romantics, as Tzvetan Todorov has pointed out, a decisive contrast had been made between *belles lettres* or creative writing on the one hand, and the utilitarian or practical use of language on the other (Todorov 1987, 17–18). *Belles lettres* found its justification within itself (was autotelic), while the practical use of language subordinated itself to external goals (was heterotelic). The autotelic view was accepted by Ukrainian modernists and symbolists for whom literature dealt with symbolic facts, mythical and metaphorical frameworks that rearranged patterns of experience and revealed the world by transcending reality. In their first collection, *Sbornik po teorii poeticheskogo iazyka* (The Anthology of the Theory of Poetic Language, 1916), the Russian formalists also contrasted the "autonomous value of linguistic representations" with the "practical goal" of language (Todorov, 11). Literature, according to them, foregrounded the use of language as device.

The counterposition that became hegemonic in the thirties stressed the primacy of social function: literature and the arts were to serve the party's educational and agitational tasks. Any foregrounding of artistic devices was condemned as "formalism." To a degree, this position had indeed been prepared earlier by avant-garde groups. Mikhail Semenko, the leader of the Ukrainian futurists, had early in the twenties called the notion of art as a "self-serving category" both "inappropriate and dangerous." According to him, it was permissible only to "exploit" the devices of art with the goal of agitating for the ideals of the working class (Semenko 1924, 227). He put forward a harder version of this line in April 1929 in a debate entitled "Who Needs Art?" when he insisted that art as an emotional category was dying: it had to be subordinated to reason and forced to perform socially useful tasks (Semenko 1929).

Nonetheless, most avant-gardists found the concept of political education espoused by the party in the late twenties to be far too narrow. Writers and artists were at this time instructed to serve the party in immediate, practical ways: they were told to praise industrial projects, hail the Five-Year Plan, or denounce the regime's critics. A crude "political" interpretation of texts and art works was used to assess "class sympathies." Overt propaganda, absolute loyalty and a militant posture were demanded. In 1930 the declaration of the All-Ukrainian Federation of Revolutionary Soviet Writers stated: "Every revolutionary Soviet writer should be an active builder of socialism, a disciplined fighter on the front of class war—this is our slogan and our command to the Army of Ukrainian Revolutionary Soviet Writers" (*Deklaratsiia* 1930, 124).

Toward an art-politics

Although neither the intransigent tone, the mandatory optimism, nor the parade-ground rhetoric were new, to be accused of "Hamletism," or "psychologism" or "tearful lyricism" could now, in the new atmosphere prove fatal. A political charge expressed in poetry or prose carried a deadly menace, making even apparently harmless literary exchanges dangerous. This was a departure from all recent practice. At some deep level a break had occurred from the humanist tradition that celebrated the blossoming of the individual personality, and welcomed the excitement produced by original, even transgressive, thought and feelings. Whereas most "civic" writers and artists had previously attempted to assimilate political awareness to a wider spiritual culture, to integrate politics into art, from 1928 the move was to entirely assimilate literature and art to politics. The structuring of human perceptions and feelings around slogans became a conscious aim, affecting the tone, diction, imagery, and rhetorical devices of poetry, prose, drama, and the visual arts. The demand was for a simple message, narrative closure, conventional psychological portrayal, and plot structure.

Works that could not be reduced to easily demonstrable political categories, that remained puzzlingly complex or sophisticated, or that challenged simple categories and schemes came under attack. After the last burst of formal innovation by the avant-garde in 1929–30, stylistic novelty and parody were eschewed. In this last fling, it appeared to many that "left art" had been used by the party in order to complete the task of "destroying" previous systems; from this moment on "left art" could be harnessed to the purpose of "constructing" whatever the regime judged to be new and useful. Ironically, both in Russia and Ukraine writers and artists who had been educated on revolt and iconoclasm appeared suddenly to have been transformed into conformist political instruments. Some, of course, refused the role. Others, although they managed to produce what Jacques Ellul has called the "overt" forms of propaganda, seemed genuinely incapable of producing the "covert," spontaneous or subconscious ones (Ellul 1973, 61–87). Indeed, the literature and art of the late twenties and early thirties, as well as much later Soviet cultural production, can profitably be analyzed as revealing a tension or conflict between these overt and covert messages. Dovzhenko's film *Zemlia* (Earth,

1930), on the surface a call for collectivization, is at a deeper level a hymn to the countryside and ancient ways. Yurii Yanovskyi's novel *Chotyry shabli* (Four Swords, 1930), which treats the revolution as national resistance, Volodymyr Gzhytskyi's novel *Chorne ozero* (Black Lake, 1929), which views Soviet expansion as the spread of Russian hegemony, and Les Kurbas's deflating production of Ivan Mykytenko's play *Dyktatura* (Dictatorship, 1929)—all are prominent examples of works with ambiguous and subversive messages. Kazimir Malevich's peasant portraits of 1928–30, as will be argued later, also resound with subversive undertones.

Another category of works shuffled the evaluative signs to make it difficult for a reader to identify positive and negative characters, thus demanding of the reader a more thoughtful assessment of events. Hryhorii Epik's novel *Persha vesna* (First Spring, 1931) is an example. But almost all writers knuckled under in some way, even rewriting their works to fit the new requirements. A much-lauded classic of socialist realism and a work given the status of a patristic text, Andrii Holovko's *Maty* (Mother) now exists in two editions, the 1932 original and the 1935 revision. The same hold true for his *Burian* (Weeds, 1927 and 1932), Petro Panch's *Holubi eshelony* (Blue Echelons, 1926 and 1928), and Gzhytskyi's *Chorne ozero* (1929 and, after many rejected revisions, 1956). Yanovskyi's *Chotyry shabli* was criticized so strongly that the author felt obliged to write *Vershnyky* (Riders, 1935) as an act of literary-political contrition. Students of the literary heritage today often have to deal with several possible versions of the same book—palimpsests in which imposed political sentiments and stylistic features obscure the original inspiration.

Before the late 1920s the introduction of a radically new sensibility had been interpreted by most avant-gardists in a broad aesthetico-cultural and philosophical sense. It was seen as the awakening and refinement of the mind and emotions, and involvement in politics as a response to perceived inadequacies. Writers and artists criticized narrow-mindedness, backwardness, obscurantism, and prejudice. However, they were gradually compelled to voice some concerns and avoid others. For instance, the attitude to the past—a crucial indicator of political preference—went through a rapid change. Many avant-gardists who earlier appeared prepared to jettison all past values, had by the late twenties begun to conform to Moscow's demands and refrained from criticizing the Russian imperial past.

In Ukraine, the political situation was defined by the existence of two powerful revolutionary political movements—socialism and nationalism. Each claimed a different kind of awakened and transformed consciousness. Writers and artists contended with the two competing visions of liberation.

In fact, in the early twenties they often found themselves attempting to reconcile them. By the end of the decade any suggestion of ambiguous and divided loyalties had been suppressed by the Soviet regime. The involvement in the struggle to create an independent Ukrainian People's Republic (1917–20) of most intellectuals, including prominent figures like Dovzhenko and the poet Volodymyr Sosiura, could not be mentioned.

National difference

The Ukrainian avant-garde negotiated four political transitions in the 1920s: the national revolution (1917–19), the establishment of bolshevik power (1919–23), the period of Ukrainization (1923–28), and the imposition of Stalinist rule (1928–33). Most individuals prudently shifted their ground, aligning their views and artistic production with changing political imperatives. Accordingly, some supported the national movement, then Ukrainization movement, and then attacked prominent figures in this movement for "bourgeois nationalism" and "formalism" in the years 1928–33.

It was convenient for cultural workers to forget that prior to 1917 a nationally conscious public had emerged, which had then participated in building the UNR by lending support in turn to the Central Rada (1917–18), the German-backed Hetman Pavlo Skoropadsky (1918) and the Directory (1918–19). This public had supported the creation of cultural institutions such as the Academy of Sciences and the Academy of Arts, and had provided the readers, viewers and audiences for publications, visual and performing arts. The legacy of state and nation-building in these years was unwillingly inherited by many bolsheviks who had initially rejected the call for an independent or even autonomous Ukrainian state as counter-revolutionary. Some had even disputed the fact that a separate Ukrainian nation existed. Many had, in fact, regarded the revolution as primarily a war against separatism and considered Ukrainian culture subversive almost by definition, denouncing it as "counter-revolutionary," "Petliurite," or "a German invention." Others dismissed it as derivative and incomplete, merely a branch of Russian, or condemned it as fundamentally flawed: inchoate, unrefined or antisemitic.

Moreover, in the early years of Soviet rule some bolsheviks felt entitled to repress all expressions of Ukrainian identity as an act of revenge against what they had been conditioned to see as "counter-revolution." This was relatively easy in the early years of Soviet rule because the composition of the Communist Party (bolsheviks) of Ukraine (CP(b)U) was predominantly Russian and contained a substantial number of non-Ukrainians, among whom Jews constituted the largest component.[2] Moreover, until 1926 Ukrainians made up less than half, and often less than a third, of the population in major cities. Not surprisingly, therefore, from 1919 until April 1923 one group in the CP(b)U leadership put forward a "struggle of two cultures" theory, according to which Russian was viewed as the "culture of the city" and Ukrainian as the "culture of the village." The latter was branded as representing the backward, peasant element. According to this theory the two cultures would compete for supremacy until the final inevitable victory of the higher and more progressive culture, which was, naturally, assumed to be Russian. This view was most closely associated with Dmytro Lebed, a secretary of the CP(b)U, but it had strong support in Moscow. Grigorii Zinovev, for example, raised the same arguments repeatedly throughout the 1920s. As a consequence of this ideological influence, Ukrainian institution-building was severely hampered in the early years of Soviet rule; support for Ukrainian newspapers, publishing houses and schools was withdrawn or withheld; and Ukrainian activists within the party were frequently treated with suspicion. In fact, long after the "struggle of two cultures" theory had been officially rejected, much of the party leadership still espoused it and continued to oppose the development of Ukrainian cultural and educational institutions. Their revolutionary experience had convinced these individuals that all Ukrainians were potential nationalists and separatists. In his memoirs Nikita Khrushchev recalled that Stalin's henchman in Ukraine, Lazar Kaganovich, "was fond of saying that every Ukrainian is potentially a nationalist" (Khrushchev 1970, 172).

The situation began to change gradually. First, when the Ukrainian Soviet Socialist Republic was proclaimed a constituent member of the Soviet Union (on the last day of 1922 and the first of 1923), and then when Russian chauvinism was condemned at the Twelfth Congress of the Russian Communist Party (bolsheviks) in April, 1923. On August 1, 1923, the CP(b)U announced a policy of Ukrainization, which included support for the development of Ukrainian language in schools, educational

2 The party census from 1922 gave the total figure of CP(b)U members as 54,818. Out of these 4,647 had come from Russian and Jewish parties, while the Ukrainian parties, namely the so-called Borotbists and the Ukrainian Communist Party (UCP, which had emerged from the Ukrainian Social Democratic Party), contributed only 118 and 34 members, respectively. The breakdown of the CP(b)U's total membership in 1923 was 51,236. Of these 27,490 (53.6%) were listed as Russians, 11,920 (23.3%) as Ukrainians, 6,981 (13.6%) as Jews, 1,241 (2.6%) as Poles, and 3,604 (7.1%) as belonging to other nationalities. See Ravich-Cherkasskii 1923, 239.

institutions and government. These concessions, Moscow realized, were required in order to obtain peace in Ukraine and to win over large sections of the population. Little, however, was done to implement the policy until 1925. During that year Ukrainians became a majority within the CP(b)U and the pressure for change increased. In May, Stalin dispatched Lazar Kaganovich to the new capital, Kharkiv, to become the First Secretary of the CP(b)U. His instructions were to instill life into the Ukrainization policy, but to keep it under close political supervision. A number of commentators have suggested that a deal had been struck between Stalin's faction in the Communist Party of the Soviet Union and the leaders backing Ukrainization in the CP(b)U, with the latter agreeing to support Stalin on all-Union issues in return for a faster pace of Ukrainization.

In June 1926, the Central Committee of the CP(b)U adopted further measures, which proved to be the government's most sympathetic statement on the national question in Ukraine. However, a crucial issue emerged: the need for decisive results in Ukrainianizing the party itself.

In the view of many communist party members, Ukrainization meant an "indigenization" (*korenizatsiia*) that would draw the local population into the party and the work of government. This would be accomplished by nourishing a Ukrainian culture that was national in form but socialist in content; in other words, one that differed only in language and modes of delivery, but whose content would be formulated in and broadcast from Moscow and Leningrad. Those who held this view were soon disappointed. In fact, as soon as the schools, media and government institutions began to actively support the use of Ukrainian, the pressure for transferring real decision-making to Kharkiv became unstoppable. Moreover, Ukrainian culture began to exhibit great vitality and assimilative power. Instead of willingly assimilating to the "superior" Russian culture, a scenario that many party leaders had assumed to be the inevitable outcome, the population began to develop cultural institutions that challenged their local Russian competitors. Those who had until then been educated in a Russian cultural environment were confronted with an identity whose existence they had never suspected and whose presence seemed foreign to them.

The twenties can therefore be characterized as a struggle between Russian centralizing and hegemonist views on the one hand and demands for autonomy among national republics on the other. When, in mid-decade, Ukrainian leaders insisted upon a full emancipation of their cultural life, a conflict with russificatory tendencies came to a head. The Literary Discussion of 1925–28 was the critical turning point. In its final stages Mykola Skrypnyk, the powerful Commissar for Education in Ukraine, urged participants to behave with decorum, devote themselves to artistic production and avoid politics. By then, however, the political atmosphere had deteriorated, and the final debate (which was devoted to the theater and held in Kyiv on May 29 and Kharkiv from June 8 to 11, 1929) bore the character of an inquisition. During this debate the theater director Les Kurbas and the playwright Mykola Kulish faced a hostile gallery of condemnatory critics.

By 1928, the party had closed down *VAPLITE* (the acronym for the Vilna Akademiia Proletarskoi Literatury; Free Academy of Proletarian Literature), an organization and eponymous journal that had conducted a vigorous critique of Soviet policy and party attitudes. The group's leader Mykola Khvylovyi signed an admission of political errors and destroyed the second part of his controversial, still unpublished novel *Valdshnepy* (Woodsnipes, 1927). To many observers this was a signal that the tide had turned against the Ukrainization policy and the "national communists" who championed it. The show trials of 1928 signaled the beginning of a frontal attack on the entire Ukrainian intellectual and creative strata. The most famous of these trials took place in 1930. It was a kangaroo court staged in a public theater in Kharkiv, then the Ukrainian capital. Forty-five academics were accused of belonging to an underground counter-revolutionary organization, the Spilka Vyzvolennia Ukrainy (Union for the Liberation of Ukraine). The charges were entirely trumped-up and the forced confessions served as pretexts for a massive wave of arrests. By 1932–33, as collectivization, grain-requisitioning and hunger took four million lives, almost anyone could be accused of "bourgeois nationalism" and summarily executed or exiled to Siberia. Thousands of cultural activists met this fate. Skrypnyk, Khvylovyi and several other prominent Ukrainian communists committed suicide in 1933.

Skrypnyk had stressed the parallel and equal development of Russian and Ukrainian languages and cultures in Ukraine. In his final years he had tried to continue Ukrainization by supporting, for example, the opening of Ukrainian theater and opera companies. However, when "local nationalism," rather than "Russian great-nation chauvinism," was singled out in 1928 as the principle enemy (a reversal of the stance taken in 1923) it was clear to all that a major shift in policy had occurred.

Avant-gardists in the political cross-fire

It was still possible in the mid-twenties to criticize imperialism and chauvinism as vestiges of tsarist rule, but attention to these issues began to draw sharp rebukes from authorities, particularly in Ukraine. Mykola Kulish's plays, which ridiculed psychological servility and contempt for Ukrainian culture as hangovers from imperial rule, produced an orchestrated response. Kurbas's theater was closed in 1933 and the director disappeared in the gulag.

At this time, Soviet Russia began "rediscovering" its own national history and traditions, revising, for example, its negative attitude toward imperial conquest, state expansion and Russian nationalism. Symptomatic of this reassessment was the enormous success, due to the sympathetic portrayal of tsarist forces, of Mikhail Bulgakov's novel *Belaia gvardiia* (The White Guard, 1925) and his play *Dni Turbinykh* (Days of the Turbins, 1926) in the Moscow Art Theater, and the publication of Aleksei Tolstoi's *Petr Pervyi* (Peter the First, 1929).

The success of Kurbas and Kulish was part of the issue. In the years 1926–33 when they collaborated with the designer Vadym Meller and the composer Yurii Meitus, the Berezil Theater's productions dazzled Kharkiv audiences, altering perceptions of Ukrainian culture. Berezil became the city's leading theater. Entertaining, politically relevant and avant-garde, it eclipsed the achievements of Nikolai Sinelnikov in Kharkiv and Nikolai Solovtsov in Kyiv, the two Russian directors who had set the tone with their productions of Ibsen and Hauptmann. This was an unexpected and unwelcome development for those who had assumed that the Russian stage would be the sole producer of serious talent. In fact, after Kurbas's theater was forcibly disbanded in 1933, the aging Sinelnikov was again instructed to head Kharkiv's Russian theater—a symbolic attempt, it appeared to many, to restore pre-revolutionary Russian cultural hegemony (Revutskyi 1955, 17).

Kurbas's productions of Kulish's "national trilogy"—the plays *Narodnyi Malakhii* (The People's Malachii, 1929), *Myna Mazailo* (1929) and *Sonata Pathétique* (1930)—carried a forceful anti-colonial message. Here is how one viewer described their successes in 1931:

> The Ukrainian theater learned to mock the living lord [*pan*]. The theater used a language that cultured families of former Russian officialdom [*chynushi*] had employed only in barber-shops and at the Central Workers' Cooperative. In the past, theater had tried to amuse the all-powerful russifiers, and had brought sentimental tears to the eyes of those who represented beekeeping/melon-growing capitalists. Suddenly, this same theater recalled that Ukrainian carvers had once been the equals of the Venetians and dared to

> compete with the theatrical culture of its time. Could Sinelnikov's apologists forgive this? (Khmuryi 1948, 15)

According to this account, the despised national backwardness was being presented in the theater as the product of national oppression and hegemonist views—attitudes that were still richly present in ruling circles. If we accept such an assessment, the role of the Ukrainian avant-garde should be seen as negotiating different views of modernity among viewers and audiences, attempting to create a new Soviet culture while nurturing a positive attitude toward Ukrainian culture. The dual imperatives of national and social change therefore gave the Ukrainian avant-garde a unique profile, but at the same time made its situation particularly complex.

With or without the past?

The avant-garde's aesthetico-cultural positions expressed a rejection of and simultaneously a dependence on links with the past. The struggle for the new involved eradicating aspects of tsarist rule, such as the colonizer's contemptuous attitude and the local's inferiority complex. Counterposed to this, however, was a celebration of the primitive and exotic, as thrilling to Ukrainian avant-gardists as the African and tribal was for French cubists. Moreover, for some an allure of the politically forbidden was attached to the repressed national past.

There were avant-gardists who appeared to reject the past entirely. Mikhail Semenko and the futurists, for example, aligned themselves with those aspects of international modernism that embraced "rational" ways of perceiving and changing the world. They admired the analytical mind capable of dismantling and then recombining elements in a deliberate process. In the later twenties they were even attracted to the idea of humanity's liberation from its own biological nature, an issue raised in Viktor Domontovych's *Doktor Serafikus* (written in the twenties but published in 1947) and in Leonid Skrypnyk's *Intelihent* (Intellectual, 1929). The subtext to this attraction was the belief that civilization could be transformed through a rational, planned process.

However, the faith in political rationality and, even less, in forced radical social-biological experimentation was not widely shared. Most Ukrainian avant-gardists felt a stronger ownership of the "primitive," to which in their opinion they had privileged access in their rich folk creativity. In Kharkiv, the capital of "proletarian" Ukraine, Maria Syniakova produced childlike paintings and sought inspiration in the tradition of tile painting which dates back to the seventeenth and eighteenth centuries. She enjoyed presenting herself as an unschooled student of nature, although her entourage was sophisticated, including the poets Boris Pasternak and Velimir Khlebnikov, and the painter Mikhail Matiushin. Like Boichuk, Burliuk and Malevich, she linked her art to folk creativity. These artists were not depicting an encounter with a foreign Other, but rather were expressing admiration for the creativity of their "own" peasantry.

A number of scholars have underscored the idea that European "primitivism" had a deeply ambivalent relationship with Western imperialism and capitalist modernity. It has been noted that Picasso's *Les Demoiselles d'Avignon* is riven by a conflict stemming from "an internal psychological division between attraction and repulsion, classical superego and primitive libido, and results in an aggressive attack on the image of women which may disguise a deep fear" (Butler 1994, 108–9). Richard Sheppard has argued that "whichever way one reads the painting, its violence and shock derive to a considerable extent from Picasso's experience of the loss of tradition within which he had previously been able to work but which a part of him was trying, unsuccessfully, to retain" (Sheppard 2000, 28). The Ukrainian variant of primitivism did not suffer these complexes because it saw itself as rediscovering its own tradition. Its intimate relationship with primitivism is an additional reason why the leap to a conceptual and abstract art was quickly achieved by many artists in these years: color symbolism and simplified, abstract forms were already familiar to most artists from icon and folk art. As has been seen in the case of Exter, the search for inspiration in native traditions was also stimulated by the belief that Slavic civilizations displayed unique, non-Western features.

Democratic, multi-disciplinary spirit

The Ukrainian avant-garde embraced a large range of Western cultural experiments. Osip Mandelshtam, while living alongside the Berezil company, noted that "in Berezil's work there is something that is common to the work of all founders: it tries in the shortest possible time to give examples of the most varied genres, to outline all the possibilities, to master all the forms" (quoted in Hirniak 1982, 225).

An exploration of Western cultural forms was linked to a strong belief among Ukrainians in democratic norms. One historian has argued that Ukraine's political culture is defined by a Western attitude toward individual rights and the separation of church and state. For this reason its territories in the nineteenth century were the strongest supporters of liberalism and constitutionalism. By contrast, the grafting of Byzantine theocracy onto Muscovy, a state already organized along the lines of the Golden Horde, produced in Russia a political culture defined by a centralizing, despotic state (Lysiak-Rudnytskyi 1973, 15). The result, as more than one scholar has argued, was a Russian messianism that left its mark on the Slavophiles, the radical intelligentsia and the bolsheviks in the form of an inverted religiosity and maximalism (Sinyavsky 1990, 4–13).

For this reason, it might be argued, the aggressive, maximalist-utopian strain was less prevalent in the Ukrainian avant-garde, even during the revolutionary years. A coexistence of different schools and tendencies could be observed in the art community, including the avant-garde: in the Academy of Arts formed in 1917–18 and in its later reincarnation as the (avant-gardist) Kyiv Art Institute during the 1920s, in the Berezil Theater's deliberate policy of continual experimentation and their welcoming of all political groups, and in Boichuk's collective and collaborative work within his studios of monumentalism.

Developing a local idiom

Myroslava Mudrak has argued that the Ukrainian avant-garde exhibited a principled localism, a determination to develop its own idiom out of locally available resources:

> The avant-garde art of Ukraine of the 1910s to 1930s was precariously hinged on an oscillating pendulum between the present and past, local traditions and cosmopolitan practices. Abstraction helped to identify the problematic and to explore and experiment with artistic systems that could direct this process into the future. What is avant-garde about Ukrainian art, then, is not its inventiveness in 'breaking the mold' but in its deliberate and conscious re-education and reformulation of art's function in a national culture. By not placing novelty as a premium, but operating instead within the framework of the enduring qualities of tradition, the Ukrainian avant-garde made claims on the aesthetic past to restore it to the dignity deserving of a modernist present (Mudrak 2001, 29).

The tendency among Ukrainians was to make wider use of indigenous art forms and also to assert independence from cultural processes elsewhere, in both Russia and the West.

Escape from marginalization

The utopian project of a reformed human nature did attract Ukrainians, but primarily as a way out of their political marginalization. The visionary dreamers of Kulish's plays, Khvylovyi's disillusioned revolutionaries, Volodymyr Vynnychenko's attraction to "concordism," Pavlo Krat's utopian novel *Koly ziishlo sontse* (When the Sun Rose, 1913), or Dovzhenko's *Zvenyhora* (1927)—all present unsatisfied yearnings for, or utopian projections of a reformed human order within which the Ukrainian nation is allowed to take its respected place alongside others.

This no doubt formed a bedrock motivation for many avant-gardists and guided their concern with national and social emancipation. The combined revolutionary drives strengthened conviction that citadels of reaction required toppling, but also that individuals were free to borrow from an entire spectrum of liberationist currents in developing visions of an emancipated world. Freedom from imperialistic or chauvinistic attitudes played an important role in the avant-garde's picture of a spiritually reformed humanity. Perhaps a particular fascination with human and universal energy, limitless expanses, even "cosmic" dimensions can be linked to this emancipatory drive.

To what extent was the avant-garde—an internationalist and pan-European phenomenon—Ukrainian in inspiration? The question is never asked of writers, or cultural figures like Kurbas and Dovzhenko, because the evidence for their inspiration seems obvious. But what of artists? The answer will of course be different in each particular case. For some, Ukrainian concerns were not necessarily significant. Nor do the works of many figures require knowledge of a Ukrainian context for appreciation. Many artists, including those who emigrated permanently to Paris, Moscow, or other centers, were assimilated to various traditions and became part of other narratives. Nonetheless, the strength of the social and national liberationist currents in Ukraine in the 1910s and 1920s had a powerful effect on the entire avant-garde, as did the fascination with the past, the primitive and the locally crafted. The remarkable burst of creativity in the two decades between 1910 and 1930 can be better understood when avant-gardists are seen as reacting to the ideological and cultural debates in Ukraine and simultaneously responding to the experiences of fellow artists.

Political Posters 1919–21 and the Boichuk School[1]

Political posters played an important role in the years that followed the 1917 revolution. Between 1919 and 1921 the Red Army fought Symon Petliura, who spearheaded the struggle for Ukraine's independence, the Russian White Armies under General Anton Denikin, and Polish interventionists under Marshal Josef Pilsudski. During this period the entire country seethed with revolts as the peasantry resisted the imposition of bolshevik rule. The political poster became a political weapon by providing vivid and immediately comprehensible propaganda on behalf of the Communist Party and Red Army. However, the poster was also a powerful medium of artistic expression. It was admired for its formal qualities and quickly gained an important cultural status, which it retained over seven decades of Soviet rule. Posters were produced in tens of thousands of copies. They adorned streets and shop windows, and served as backgrounds to numerous political rituals, such as processions and public meetings. In later years the poster was used to reinforce Soviet directives and convey a positive image of the new regime.

A number of prominent Ukrainian avant-gardists were involved in designing these posters, among them Mykhailo Boichuk and Vasyl Yermilov. The question is why? Were they endorsing bolshevik power? How should we interpret their imagery? And how can their appearance be contextualized, both in terms of message and artistry?

The overarching symbolism of these posters cannot be missed. They tell the story of human emancipation—from foreign intervention, from the bourgeoisie, from capitalism, and from human want. They hold out the promise of a radiant future, signified by the rising sun, the distant perspective, and the bountiful harvest. Peace and prosperity are always the horizon

1 Sections of this essay appeared in Shkandrij, 2013.

of expectation. The road to this goal, it is made clear, requires military victory and personal sacrifices. The art illustrates a story of political liberation through struggle.

Today's viewer cannot help but juxtapose this message to the reality of what came only a few years later. The rhetoric and slogans of bolshevism appear hollow in light of the collectivization of 1929–31 and the Great Famine (Holodomor) of 1932–1933, which laid waste the country. Hundreds of thousands were deported to Siberia in these years, and millions died. There is enormous irony, therefore, in the call these posters make to the peasantry urging them to give up their grain for the revolutionary cause. At that time it was the starving cities that needed saving. As awareness of the Holodomor has spread and scholarship has analyzed various aspects of the tragedy, readers today will be tempted to decipher the message of these posters less as an enthusiastic endorsement of the bolshevik regime and more as a lesson in disinformation and population control.

The propaganda and slogans emanated of course from the Communist Party leadership in Moscow, which was then trying to impose its rule throughout Ukraine. It had defeated the armies of the UNR, Poland (which launched an invasion in 1920), and the White Armies (who wanted to restore Russian imperial rule). The posters were commissioned to serve primarily political and military imperatives. They were directed mainly at the Ukrainian peasantry—over 80 percent of the population—whom they call upon to deliver their grain and support the Red Army.

The collection of grain was accomplished by force. Food products were ruthlessly requisitioned. The regime had not established control over large parts of the country, and the posters therefore attempted to win over the population. They emphasized the message that Soviet rule represented peace and future prosperity, and that the worker was the peasant's ally. The devastation caused by years of war and repeated requisitioning, coupled with a drought, resulted in a massive famine in 1921 during which an estimated one million people died. Nonetheless, the posters from that year plead with farmers not to resist giving up their grain. As we know, ten years later the requisitioning process was repeated, leading to the Holodomor. In retrospect, the posters, therefore, raise another question: did the regime learn from this requisitioning of 1921 how to extract grain by force and how to control the population through hunger? Was this, in short, a precursor to the even greater violence and famine that came later?

Today it is difficult to estimate the reaction these posters would have elicited when they first appeared. In all likelihood there would have been a wide range of responses, depending on who stood to benefit from Soviet rule, who suffered from the imposition of a monoparty dictatorship, requisitioning, or the punitive expeditions that were putting down revolts. The contemporary viewer has the luxury of distance from these events and is more able to appreciate the artistic qualities of the works. Some of the country's best and most innovative artists were drafted into producing them. In this bleak time of hunger and unemployment, they often welcomed the assignment, for which they received payment either in currency or in food products.

The viewer will immediately notice the depiction of multitudes. The peasant crowd and the marching army form part of the language of political persuasion. Often the large-scale figure of an individual worker or peasant is superimposed or placed in the foreground. They symbolize the broad masses, who can be seen in the distance. This figure emerges from the masses, and represents the collective will. Those who oppose bolshevik rule are associated with mass exploitation and destruction, which are often symbolized by rows of gallows or a ravaged landscape.

The posters introduced the public to totems of Soviet rule: the acronyms of the new Ukrainian state (URSR, or USRR), the red flag, the hammer and sickle, the unity of proletarian and peasant, soldier and laborer. It should be noted, however, that the Communist Party's dictatorship, Lenin, or Marxist doctrine are entirely absent—an indication of how unpopular was the notion of rule imposed from outside, particularly from Moscow. In order to counteract this resistance, the symbolism in the posters underlines a specifically Ukrainian reality: yellow wheat fields, luxurious flowers, blue skies, colorful peasant dress, quotations from the classics of Ukrainian literature. The land itself is treated as sacred; it is honorable to protect it, and to die for it. The posters work in this way to emphasize objects that create a link between the land, the Ukrainian collective, and the new state. An early bolshevik slogan, after all, had promised to return "the land to the peasants."

The art makes use of abstract forms, bold lines, arresting poses, and strong colors. Traditions of popular painting are blended with a streamlined modern graphic art. Such a combination sends a subliminal message: Ukraine is moving into a new world of technology, urbanization and the machine aesthetic, but retains its links to past forms sanctified by custom.

A particular feature of these posters was the style developed in the Boichuk School. Sometimes referred to as neo-Byzantinism or monumentalism, it drew on the icon (particularly the folk icon of Western Ukraine) and Italian Renaissance painting. The School included Ivan Padalka, Vasyl Sedliar and Oksana Pavlenko. As is evident from the poster art of 1919–21 it developed a style that was used to appeal to the Ukrainian masses in an idiom they understood.

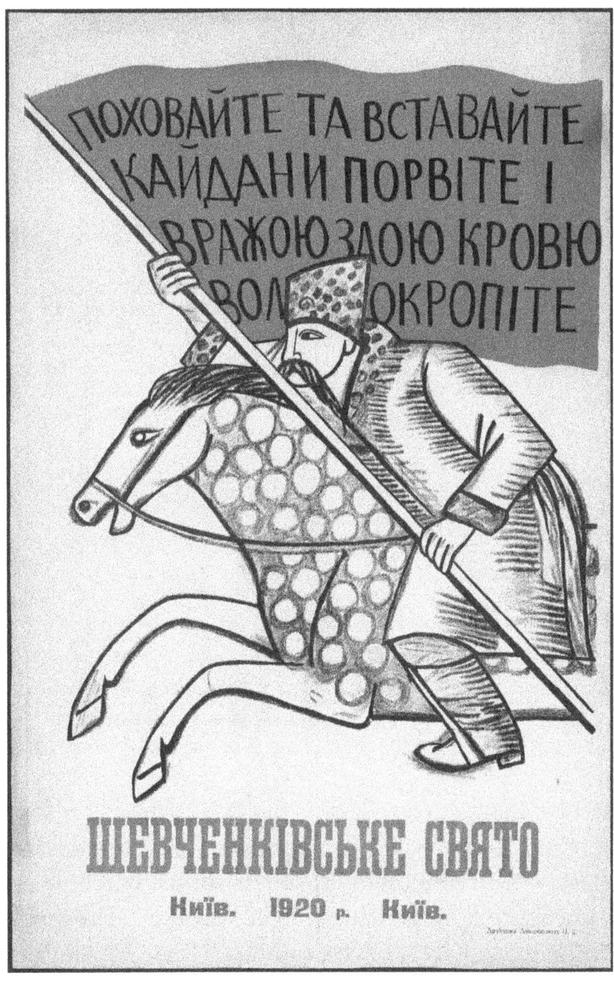

Mykhailo Boichuk (attributed). *Shevchenko Day*, 1920.

Shevchenko Day (Shevchenkivske sviato, 1920) was produced in Kyiv and is attributed to Boichuk. The words on the poster are taken from Taras Shevchenko's poem "Zapovit" (Testament), a second national anthem and frequently sung at patriotic gatherings: "Bury me and arise, break your chains and let the blood of your enemies baptize freedom." The message supports popular rebellion in the name of freedom. However, its political alignment is ambiguous. Only the red flag suggests a pro-bolshevik stance.

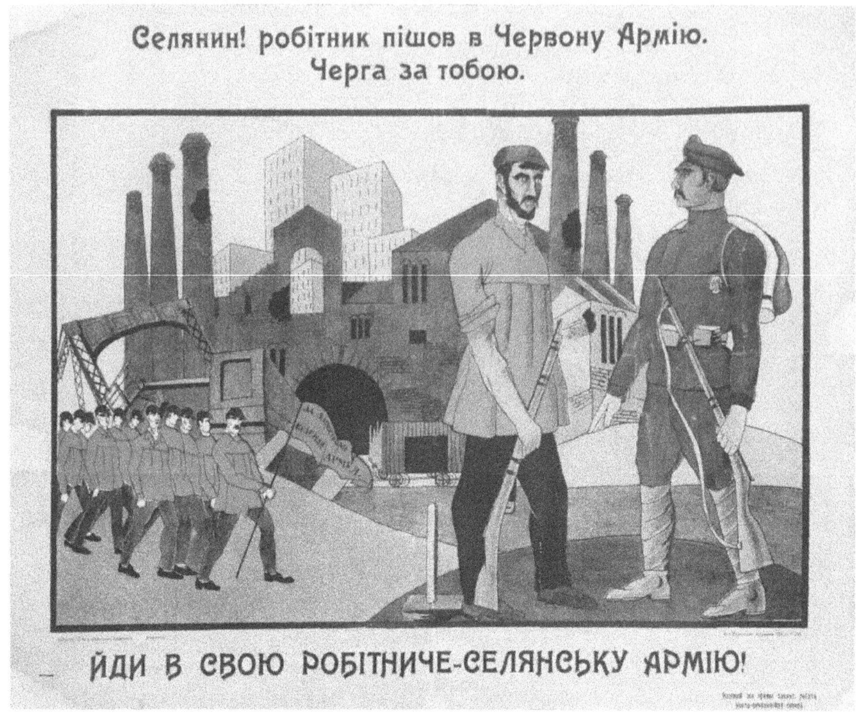

Peasant, the Worker Has Joined the Red Army. Now It's Your Turn, 1920.

Peasant, the Worker Has Joined the Red Army. Now It's Your Turn (Selianyn, robitnyk pishov v chervonu armiiu. Cherha za toboiu, 1920) was produced in Kyiv as a recruitment poster. It shows marching armies and a larger-than-life figure of what appears to be a peasant. The shirts of this figure and the other recruits resemble peasant smocks. The slogan reads "Join your worker-peasant army." The words "Long live the Red Army" are written on the banner. The representation of buildings is highly stylized. They are copied from icon art and eighteenth-century graphics. Such a distinctive style was developed by Ivan Padalka in Kharkiv in the 1920s. He would later be arrested and shot for "formalism" and "Ukrainian nationalism" in 1937, along with Boichuk and Sedliar.

On the back of this particular poster are telegram forms of the Ukrainian State Bank from the time of the UNR in 1917–19, a reminder of the fluid political situation. The city of Kyiv changed hands a dozen times during the revolutionary period.

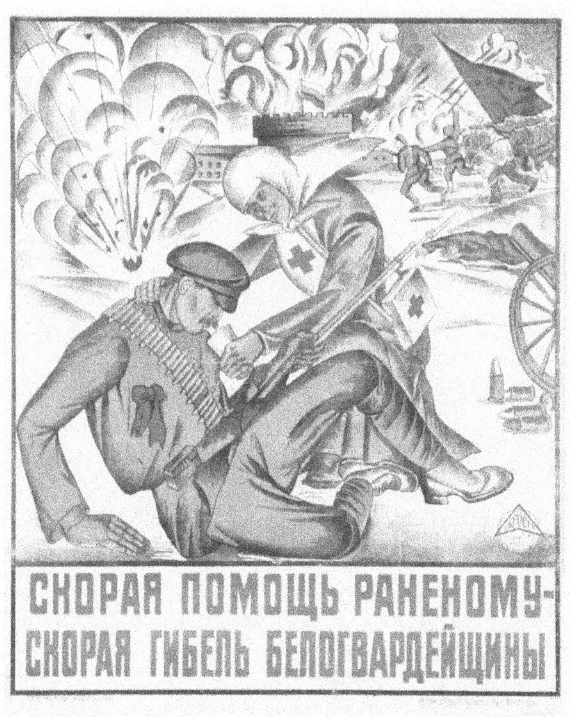

First Aid for the Wounded—A Quick Death to the Whites, 1921.

First Aid for the Wounded—A Quick Death to the Whites (Skoraia pomoshch ranenomu, skoraia gibel belogvardeishchiny, 1921) was produced in Kharkiv and also recalls the graphic art of Padalka and the Boichuk School. The poses of the woman and soldier are strongly reminiscent of icons, as is the stylized treatment of fingers and the clouds of smoke. The flag shows the army of the RSFSR (Russian Soviet Socialist Federal Republic) attacking the White forces, who fly the Russian tsarist flag. The creation of the Ukrainian Soviet Socialist Republic and of the Union of Soviet Socialist Republics (USSR) was only declared on the January 1, 1923. The language of the poster is Russian. It was issued by the Committee to Help Sick and Wounded Red Army Soldiers and created by the Art Department of the Ukrainian Rosta (Telegraph Agency).

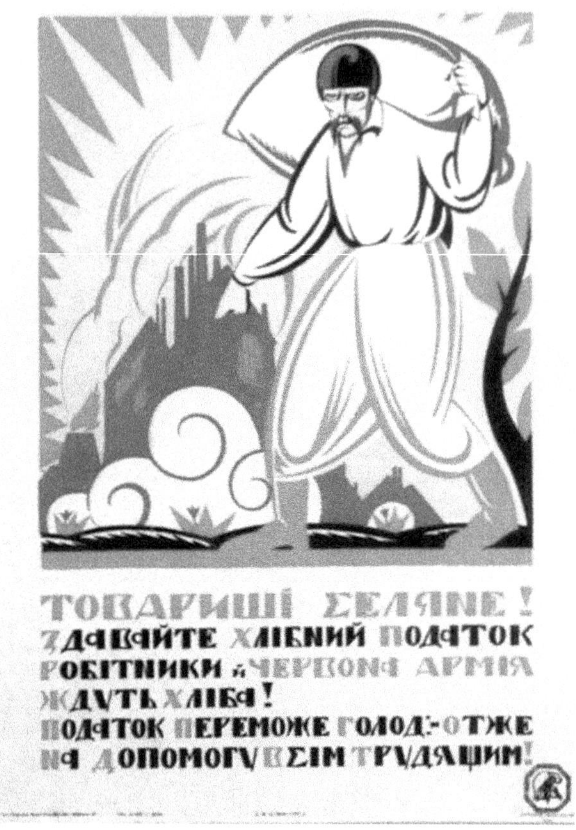

Oleksii (Aleksei) Marenkov. *Comrade Peasants! Hand in Your Grain Tax. The Workers and the Red Army Are Waiting for Bread! The Tax Will Help Overcome Hunger. Help All Laboring People!*, 1921.

Comrade Peasants! Hand in Your Grain Tax. The Workers and the Red Army Are Waiting for Bread! The Tax Will Help Overcome Hunger. Help All Laboring People! (Tovaryshi seliane! Zdavaite khlibnyi podatok. Robitnyky i Chervona Armiia zhdut khliba! Podatok peremozhe holod. Otzhe na dopomohu vsim trudiashchym!, 1921) was produced in Kyiv and is attributed to Oleksii (Aleksei) Marenkov. It is notable for its elegant composition, harmonious use of color, and stylized lettering that recalls wood carving. This style of graphic art strongly influenced by wood carving was a distinct feature of Ukrainian art. In the interwar period it was popularized in the book design art of Lviv and among émigrés in Prague by artists such as Pavlo Kovzhun and Robert Lisovskyi, both of whom began as avant-gardists in Kyiv.

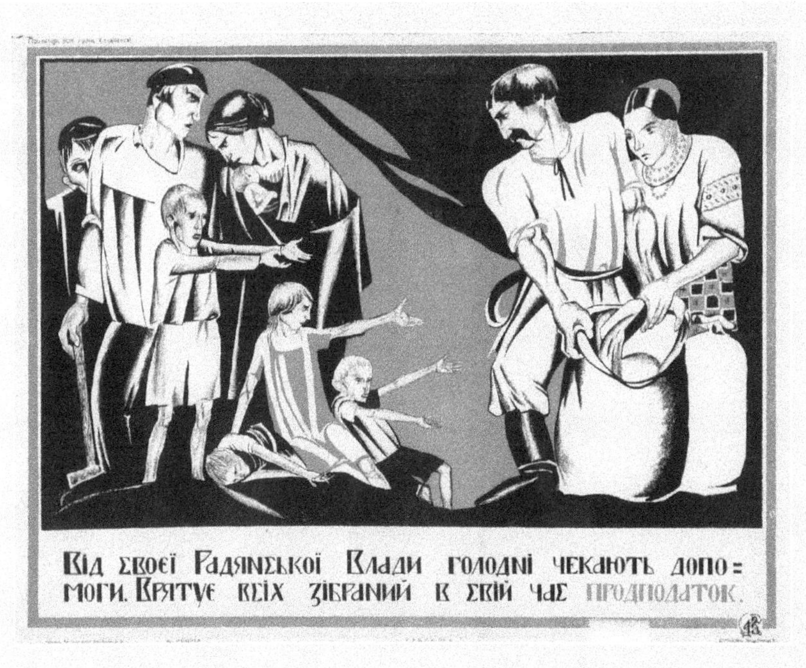

The Hungry Await Help from Their Soviet Rule. Timely Collection of the Food Tax Will Save Everyone, 1921.

The Hungry Await Help from their Soviet Rule. Timely Collection of the Food Tax Will Save Everyone (Vid svoiei radianskoi vlady holodni chekaiut dopomohy. Vriatuie vsikh zibranyi v svii chas prodpodatok, 1921) was produced in Kyiv. An eye-catching example of graphic art, it is notable for the unexpected poses, and an unusual and arresting composition. Facial expressions offer psychological insight into the suffering of individuals, and the use of color adds drama.

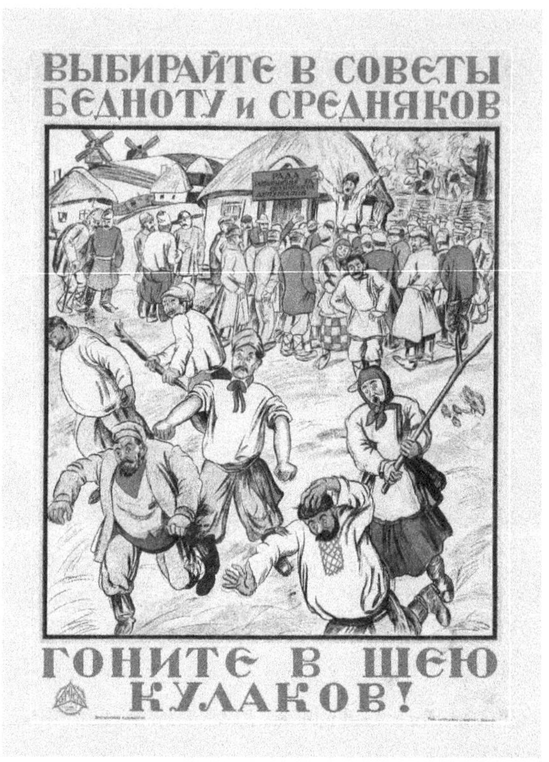

Oleksandr Khvostenko-Khvostov. *Drive Off the Kulaks!* 1920.

Drive Off the Kulaks! (Gonite v sheiu kulakov!, 1920) was produced in Kharkiv and is the work of Oleksandr Khvostenko-Khvostov. Its subject is "class war" in the village. The bolshevik regime attempted at the time to split the village community by mobilizing poor peasants against their neighbors. The Council ("Rada" in Ukrainian, "Soviet" in Russian) of Worker and Peasant Deputies is shown meeting in the background. This is indicated by the plaque over the entrance to the building, written in Ukrainian. However, the language of the rest of this poster is Russian. The slogan reads: "Elect the poor and middle-peasants to the Council." The Art Department of the Ukrainian Rosta (Telegraph Agency) is identified as the poster's producer. It made many agitational posters at the time. Khvostenko-Khvostov became a well-known theater artist in the 1920s.

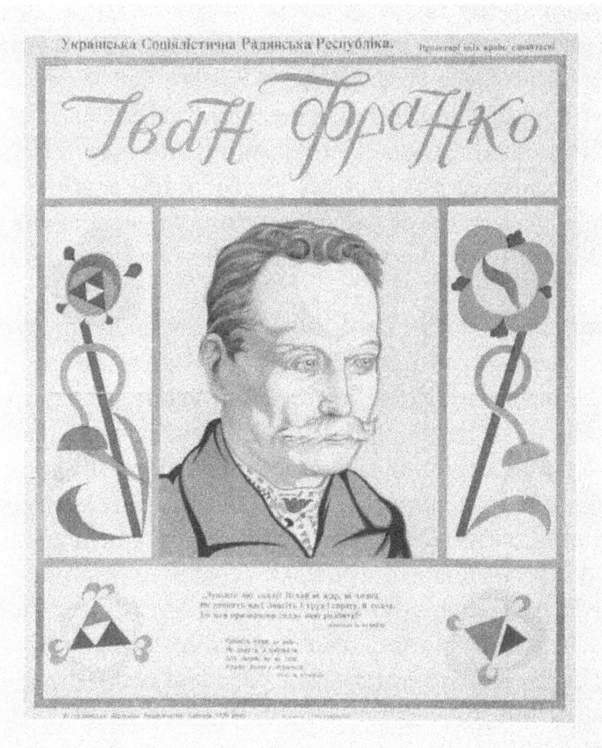

Vasyl Yermilov. *Ivan Franko*, 1920.

Ivan Franko (1920) was produced in Kharkiv by Vasyl Yermilov. The quotations from Franko's popular poem "Kameniari" (Stone Masons) are used as encouragement to work for a better future. The graphic design is typical of Yermilov, a Kharkiv artist well-known for his love of clean, light and polished surfaces. Noteworthy are the innovative lettering and the manner in which graphics representing flora approach abstract designs. Both are signatures of Yermilov's work. The words Ukrainian Socialist Soviet Republic (USRR) appear at the top of the poster along with the slogan "Proletarians of all countries unite!" The poster was issued by the All-Ukrainian State Publishers in Kharkiv. The city was the capital of the Ukrainian Republic from 1923 to 1934.

Since the Boichuk School was the inspiration behind many of these posters, it is useful to glance at the artist's career. When one does so the School's involvement with bolshevik poster art in 1919–21 appears paradoxical. In pre-revolutionary years Boichuk attempted to produce a synthetic national art. He drew on sources which, in his opinion, had the deepest roots in Ukrainian culture, in particular Byzantine art and folk creativity in its many manifestations. In these he saw the best expression of Ukraine's unique cultural profile: a fusion of both Eastern and Western influences. He explored Egyptian and Assyrian art, which he felt had left their mark through monumental classical and Byzantine art on early Ukrainian culture. He also examined reflections of the Byzantine tradition in the early Renaissance, especially in the Italian quattrocento, when, following the fall of Constantinople to the Turks, escaping artists had brought their talents to Italy.

The continuities Boichuk sought were in the millennium of recorded Ukrainian history, which began with the first great culturally formative period of the princely era, the tenth to fourteenth centuries in Kyiv and Galicia. It was then, he thought, that disparate elements had first come together to form a recognizable cultural entity. This privileging of the medieval period marked a departure from the self-image favored by Ukrainian populists in the last third of the nineteenth century, who tended to associate the period of Kyivan Rus with the Russian state tradition more than with the Ukrainian past. In envisioning a thousand-year-old culture centered in Kyiv and Lviv, Boichuk was following the historiography of Mykhailo Hrushevskyi, the historian who became president of the Ukrainian People's Republic when the Russian Empire disintegrated in 1917. Boichuk was indebted not only to Hrushevskyi, but also to the Metropolitan Andrei Sheptytskyi, and the Shevchenko Scientific Society of Lviv for his education.[2] The UNR initiated many of the political and cultural transformations which, even after its collapse three years later, continued to shape Soviet rule. In emphasizing continuity with the medieval past, Boichuk was also breaking ranks with Russian historians who, in their almost unanimous adherence to accepted imperial teleology, appropriated this period exclusively for Russia. Because he linked contemporary cultural forms to the medieval past through the channels of Byzantine painting and folk creativity, in the 1930s Boichuk would be branded a nationalist and his School destroyed. In this decade, while members of the School were being arrested

2 The Shevchenko Scientific Society, which Hrushevskyi directed from 1897, provided financial support for Boichuk's studies. In 1899 the artist traveled to Vienna, where he was enrolled in a private studio. After his return to Lviv, on the recommendation of the painter Ivan Trush, he enrolled in the Krakow Academy of Arts, again with a scholarship from the Society, and spent the following five years in Poland. In 1905, after contributing a number of portraits to the First All-Ukrainian Art Exhibition organized by Ivan Trush in Lviv, he left for Munich, where he studied with Franz Herterich and Franz von Stuck, the teacher of Kandinsky and Klee. In the Spring of 1907, thanks to Sheptytskyi's support, he spent the next four years in Paris.

and shot, many of Kyiv's earliest monuments, such as the Monastery of St. Michael of the Golden Domes (to which Boichuk had taken students to study the unrivaled collection of mosaics and frescoes) and the Mezhyhiria Monastery (on the site of which his students revived a famous ceramic factory), were demolished and their treasures destroyed.

The second important factor in Boichuk's cultural program, the connection with the international art movement of the twentieth century, has not attracted the attention it deserves. In Munich and Paris, Boichuk studied with and was influenced by some of the major teachers and artists of the early twentieth century—figures such as Franz von Stuck (the teacher of Wassily Kandinsky and Paul Klee), Paul Serusier and Maurice Denis. His connection with modernism's high-minded cult of form and his competitive but close relationship with avant-gardists such as Malevich are frequently overlooked. Boichuk's work can be seen both as a strand in the modernist exploration of form and a foil to the avant-garde's aesthetic of rupture.[3] In short, he was a product both of the national revival and the contemporary art movement, and searched throughout his career for forms that would draw upon ancient roots but still speak to a modern viewer.

Boichuk sought epic, monumental images representing Ukraine's princely past (suggesting lost statehood and majesty), the peasantry (signifying the eternal, natural world), and ideal characters (archetypes of devotion, mercy and industry). The purpose was to develop a concept of Ukrainianness that embraced the past, present and future. Accordingly, his aesthetic of harmony, synthesis and moderation shunned the eccentric or accidental in favor of the significant, representative, and unchanging. His quest was for the essential that lay beneath the shimmering surface of modernity.

There was another important feature to Boichuk's art. He had been born into a peasant family, and endeavored to elevate village culture by celebrating its life-affirming qualities, and affirming the wisdom encoded in its traditions and relationship to nature. His village roots not only accounted for his interest in the arts and crafts movement, but also explain his strong social conscience and ecological sensitivity.

After living through the revolution years of 1917–21, Boichuk would witness the industrialization and modernization drive of the 1920s and 1930s. In these decades the bolshevik attitude to the peasantry could be characterized by two beliefs. The first was "victory" of the city over the village. The second, which became increasingly prominent in the 1930s, was

3 For Boichuk's relationship to modernism and the avant-garde see Shkandrij, 1994.

the primacy of Russian culture over Ukrainian. In the minds of some bolshevik leaders and many urbanites the two dogmas were connected.

In the political context of the late 1920s and early 1930s many observers felt that the avant-garde's aesthetic of rupture, with its celebration of mastery over human biology, nature, the countryside, and national particularity, spoke a dangerous language of hegemony, subordination and control. Bolshevik leaders in the 1930s turned this language against the countryside. Raymond Williams has spoken of "certain metropolitan intellectuals" who had inherited "a long contempt [...] of the peasant, the boor, the rural clown [...] How many socialists, for example, have refused to pick up that settling archival sentence about the 'idiocy of rural life'?" (Williams 1973, 36). It was in large degree the easy collusion between communist industrialization and a Russian imperial reflex that set the stage for the horrors of the 1930s. At that time the assumption that Russian, "advanced" urban society was beseiged by "rural idiocy" and "barbarism" was used to justify the violence against rural and non-Russian populations. This explains why the war against "reactionary" Ukrainian intellectuals in the 1930s coincided with a war against the Ukrainian village. The fact that so many Western intellectuals for many decades avoided discussing, or even registering, these events is a reminder of how powerful the bolshevik propaganda campaign was and how deeply rooted were prejudices against peasantry. Because Boichuk's aesthetic challenged people to see the world through different eyes, his works and School suffered destruction and for many decades was expunged from cultural memory.

The School existed in three separate periods: in Paris (1907–11), prewar Lviv (1911–14), and postwar Kyiv (1918–36).[4] In Paris, after attending the Académie Vitti (1907), and the Académie Ranson (1908), he created his own studio in 1909, which was attended by Mykola Kasperovych from the Chernihiv region and the three Sophias from Saint Petersburg: Nalepinska (whom he later married), Segno and Baudouin de Courtenay. They had recently arrived after completing their studies in Munich. Soon afterwards they were joined by Helena Szramm, Janina Lewakowska, Olga Shaginian, Yevhen Bachynskyi, and Yosyp Pelenskyi. The School exhibited in the Salon d'Automne in 1909 and the Salon des Indépendants in 1910. At the end of 1910 Boichuk returned to Lviv.

4 For an overview of his life and art see Ripko and Prystalenko, 1991.

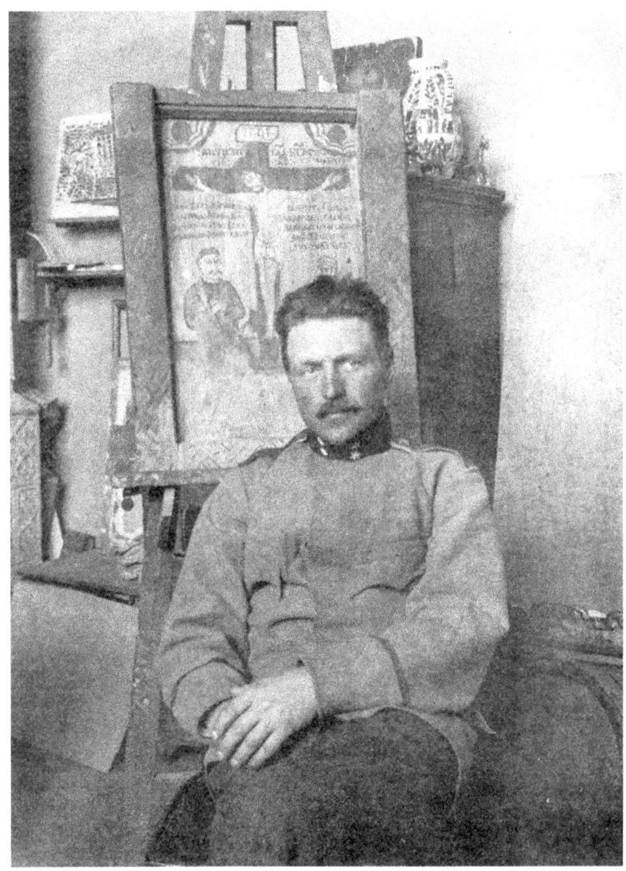

Mykhailo Boichuk in the restoration studio at the Lviv National Museum, 1911–12.

In Lviv societal expectations for him were formidable. He was seen as a chosen son, destined to produce a civic art of enormous didactic value for the national movement. Metropolitan Sheptytskyi commissioned him and Kasperovych to produce a series of paintings in the Chapel of the Holy Ghost, in the Cantors' Residence of St. George's Cathedral in Lviv. The icons *Prophet Isaiah* and *The Last Supper* were made by Boichuk for the chapel interior in 1911–13. He created idealized images that personified the national character, stressing its spiritual vitality, moral uprightness, dignity and sincerity. The director of the National Museum, Ilarion Svientsitskyi, offered him a position as icon restorer, which Boichuk accepted. Together with Kasperovych and Nalepinska he worked on a number of icons dating from the fifteenth to the seventeenth centuries in the museum's collections.

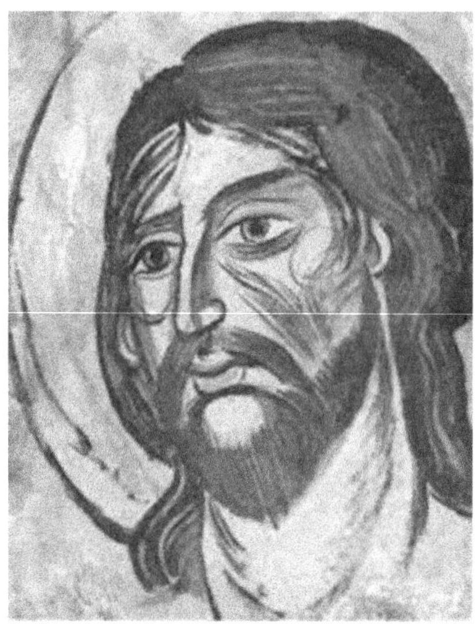

Mykhailo Boichuk. *Head of the Savior*, 1910s.

In 1917, when Mykhailo Hrushevskyi and the Central Rada created a Ukrainian State Academy of Arts, Boichuk was selected to lead the studio of monumental painting.[5] The Academy officially opened on December 5, 1917 (November 22 according to the old-style calendar).

Given this earlier history the involvement with the Soviet regime requires some explanation. The regime gave commissions to artists and purchased their work, in this way saving many from hunger. Its relationship with artists was defined by the need to integrate their work into propaganda campaigns, which soon became a way of life in the new society. The state enlisted artists to produce a new visual language, a sense of cultural revival, and to stimulate political support within the population. The Boichuk School could only compromise and retreat from its original principles. It was gradually compelled to work within the framework of the new "class" ideology, to select images and themes dictated by the Bolshevik Party for the decoration of streets, squares and architectural objects during revolutionary festivals, the painting of agit-trains and agit-ships, and the

5 Fedor Krychevsky, the elected president, headed the Studio of Historical and Scenic Painting, Engraving and Sculpture; Oleksandr Murashko, portrait painting; Mykhailo Zhuk, decorative painting; Vasyl Krychevsky, Ukrainian architectural and folk arts; Abram Manevych, decorative landscape; Mykola Burachek, lyrical landscape and lithography; Heorhii (Hryhorii) Narbut, graphic art. Boichuk's studio was to teach religious painting, mosaic, fresco, and icon painting.

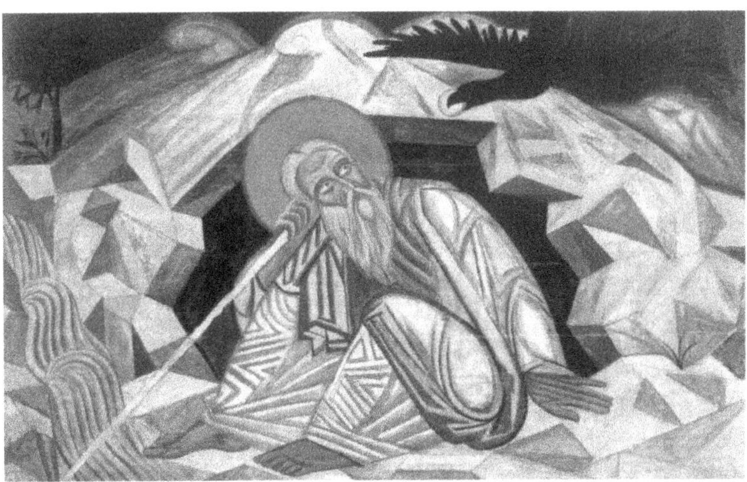

Mykhailo Boichuk. *Prophet Isaiah*, 1912–13.

reproduction of countless posters on topical issues. Boichuk used every opportunity to develop the practical work of his students. Oksana Pavlenko recalls that he called upon students to regard this kind of work not as a "distraction" that interfered with the study process, but as a required practicum aimed at strengthening their theoretical knowledge

Early in 1919 his students prepared the Kyiv Opera Theater for the First Congress of Regional Executive Committee Representatives. Numerous large tableaux decorated the building externally and internally, celebrating the event in brightly colored, allegorical subject-matter generally taken from village life. These propagandistic paintings on boards were in practice the first public exhibition of Boichuk's Kyiv School, which was linked to the earlier one in Paris in its general conception and formal principles, but focused more attention on scenes from the daily life of contemporary society. Some idea of the paintings can be gleaned from an examination of surviving sketches and black-and-white reproductions of tableaux by Taisa Tsymlova, Maria Trubetska, Padalka and Tymofii Boichuk.[6]

In the Spring of 1919, Boichuk's students decorated the premises of the Lutsk Army Barracks.[7] Fourteen thematic compositions, some in an ornamental framework, and two figures—a woman in traditional Ukrainian dress, symbolizing the revolution, and a Cossack, her

6 The sketches were obtained by Oksana Pavlenko from the sculptor F. Balavensky and donated by her to the Zaporizhia Art Museum. Some black and white reproductions of the art were published in Khmuryi 1932.

7 They were destroyed during a renovation which in 1922 demolished the rooms.

protector—illuminated the walls of rooms, staircases and arches. The political slogans, which had been commissioned, were transformed by the artists into accessible subject-matter: the collective *Workers Beating the Hydra of Counter-Revolution*, *The Internationale*, *The Red and the White*, *The Demonstration*, Tymofii Boichuk's *The Red Army Camp* and Tsymlova's *The Workers*. Students were encouraged to rework the vocabulary of folk painting with which they were familiar. Accordingly Tymofii Boichuk produced *By the Apple Tree*, *Ploughing*, and *From the Meadow*, Padalka produced *Return from the Fields*, and Uliana Horban produced *Women in a Field*, while the entire collective produced *Cutting of Bread*. The color scheme, Ukrainian character-types, clothing, ornaments, use of humor, and epigraphs echoed vernacular sources.

Life in the Academy of Arts was difficult. Pavlenko later recalled "sitting in the studio, painting, to the accompaniment of heavy cannon-fire [...] the street seemed to have been swept clean by some gigantic broom—not a person anywhere. And one would just continue painting." Food shortages made the physical survival of each student a concern: "On one occasion, Dmytro, the middle Boichuk brother, brought a sack of wheat from home. We soaked it until it swelled, ground some poppyseed for flavor, and that's how Boichuk fed us" (Cherevatenko 1987, 370, 372). Illness and deprivation caused the death of Taisa Tsymlova, Oleksandr Lozovskyi and Tymofii Boichuk.

It was in these years that Boichuk produced several posters, two of which have survived: *Shevchenko Celebration* and *Bring Presents for the Red Army*.[8] After that his integration into Soviet art proceeded rapidly. Early in 1921 he received a commission to decorate a Kharkiv theater for the Fifth All-Ukrainian Congress of Soviets that was to take place on March 2. He set out from Kyiv with his students on a trip that took almost two weeks because of frequent stoppages during which the group would cut wood to feed the train's steam engine. When they reached Kharkiv there was only enough time to hurriedly produce several slogans and ornaments.

Then in mid-1921, during their final practicum year at the Academy, Sedliar, Pavlenko and Ivanchenko came to Mezhyhiria to restore a ceramics factory. Living in penury, with little equipment and few instructors, they spent months of hard work setting up the facility.[9] Their vision was to make

---

8 These posters are now held in the National Art Museum of Ukraine (NKhMU).

9 In 1919 an initiative had been put forward to reorganize the Myrhorod School of Ceramics into an Institute. As a result, the Hlynske Ceramic School was reorganized with Lev Kramarenko as its new director, and early in 1920 was transferred from Hlynske to ancient Mezhyhiria (now Novi Petrivtsi), a village situated on a high bank of the Dnipro about thirty kilometres north of Kyiv, near Vyshhorod. In the years 1798 to

Mezhyhiria a school of industrial arts producing both artists and technologists of ceramic manufacture. Early in 1922 they began producing decorated tableware of majolica in designs that appealed to the tastes of the mass consumer. In September 1922, the first exhibition, containing more than a thousand products, took place in Kyiv, featuring dippers, dishes, plates, pots, wheel- and barrel-shaped jugs, candle-holders, pipes, toys, whistles, and other items. The Ukrainian agency, Zovnishtorh, began ordering works for export, paying in food products, which at the time served as currency. Ivanchenko later recalled that this enabled them to survive the famine of 1922: "Zovnishtorh began periodically sending us either a large sack of rye flour or grain, or a barrel of fish oil, and we began to eat rye dumplings with fish fat."[10]

In 1925 the Boichuk School was instrumental in creating ARMU (the Association of Revolutionary Art of Ukraine).[11] In public debates Sedliar, the organization's main theorist, maintained that the creation of Soviet artistic culture could only be achieved through the study, development and elevation of Ukrainian artistic forms. ARMU's main opponent in these debates was AKhRR (the Association of Artists of Revolutionary Russia), which denounced formal experimentation and refused to recognize contemporary and past European achievements. By 1929 a campaign of criticism against Boichuk was coordinated with the overall attack upon the Ukrainian intelligentsia and village. The baiting of Boichuk began early that year on the pages of *Vechirnii Kyiv* (Evening Kyiv) and soon spilled out into public discussions.[12] Eventually Boichuk was arrested in the mid-thirties and shot in 1937, along with the other leading members of his School.

This background enables one to see the bolshevik propaganda posters of 1919–21 as the products of a transitional time. The difficult circumstances and ambiguous situations in which artists worked, along with the compromises they had to make, are reflected in the tensions and subtexts that the viewer can read into these works.

1874 its rich variety of clays had served a factory that produced household items famous for their quality, their relief ornaments, their malachite and turquoise glazes, and their yellow to violet spectrum of colors. The old equipment had been sold off in 1880, leaving nothing behind.

10 Pavlo Ivanchenko's letter dated 4 November 1988 was addressed to Nelli Prystalenko and was in the latter's archive.

11 ARMU included some of the best known figures in Ukrainian art, including Bohomazov, Yermilov, Khvostenko, Meller, Viktor Palmov, Andrii Taran, Pavlo Holubiatnykov, Vasyl Kasiian, Bernard Kratko, and Semen Prokhorov. Boichuk's students were the most influential part of ARMU. They defined the direction of its work and insisted upon the importance of understanding social psychology.

12 See Shkandrij 1992, 163–68.

Jews in the Artistic and Cultural Life of Ukraine in the 1920s[1]

Jews have lived on the territory of today's Ukraine for over a millennium. Their interaction in the eleventh century with the local population was already recorded in one of Kyiv's earliest written records, the *Paterik* of the Kyivan Caves Monastery. Throughout this long history the Jewish and Ukrainian communities were not always "two solitudes," as sometimes described. In fact, at various points in history they were allies in the struggle for civil rights and national emancipation. This was particularly true of the years preceding the February 1917 Revolution, when the Ukrainian and Jewish intelligentsias worked together politically, motivated by the realization that both peoples "had to mend their mutual relations, because circumstances had dictated that they were to live side by side" (Goldelman 1921, 5). When the Russian Empire fell, the Ukrainian government (first the Central Rada and then the Ukrainian National Republic) proclaimed and built national-cultural autonomy for Jews. The Jewish population was given freedom in matters of self-government, education and culture. A minister (called a secretary) for nationality affairs was established, with three vice-ministers for Jewish, Russian and Polish affairs. After the declaration of independence, the vice-minister for Jewish affairs became a full minister responsible for community self-government, education and culture. Even Ukrainian banknotes included wording in Yiddish.

The UNR hoped that support for Jewish education would help to counterbalance the influence of Russian culture, which had been dominant in

1 This article first appeared in *Jewish Life and Times: A Collection of Essays*, Vol. 9, edited by Dan Stone and Annalee Greenberg, 85–99 (Winnipeg: Jewish Heritage Centre of Western Canada, 2009).

urban centers for close to two centuries, during which time the Ukrainian written word had been banned. Two networks of Jewish secular schools were created, one using Yiddish, the other Hebrew. Jewish research sections were created within Ukrainian academic institutions. Private, religious Jewish organizations, such as the heders, Talmud-Torahs, and yeshivas, were not subordinated to the Ministry. It is worth recalling that in 1917 most Jews supported the Ukrainian government. They were "united on the question of the right of the Ukrainian people to determine their ultimate political destiny" and delighted that parliament showed "more willingness to grant concessions to Jews than had any other constituent assembly in history" (Margolin 1922, 18). In 1917 Yosef Shekhtman, one of Jabotinsky's closest allies, published *Ievrei ta ukraintsi* (Jews and Ukrainians) in which he wrote:

> Who if not we, children of an oppressed people, are capable of understanding the feelings and sufferings of a neighbor, who along with us has endured the cruelty and abuse of the old regime! We have been united by common aspirations and common goals. The moment has arrived when these aspirations are close to realization. Our common path is still a long one, but we believe, that a free Ukrainian people will support us on this path! (Quoted in Kleiner 2000, 61)

One important reason for this alliance lay in the fact that Ukrainians formed a minority of the urban population. Realizing that neither the Polish nor the Russian minorities were well disposed toward it, the new government looked for allies in the Jewish minority. Several commentators have described the pervasive optimistic faith in the fruitfulness of the Ukrainian-Jewish accord (Vynnychenko 1920, 297–8; Goldelman 1967, 21). The Ukrainian leadership viewed the parallel development of Jewish cultural autonomy and Ukrainian national-territorial autonomy as a linchpin in its political strategy. Loyalty to the territory and its people, not to Ukrainian nationality or ancestry, was proclaimed as the new government's principal requirement of the residents of Ukraine by Mykhailo Hrushevskyi, the first head of state. With the declaration of that principle, "Hrushevsky was laying the cornerstone of Ukraine's proposed relations with its national minoritites" (Plokhy 2005, 77). Prominent Jewish figures served in the government, among them Solomon Goldelman, Arnold Margolin, who was vice-minister for Foreign Affairs, Moisei Zilberfarb, who was minister for Jewish Affairs, and the historian Mark Vishnitzer, who was a secretary of the English mission (Margolin 1922, 18–9). Jews were also part of the press and secretarial sections of the government missions to France and the Netherlands. In November 1918 Margolin personally read "proclamations issued by the government strongly condemning pogroms, explaining to the people that the Jews were fellow-citizens and brothers who were helping in the evolution of the Ukrainian state, and to whom the fullest rights were due" (Margolin, 19). He tendered his resignation in March 1919 because although he "was aware that the government was not to blame for the pogroms," as a Jew, he could not retain an official position in a country where his "bretheren were being massacred" (Margolin, 19). When asked to stay on and work abroad as a diplomat for the UNR, he accepted, attending international conferences and serving as the government's representative in London. The Folkspartei, Poale Zion, and the United Bund worked with the Jewish ministry. However, events leading up to the defeat of the UNR, and, in particular, the appalling wave of pogroms in 1919, in which demoralized units ostensibly loyal to the UNR participated, badly damaged this rapprochement.

Under Soviet rule in the years 1923–28 the policy of Ukrainization or indigenization—a concession that the bolsheviks had to make to gain support in Ukraine—was accompanied by a great surge of interest in Ukrainian culture, a fact that shocked Russian urbanites, who had expected Ukrainians to willingly dissolve their identity in Russian. Instead they witnessed a great, spontaneous cultural revolution. Ten thousand people gave "poet" as their occupation during a census in Kyiv. In 1927 the newspaper *Kultura i pobut* (Culture and Life) claimed there ware 6,000 dramatic groups in Ukraine serving 12 million spectators. In the following year the journal *Nove mystetstvo* (New Art) informed that 70,000 people were involved in amateur theatricals and over 5,000 laid claim to being dramatists (Makaryk 2004, 143).

The indigenization policy allowed for the continued development of not only Ukrainian, but also of Jewish secular cultural life, including the formation of Jewish institutions and structures. In the pre-revolutionary and immediate post-revolutionary years, Jews made up the second-largest urban population in Ukraine, second only to the Russian. In Kyiv, for example, where before 1903 Jews had practically been forbidden permanent residence, their numbers grew from 50,792 (10.84 percent) in 1910, to 117,041 (21.04 percent) in 1919, and to 128,041 (31.95 percent) in 1923 (Khiterer 1999, 143) Whereas other populations fled the city for the villages during the Revolution and its aftermath, or emigrated, the Jews often stayed. By 1926 they made up 26 percent of the city's population. The Soviet Ukrainian government, like the UNR before it, sought the support of this population and continued, in modified form, the UNR's policy of developing

Jewish institutions and cultural life, also as part of the effort to win over the local population. The government in Kyiv hoped for Jewish support in the Ukrainization movement it had initiated. Jewish newspapers, libraries, clubs, and theaters were created. Although religious schools were banned, national schools for Jews were at first continued. The authorities set up a network of Jewish secondary institutions (technicums, or professional-technical schools). All this came to an end, however, in the late twenties, when Stalin came to power and declared local nationalism (as opposed to Russian "great-power chauvinism") the "main enemy." This became the signal to curtail both the Ukrainization movement and the movement for Jewish cultural autonomy.

Nonetheless, in the twenties, as a result of the indigenization policy, Ukrainians and Jews became cultural allies. Interaction was intense as parallel institutions were created and parallel tasks embarked upon. A flowering of both Ukrainian and Yiddish literatures and cultures took place in Ukraine in this decade. Relations between Ukrainian and Yiddish writers were often cordial and close. Skuratovskyi has described the two literatures as "pointedly loyal in their mutual relations" (Skuratovskyi 1998, 54). Some important friendships were forged. For example, the two poets Leib Kvitko and Pavlo Tychyna worked together from 1926. Kvitko was also close to Andrii Chuzhyi (pseudonym of Andrii Antonovych Storozhuk) and the Kharkiv journal *Avanhard* (Avant-Garde). Der Nister (Pinchus Kahanovich) was a close friend of the writers Yurii Smolych and Maik Yohansen. The famous actor Solomon Mikhoels and a number of Jewish theater directors worked with the theater director Les Kurbas.

Smolych has pointed out that many Jews in the 1920s were "native speakers" of Ukrainian. They came from Ukrainian villages and towns, lived and grew up among Ukrainians, were born of parents who knew only Yiddish and Ukrainian. If they knew Russian, they did so badly. It was, writes Smolych, only the later, post-Stalin generation of Jews that grew up without speaking Ukrainian and was prejudiced toward it: "Along the way," he writes, "we lost a good colleague in our cultural process" (Smolych 1990, 161). During the twenties many Jews played prominent roles in the creation of a modern Ukrainian culture and identity, making major contributions to literature, art, cinema, and scholarship, "creating a home" for themselves in the culture and simultaneously helping to define the culture itself as diverse and complex. Olena Kurylo, for example, was a leading linguist who explored Ukrainian dialects and folklore. Osyp Hermaize was a leading historian. Abram Leites, Samiilo Shchupak, Volodymyr Koriak, and Yarema Aizenshtok were important critics. The last worked on the complete edition of Shevchenko's *Diary*, wrote on Shevchenko and folklore, and produced studies of Ukrainian classics such as Kvitka, Koliarevskyi, Kotsiubynskyi, and Franko. Accused of Ukrainian nationalism in the thirties, he was forced to move to Leningrad (Revutsky 1985, 164–65). Important figures of Jewish origin entered and made a name for themselves in Ukrainian literature in the 1920s, among them Leonid Pervomaiskyi (Illia Hurevych), Sava Holovanivskyi, Ivan (Izrail) Kulyk, Aron Kopstein, and Raisa Troianker. These and other Jewish writers contributed heavily to a number of literary journals, in particular *Molodniak* (Youth), the organ of the Komsomol or communist youth organization, and Hart (Tempering), which defined itself as the organ of proletarian writers.

Many talented individuals of Jewish origin participated in the Ukrainian film industry. Oleksandr Voznesenskyi, who was also know as the writer Ilia Rents, in 1918–23 created a Kyiv film studio called "Art Screen." Arrested in the thirties, he died in Kazakhstan in 1939. Mykhailo Kapchynskyi headed the Odesa film studios, which began construction in 1922. He reorganized film theaters, helping to create the cinema boom of the twenties. By the middle of the decade Ukrainian film production, headed by the All-Ukrainian Film Photo-Cinema Management (*VUFKU*) was enjoying rapid growth. In the years 1925–30 it produced outstanding films and laid the foundation of a national industry. By the end of the decade the Odesa and Kyiv factories expected to produce a hundred films each year. A push was made for films that would be appreciated by the large Jewish minority of 1.5 million in Ukraine, and also to make films about Jews for the Ukrainian public. As a result, a range of films describing Jewish life were made. Screen versions of the works of Sholem Aleichem, who was canonized by the regime as an "official" classic of Jewish literature, depicted the poverty of Jews in the Russian Empire. Other films depicted Jewish life under the Soviet regime, and propagandistic films were also made about enemies of the regime. *Tini Belvedera* (Shadows of Belvedere, 1928), for example, tells the story of a love affair between an aristocratic Polish officer and a poor Jewish girl, depicting aristocratic Poland as antisemitic. All films on Jewish themes were stopped in 1930, when *VUFKU*'s autonomous status was liquidated.

Perhaps the most important Jewish organization in Ukraine was the Kultur-Lige. It represented, more than any other institution, the face of Jewish cultural autonomy. Headquartered in Kyiv, in the years 1918–25 it actively promoted Jewish cultural life, publishing, organizing musical and theatrical performances, art exhibitions, an art school, a school of music, libraries, museums, university courses, and kindergartens. Created in January 1918 in Kyiv under the UNR government in order to develop Yiddish language culture, the organization initially emphasized the creation of evening classes and clubs. By the end of 1918 it had 120 branches throughout Ukraine. More branches were later created in Russia, Lithuania, Romania, and Poland. Kyiv's role in the Eastern European Jewish world became particularly important at this time because of the isolation and relative decline of cultural activity in such traditional centers of Yiddish culture as Warsaw and Vilnius during the First World War. Kyiv also attracted some of the most active figures in Jewish culture and politics as they escaped from Petersburg and Moscow in the wake of the Bolshevik Revolution. They contributed to the flourishing growth in the Ukrainian capital of Yiddish-language culture in education, theater, book publishing, and art. The main organizers and literary figures in the Kyiv Kultur-Lige were David Bergelson, David Gofstein, Moishe Litvakov, Yokhezkel Dobrushin, Der Nister (Pinchus Kahanovich), and Nakhman Maizil. Others included Perets Markish, Leib (Lev) Kvitko, Nakhum Oislender, and Lypa Reznik. In the mid-twenties a younger group appeared that included Itsyk (Itzik) Fefer, Itsyk (Itzik) Kipnis, Noiakh Lurie, Zinovia Tokachev, and Shloimo Cherniavskyi. Since it grouped together leading individuals from a number of Jewish political organizations, the Kultur-Lige also acted as a kind of inter-party association. It was an independent organization from 1918 until 1920. However, after Soviet rule had been imposed, its central committee was dismissed by a decree of 17 December 1920 and replaced with communists who saw it as merely an instrument of Soviet rule. In 1924 all the organization's educational institutions were subordinated to the government, although the publishing house survived until 1930.

The organization was committed to preserving and furthering the autonomous national life of Jews as a diasporic people by developing a contemporary Jewish culture in Yiddish, which at the time was the conversational language of most East European and American Jews. The Kultur-Lige saw the Yiddish language not simply as a means of communication, but as a unified cultural phenomenon, the product of a collective national creativity. It aimed at developing a modern Yiddish culture that would be a synthesis of the old and new, the national and universal, a culture of the whole Jewish diaspora "from Moscow to New York and from London to Johannesburg."

The artistic section was particularly successful. Formed in July 1918, it promoted a "Jewish style" in art, one that fused leanings toward abstraction with the devices of folk art. It included Boris (Barukh) Aronson, Mark (Moisei) Epstein, Issakhar-Ber Rybak, Aleksandr (Oleksandr) Tyshler, Yosyf Elman, Isaak Rabichev, Solomon Nikritin, Yudel Ioffe, Isaak Pailes,

Mordekai (Maks) Kaganovich, Nisson Shifrin, and Sara Shor. They were soon joined by El (Lazar) Lissitzky, Yosyf Chaikov, Polina Khentova, and Mark Sheikhel, who arrived from Petersburg and Moscow. Abram Manevych joined early in 1919. In spite of all the difficulties posed by the political situation, the period 1918–21 was the most productive. Artists decorated theater studios of the Kultur-Lige, participated in discussions on the nature of national art in the Jewish Literary-Artistic Club. Chaikov and Rabinovich taught drawing and sculpture in the Kyiv Jewish High School of the Kultur-Lige. In 1919, a Jewish art and theater studio was opened in Kyiv which continued to exist as a part of the Kultur-Lige until 1924, when it became the Jewish Art-Industrial School. With Mark Epstein as director, it was one of three Jewish art institutes in the world—more leftist than the Bezalel Arts Academy in Jerusalem, and more focused on the national tradition in art than the Educational Alliance Art School in New York. Children's books were published in the Kultur-Lige's own printing house during the 1918–20 period and were illustrated by artists such as El Lissitzky, Natan Rybak, Sara Shor, and Mark Chagall. These illustrations are today considered some of the best of Jewish book art in the twentieth century. An exhibition of the artistic section opened in Kyiv on February 8, 1920 and a second exhibition in April–May, 1922. A museum exhibition opened on September 10, 1921. Influenced by Exter, whose studio most had attended, these artists showed a love of geometrical, flattened forms. They contributed to a variant of Ukrainian cubo-futurism that was less static and monochrome than the French. Like the art of Ukrainian modernists and avant-gardists, their work combined cubism with the archaic, and gravitated towards simplified monumental sculptural forms.

The dream of the Kultur-Lige artists during this period was the creation of a new Jewish national art, one that would "fuse Jewish artistic traditions and the achievements of the European avant-garde" (Kazovsky 2003, 91). To this end, they explored ethnography and folk art. They were inspired by the contemporary rediscovery of folk creativity in Ukraine, which owed much to the great ethnographic expeditions through the Pale of Settlement directed by S. An-sky (Shlome Zanvla Rappoport) in 1912–14. In 1913 Nathan Altman copied ancient tombstones in Jewish cemeteries, while in 1915–16 Lissitzky and Rybak studied wooden synagogues along the Dnipro, making about 200 drawings of their interiors for the Jewish Historical-Ethnographic Society. Solomon Yudovyn had participated in ethnographic expeditions in which he painted tombstones and ritual objects. Elman, Chaikov and Kratko had studied the designs on Jewish silverware. This work allowed the artists to discover the shtetl as a distinctive topos in art. Jewish primitive art and children's art became topics of special investigation. One commentator has written: "*Lubok* and gingerbread figures, toys and stencils—all these offer a complete program of contemporary applied aesthetics" (Efros 1918, 301; quoted in Kazovsky 2003, 87) Like Ukrainian artists, they linked the new abstract art to what they described as their own "national sense of form" (Rybak and Aronson 1919, 123; quoted in Kazovsky 2003, 91). The remarkable graphic art produced for the Kultur-Lige's publications testifies to the surge of creativity in the years 1918–22.[2] In these years of intensive work, El Lissitzky illustrated around ten Yiddish publications, while Rybak worked as a book illustrator and a decorator for Jewish theaters.

The influence of this Kyiv milieu was soon felt abroad. Aronson, the son of Kyiv's chief rabbi, who had studied set-design in Exter's studio in 1917–18, subsequently worked in over a hundred productions in the United States. Shifrin and Tyshler, who also studied in Exter's studio, moved to Moscow in the twenties, where they became well-known theatrical designers. A number of artists emigrated to Europe. Issakhar-Ber Rybak moved to Berlin and then Paris in the twenties, where he published albums of lithographs (in 1923 and 1924) that brought him fame. The images in these albums are of the Ukrainian shtetl and its Jewish figures. After a visit to study the Jewish agricultural colonies in Ukraine, he published an album on them (Paris, 1926), and his final album (1932) was based on his reminiscences.

There was also a large contingent of Jewish artists in the largest and most important Ukrainian school of the twenties, that of Boichuk. The need to combine the international with the national, the universal with the folkloric, was common to both Jewish and Ukrainian artists and explains the presence of artists such as Nisson Shifrin, Emanuil Shekhtman and Teofil Fraierman in Boichuk's School. Their works often depicted Jewish life in small towns and villages. The search for types (sometimes even archetypes) was also a common interest of Boichukists (such as Antonina Ivanova, Vasyl Sedliar, Oksana Pavlenko), and for artists close to the Kultur-Lige (such as Rybak and Mark Epstein). These portraits today constitute a gallery of types, a record of the appearance and behavior of Ukrainian and Jewish villagers and townspeople.

It has generally gone unrecognized that the brief but powerful artistic ferment of 1919–21 made Kyiv the center of both a Ukrainian and a Jewish avant-garde art that radiated an international influence. Moreover,

2 For reproductions of these works see Kazovsky 2007.

throughout the 1920s both Ukrainian and Jewish avant-gardists continued to produce significant work.

As has already been suggested, one reason for the remarkable artistic achievements in Ukraine in the immediate pre- and post-revolutionary years was the Kyiv Art School, which from 1901–20 developed many great talents, among them Exter, Meller, Kavaleridze, Archipenko, Bohomazov, Manevych, Pevzner (Antoine Pevsner), Tyshler, Epstein, Aristarkh Lentulov, Isaak Rabinovich, Solomon Nikritin, Issakhar-Ber Rybak, and Anatolii Petrytskyi. Another was the creation in 1917–18 by the Ukrainian People's Republic of a Ukrainian Academy of Arts. Although this institution went through two name changes under Soviet rule, it continued to exert a strong influence on artistic life in Ukraine throughout this period.[3] A third was the Kultur-Lige. Although, after its Sovietization in 1920, some prominent figures left, the organization continued to exist until 1925 and the art school it created survived into the thirties.

The subsequent fate of both Jewish and Ukrainian artists of the avant-garde is in almost all cases a tragic story. The Jewish intelligentsia was split between those who were more concerned with promoting cultural and national values, and those who gave pride of place to political-ideological issues. The most important figures in the Kyiv Kultur-Lige, for example, leaned in the former direction—toward the spreading of secular Jewish culture in Ukraine. They were challenged by the second group. One historian has written: "Those members of the Kyiv group who had nothing to express but their ideological orthodoxy looked for support from the so-called Jewish sections [*evsektsii*—national sections of the various communist organizations] and acted in their name, according to their instructions" (Petrovskii 1996, 239). When the communist groups demanded complete subordination to themselves, the conflict between the two tendencies among Jewish intellectuals in Kyiv flared up. Nakhman Maizelson and other leaders left for Warsaw. Many activists (for example, most of the artistic section) moved to Moscow. Lev Kvitko and Perets Markish left for Germany; David Gofstein, the oldest and best known poet of the Kyiv group, went to Palestine. Disillusioned by the situation abroad, most soon returned to Ukraine, where they shared the same fate as the rest of the Ukrainian intelligentsia. Many were killed in the thirties. Some who survived the purges, such as Lev Kvitko and thirteen other members of the Jewish Anti-Fascist Committee, were murdered by the KGB in 1952.

3 The Ukrainian State Academy of Arts was created in 1917. It was renamed the Kyiv Institute of Plastic Arts in 1922, then renamed the Kyiv Art Institute in 1924.

Although the Soviet government made attempts in the 1920s to deal with antisemitism, its own fierce anti-religious agitation, which specifically targeted Judaism and Zionism, only served to exacerbate the problem. In the post-revolutionary years synagogues were forcibly closed and Judaism was branded as the most reactionary of religions. The struggle between Hebrew and Yiddish was presented as a class war. In August 1919 the bolsheviks prohibited the teaching of Hebrew (Orlianskii 2000, 43). In June 1919, a law was passed liquidating all Zionist organizations, as well as all Jewish party, political, professional, and cultural organizations created under the UNR. Immediately afterwards the confiscation of the money and property of local Jewish communities began. In spite of, or perhaps because of this, the growth of Zionist parties mushroomed. Show trials against the "Jewish counter-revolution" began in 1922 and sentenced over a thousand individuals to prison terms or Siberian exile. The anti-religious campaign was spearheaded in 1921–22 by the Jewish sections of the communist party. A strong reaction to these measures made the sections retreat temporarily, but they went on the offensive again in the late twenties and early thirties. Severe limitations on expressions of religious life were made law in 1929, and all non-government organizations were liquidated in the 1930s. The last synagogue in Kyiv was closed in 1936. Many of the closings have been preserved on newsreel in Ukrainian archives (Khiterer 2002, 10).

Under Soviet rule, all Jewish educational institutions were subordinated to the People's Commissariat of Education of the Ukrainian SSR. In the mid-twenties and early thirties Soviet authorities set up a network of Jewish secondary institutions (technicums, professional-technical schools) all of which were shut down in the second half of the thirties. By that time the policy of supporting Jewish schools was associated with nationalism.

Most Jewish political parties and organizations that had been formed in the revolutionary years or under the UNR were liquidated in the twenties. Almost all underground Zionist organizations were destroyed. Only the Jewish sections of the communist party were allowed to exist in the twenties in order to build a loyal communist Jewish culture in Yiddish. After 1930, this initiative was not supported by the government. At that time many members of the Jewish sections were treated with suspicion because their non-communist affiliations prior to 1919.

Many Ukrainians in the Soviet leadership in Kyiv had also held non-communist affiliations prior to 1919. In the twenties these figures frequently supported Ukrainization, saw Jewish culture as an ally, and supported Jewish scholarship. For example, in 1918 the newly created Ukrainian Academy of Sciences formed two research centers for the collection and study of Jewish materials: the Jewish Historical-Archaeographical Commission (1919–29) headed by Ilia Galant, and the Jewish section at the National Library of Ukraine. They continued their work under Soviet rule. In 1928–29, when the Society for the Spreading of Enlightenment among Jews in Russia (Obshchestvo dlia rasprostranenia prosveshcheniia mezhdu evreiami v Rossii—OPE, 1863–1929) and the Jewish Historical-Ethnographic Society (Evreiskoe istoriko-etnograficheskoe obshchestvo—EIEO, 1908–30) were closed down, their valuable collections were sent from Leningrad to the National Library in Kyiv.

At the end of the twenties the Institute of Jewish Proletarian Culture in Kyiv (1929–36) became the main research center for Jewish history and culture in the USSR. By the mid-thirties its library and archives had 100,000 items. In 1936 it was told to transfer its holdings to the National Library in Kyiv. Evacuated to Ufa during the Second World War, this collection was returned to Kyiv but not made available to readers. It contained unique collection of folk music and recordings made by S. An-sky during his famous ethnographic expeditions (1911–13), and by Yu. Engel and M. Berehovsky made between 1911 and 1948. In 1950 the Soviet government closed the collection and destroyed the catalogues. Until 1990 it was kept in reserve vaults, where it survived almost entirely intact thanks to the staff.

From 1929–30 the Soviet authorities began to close all non-communist academic institutions, and to throw out of work all academic experts of pre-revolutionary training. Soon afterwards, in the thirties, the pro-communist Jewish scientific organizations were also shut down. The only exception was the Cabinet for the Study of Soviet Jewish Literature, Language and Folklore (later called the Cabinet of Jewish Culture) in the Academy of Sciences of Ukraine, which survived until 1949.

The preconditions for an extended Ukrainian–Jewish dialogue existed in the post-revolutionary decade, but political circumstances intervened to cut short the rapprochement. As Russian hegemony was reasserted under Stalin, the dream of an independent, albeit communist, Ukraine collapsed. Along with it died the vision of Jewish cultural autonomy. By the end of the twenties, Jews were no longer drawn into the work of Ukrainization, Jewish education and scholarship in Ukraine were liquidated, and the development of Jewish literature and culture was undermined. The achievements of Jewish artists and writers in the 1920s is now being researched by a new generation of scholars.

National Modernism in Post-Revolutionary Society: Ukrainian Renaissance and Jewish Revival, 1917–30[1]

In the early twentieth century Ukrainians and Jews struggled to establish their cultural and political identity. Both were heavily concentrated in bordering empires—the Austro-Hungarian and Russian. Their increasing assertiveness at this time expressed itself in a growing number of publications, and a sharper focus in their literature and art on national self-representation and self-definition. One reflection of this assertiveness was the promotion of an identity that combined a modernist style with elements of the national tradition, a development that arguably reached its peak in Ukraine in the years immediately following the 1917 revolution. Revolutionary Ukrainian society—first the Ukrainian People's Republic (UNR) in the years 1917–20 and then the Soviet Ukrainian state from 1923—conducted a policy of Ukrainization that created what is often referred to as a "Cultural Renaissance." Simultaneously the Jewish Kultur-Lige, which was headquartered in Kyiv, pioneered a Jewish "Cultural Revival." The two movements were connected: both came out of the Ukrainian revolution, and both embraced modernism (often in its most radical, avant-garde forms). The emergence of this "national modernism" was an important aspect of post-revolutionary life, and one that offers the possibility of reconceptualizing cultural developments in the 1920s.

---

1 This is an adaptation of an article originally published in *Shatterzones of Empire: Coexistence and Violence in the German, Habsburg, Russian, and Ottoman Borderlands*, 238–48, edited by Omer Bartov and Eric D. Weitz, Indiana University Press, 2013.

The collapse of the tsarist state provided Ukrainian and Jewish intellectuals with a hitherto unavailable opportunity to explore and develop the idea of their cultural uniqueness. At the same time, the rapid pace of revolutionary transformations demanded an immediate and radical re-imagining of all identities, including the national-cultural. When Mykola Khvylovyi formed his organization *VAPLITE* (Free Academy of Proletarian Literature) and initiated the great Literary Discussion of 1925–28, his aim was to accelerate the Ukrainization process, which had been proclaimed by the Soviet Ukrainian government in 1923 and which, he felt, had stalled. But it was also to promote a new Ukrainian identity. How to achieve both these aims is the question that dominates his polemical pamphlets and fiction.[2] These writings represent one of the best expressions of the yearning for the new in the literature of the twenties and inspired a vigorous debate on the future of Ukrainian culture. Khvylovyi argued that the culture had to be modern, European, and had to chart a course of its own, independently of Russia. This last, controversial call to escape Russian cultural hegemony has attracted most critical and scholarly attention. The party's decision to close down the debate, *VAPLITE*'s dissolution, and the writer's suicide in 1933 inevitably made him a martyr in the eyes of many commentators. By contrast, his attitude toward modernism's aesthetic of rupture and renewal, and its promise of a new community has been understudied.

Khvylovyi produced daring, innovative work in the immediate post-revolutionary years, especially two collections of short stories *Syni etiudy* (Blue Etudes, 1923) and *Osin* (Autumn, 1924). They already show evidence that the nation-building imperative, especially the articulation of a new national identity, was pulling him, as it was other writers (such as Pavlo Tychyna, the major poet of these years) toward historical allusions and narratives that could serve as allegories of the nation's fate. As a result, Khvylovyi, like most other "revolutionary" writers, found himself elaborating a modernist sensibility that both rejected traditionalism and continually invented ways of including and reconfiguring within it elements of the national tradition. The ambivalent tone of these early stories emerges from attempts to reconcile rejection of the past with historical references, to balance the rational with the intuitive, and to make the urban, as opposed to the rural, the stylistic matrix of a new culture.

World revolution was linked to the dream of modernity, access to the wider world, and the triumph of justice. Many young people felt, like Lev Kopelev, that this world would have "no borders, no capitalists and no fascists

---

2 For pamphlets, see Khvylovyi, 1986. For translations into English of selected stories, see Khvylovyi, 1960.

at all," and that Moscow, Kharkiv and Kyiv "would become just as enormous, just as well built, as Berlin, Hamburg, New York," with skyscrapers; streets full of automobiles and bicycles; workers and peasants in fine clothes, wearing hats and watches; airplanes and dirigibles (Kopelev 1980, 183–84). Kopelev's picture of the future is based on the assumption that modernity would be culturally Russian, perhaps uniformly so. These sentiments were echoed by others. Benedikt Livshits has described how he thought of David Burliuk and the early futurists "who had destroyed poetical and painterly traditions and had founded a new aesthetics as stateless Martians, unconnected in any way with any nationality, much less with our planet" (Livshits 1977, 39). Khvylovyi described the early post-revolutionary years differently: "some kind of joyful alarm grips my heart. I see my descendants and see with what envy they look at me—a contemporary and eyewitness of my Eurasian renaissance. Just think, only a few years and such achievements [...] What wonderful prospects appear in the future for this country, when these courageous innovators finally overcome the inertia of the centuries" (Khvylovyi 1926, 10). It was not material but cultural achievements that inspired him, and his focus was not on some abstract borderless, geographical space, but on Ukraine ("this country') as the pathblazer of a new culture ("my Eurasian renaissance"). However, the excitement and fervor resemble Kopelev's. In his memoirs another Ukrainian writer of the twenties, Yurii Smolych, reflects this fervent faith in the arrival of the new: "This generation was called to liquidate the ruins of the war period and to create the first beginnings of the new way of life. And this took place at the break of two epochs—the destruction of the old worldly, reactionary norms and customs and the search for new customs and norms" (Smolych 1986, 384).

What fascinates in this creative excitement is the combination of the avant-gardist, revolutionary and national. A vehement rejection of the past is linked to the belief that the modern would be built on the release of long-suppressed, untapped national energies. The structure of Khvylovyi's stories is built on this kind of "argument." His characters have often emerged from the whirlwind of revolutionary ideas and find themselves thrown into confusion by the horrors of the revolution. They are dissatisfied with revolutionary society, but find no inspiration in the pre-revolutionary world, which they associate with symbolism and aestheticism, a search for self-knowledge through retreat from the world. These characters suffer from arrested inner growth. Divorced from their surroundings, they focus obsessively on a beautiful illusion, the distant future, in which, they believe, the dreams of many past generations will become reality. However, the path to this future has been blocked. The vision recedes year after year, and is eventually entirely blotted out by the corruption of urban civilization. People from the countryside who have thrown in their lot with the revolution bring freshness, innocence and idealism to the construction of revolutionary society, but soon succumb to the city's sterility and cynicism. Their vitality and excitement are extinguished. The loss of faith is caused in large part by the blocking of the national cultural movement, which authorities treat as something embarrassing, or even reactionary. As a result, Ukrainian protagonists develop a feeling of self-hatred. The same message is carried in the famous polemical pamphlets, in which Khvylovyi challenges young people to create a cultural renaissance.

There is an underlying pull of mythic structures in the stories and pamphlets: illusions are destroyed by reality, heroism is disappointed by cowardice, and idealism is stifled by cynicism. Because of this, the stories can be given allegorical or symbolic readings, to which the pamphlets hold the interpretative key. The individual who is unable to tell his story openly can be seen as the nation that is not allowed to express itself, whose dreams of cultural development have been dashed. In this way, the fictional works recount a familiar tale of national oppression and the need for emancipation, albeit in a fragmented and mysteriously allusive modernist style.

Nonetheless, the writer remained a caustic critic of conservative and populist views. He probed darkness at the heart of the village idyll, explored disturbing and anarchic forces in the human psyche, and exposed clichés such as romantic love. Like much of the literature and art of the early post-revolutionary period Khvylovyi's writings show an aversion to populism and a refusal to embrace ethnographic traditions uncritically. Inspired by a vision of a blended social and national liberation, and by the prospect of introducing a new Ukrainian culture onto the world stage, his writings draw sustenance from the palingenetic myth (the idea of rebirth, regeneration, revival) that has been widely observed in twentieth-century modernism. The crucial concept is that of genesis. Both artists and writers sought to identify key elements out of which the culture had been formed. Thus the writers who contributed to the *VAPLITE* journal and to the next journal formed by Khvylovyi, *Literaturnyi iarmarok* (Literary Marketplace, December 1928–February 1930) searched for elements of the cultural code that represented the national experience and identity as it had evolved over the centuries. They examined archetypal forms, characters, canonical images and works, and then recoded these into a new format and a new identity. Abstraction, along with the idea of investigating fundamental concepts, played an important role—whether in literature, painting, or theater. The search for the "grammatical structure" of national identity became analogous to experimentation with pure color and form in painting, or with the search for basic patterns of sound and meaning in poetry, which were also typical of the avant-garde in the twenties. It was thought that, once discovered, these basic elements could by some mysterious alchemy be transformed into a new synthesis.

Others negotiated attitudes to the past in similarly ambiguous ways. The example of art is particularly instructive. Exter's studio in Kyiv in the years 1917–20 was a good example of the modernist transformation of tradition. It blended cubo-futurism, constructivism, and folk-primitivism in innovative ways. Her interest in arts and crafts at this time led to collaboration with artists such as Yevheniia Prybylska and Nina Henke, who developed workshops in which local women mass-produced textiles and other products using patterns inspired both by folk motifs or by suprematist art. These were shown in major exhibitions in Moscow and Paris to great acclaim. Exter's studio educated many important artists, including leading Jewish figures such as Boris Aronson, Isaak Rabinovich, Nisson Shifrin, Aleksandr (Oleksandr) Tyshler, and was visited by many figures from Moscow and Petrograd who found themselves in Kyiv at the time, such as Illia Ehrenburg, Benedikt Livshits, Osip Mandelshtam, Viktor Shklovsky, and Natan Vengrov. Malevich's suprematist art can also be seen as a kind of recreation in an abstract and mystical key of the ancient and ethnographic; and Boichuk's monumentalist or neo-Byzantinist school also turned to national sources in its search for primitive, ethnographic and folk features. The Boichuk School came out of the thrilling "rediscovery" in pre-revolutionary years of the icon as not only a popular but also a sophisticated form that could be linked to cubist and avant-gardist experimentation. The artist turned to the icon and folk arts for national forms, and attempted to crystallize these traditional elements into a modern synthesis and a national style. Other artists, who were not part of the avant-garde, where also feeding this interest in the past. Heorhii Narbut and Vasyl Krychevskyi, for example, were famous for translating ornamental images into modern graphic art, particularly in book design: Narbut reworked baroque images and Krychevskyi folk art patterns. Like the "national modernist" writers grouped around Khvylovyi, they were guided by a desire to give old, often very ancient forms a new expression.

These writers and artists felt no dichotomy between "ethnic loyalty" and participation in international modernism. Their interest in the traditional aimed at uncovering its deeper generative principles. Figures such as Archipenko, Malevich, Exter, and Burliuk succeeded in bringing their discoveries to the international community. Like these artists, writers did not desire to remain strictly within the limits of their particular national tradition, but recognized the dialectical relationship between the national and international in art.

Abstracting, translating, or transforming tradition into modernist form became something of an obsession in Ukrainian culture in the following decades, and a major part of the continuing search for self-definition. In the forties, for example, Sviatoslav Hordynskyi, an artist, poet, and art critic who began exhibiting and writing in Lviv in the thirties (then part of the Polish state) before moving to the United States wrote an article in which he argued for an abstract national art in terms very close to those used in the early twenties. He suggested that international modernism's interest in form had compelled twentieth-century Ukrainian artists to abandon historical styles and genre painting and forced them to study the compositional techniques and colors of their own popular traditions. The "strong, formalist features of the old Ukrainian art, its anti-naturalism" allowed them to create in an abstract manner that simultaneously echoed traditional forms (Hordynskyi 1947, 15). Hordynskyi singled out the Boichuk School of the 1920s as an exemplary synthesis of traditionalism and formalism, and thought that the search for this synthesis continued to drive many contemporary artists.

A comparison with the key concepts of the Jewish revival is revealing. In the years 1918–20 Kyiv's Kultur-Lige championed the idea of a secular Yiddish culture that would be international and modern. Created on January 9, 1918, the organization had established a hundred and twenty branches throughout Ukraine by the end of the year. Eponymous organizations were created in Petrograd, Crimea, Minsk, Grodny, Vilnius, Bialystok, Chernowets (in Romania; today's Chernivtsi in Ukraine), Moscow, Rostov-on-Don, and the far-eastern cities of Chita, Irkutsk and Harbin. When at the end of 1920 the Kyiv center came under bolshevik control, some members left in order to reproduce the organization in Warsaw in 1921 and Berlin in 1922. A Kultur-Lige was created in Riga (Latvia) in 1922, New York and Chicago in 1926, Bucharest in 1931, and Mexico and Argentina in 1935. The Ukrainian organization was the largest and strongest in the years 1918–20, and provided the model for developments elsewhere. Claims were made for its having "four evening folk universities, twelve grammar schools, twenty large libraries with reading rooms, seventy kindergartens and orphanages, forty evening programs, ten playing fields, three gymnasiums [high schools], twenty dramatic circles, choruses, and troupes" (*Der Fraytog*, Berlin, 1 August 1919, 36; quoted in Wolitz 1988, 35) The organization opened art studios, an art museum, a teachers' seminary, and a Jewish People's University. In 1918 its press accounted for over forty percent of all titles in Yiddish produced in the lands of the former empire.[3] Kyiv at this time became the center of an international Jewish avant-garde art. The book graphic art produced in these years is today universally admired precisely for the blending of modernism and national tradition that it was able to achieve. Two major art exhibitions were held in Kyiv (in 1920 and 1922) and another in New York (in 1924).

Kultur-Lige's growth and the Jewish cultural revival took place against the background of the 1917–20 revolution. The revolutionary Ukrainian government (initially the Central Rada, then the UNR) approved a multicultural policy, offering support in particular to the Jewish, Polish and Russian minorities. The Ukrainian intelligentsia saw Jewish cultural development as parallel to its own Ukrainization policy and an ally in the struggle to reverse the process of russification that was a legacy of tsarist rule.

The Kultur-Lige was formed in Kyiv, a day before the UNR's law on national-personal autonomy was proclaimed on 9 January 1918. The organization's statue was approved on 15 January. Its creation was supported by a coalition of Jewish socialist parties: the Bund, Fareinigte, Poale Zion and Folkspartei (United Jewish Socialist Workers' Party). Since Moisei Zilberfarb, the Central Rada's Minister of Jewish Affairs was in the Kultur-Lige's leadership, the organization was effectively an auxiliary organ of the Ministry. The Kultur-Lige continued to expand its activities under Hetmanate rule (from April to November 1918 Pavlo Skoropadsky ruled as Hetman with German backing), when it "assumed the role of the organ of Jewish autonomy in Ukraine" (Kazovsky 2007, 27). At this time it created a university, a major library, and developed its program of extra-mural education. The university began operating after a circular on national higher education allowing "teaching in the languages used in schools" was promulgated on 5 August by the Minister of Education and Art. When the UNR government returned to Kyiv under the leadership of the Directory (November 1918 to January 1919), lecturers from the Kultur-Lige's teacher-training school in Kyiv formed the Department of Education in its Ministry of Jewish Affairs. The Kultur-Lige therefore embodied the concept of cultural autonomy under successive Ukrainian governments, receiving financial support from them, while at the same time also raising its own funds. In 1918 it employed around 260 people, and of the twenty one individuals on its governing board three were ministers in the governments of the UNR. When the organization was brought under the control of the Communist Party in December, 1920, the original leadership was squeezed out. By 1922 all branches throughout

3 Apter-Gabriel (1988) has provided a bibliography, and titles published in Ukraine are listed in Rybakov (2001), 163–64, and 176–87.

Ukraine had been subordinated to the Evsektsii (the Jewish Sections of the Commissariat of Education). Initially the bolsheviks supported aspects of the Kultur-Lige's work, such as the university and theaters, but the Jewish sections of the Bolshevik Party argued that the Kultur-Lige was a class enemy and nationalist. More to the point, the Kultur-Lige presented a rival to the Jewish sections, which wanted exclusive control over organized Jewish cultural life (Gitelman 1972, 273–76). The collapse of the UNR government was accompanied by the terrible wave of pogroms in 1919, in which troops ostensibly loyal to this government participated. These pogroms did much to destroy the Ukrainian-Jewish rapprochement, and encouraged some Jews to support the bolsheviks.

In spite of its short existence, the Kultur-Lige achieved astonishing successes, including the development of a network of Jewish schools throughout Ukraine, a flowering of Yiddish literature, and the creation of an avant-garde art of international fame. Even after the Soviet takeover, many aspects of its work continued under other names. The music school was sponsored by a trade union organization; the major library in Kyiv continued to function under other names; the art school was active until 1931; the Kultur-Lige's Jewish theater began working in Kharkiv in 1924; and the publishing house continued using the organization's name until the end of the twenties.

It is hard to convey today how thrilling the vision of a cultural rebirth was to participants. In his memoirs Arthur Golomb, who lived in Kyiv in the years 1917–21 describes how in January of 1918, as the bolsheviks began to sow disorder in Kyiv and the Red Army commenced an artillery bombardment of the Ukrainian capital from the left bank of the Dnipro, he was running down the street to the Jewish student kitchen when he met Zelig Melamed, who called out: "It's ready!" He had in his pocket the statute of Kultur-Lige. Both friends were so excited by the news that they stood up, forgetting entirely about the danger, and ignoring the flying bullets and the roar of the cannonade (Kazovsky 2007, 24–25)

The new culture was to be modern. For some this meant that it should be politically leftist and activist. Perets Markish, a leading figure in Kyiv's Yiddish revival, who moved to Warsaw and then to Moscow in the thirties, was remarkably pro-Soviet, even after the regime repressed the Kultur-Lige. However, other members of the organization were not. When the Kyiv organization was shut down, some of the main figures, such as I.I. Zinger, Moisei Zilberfarb, Melamed and Maizil moved to Warsaw, hoping that this city would become the base of a Yiddish cultural flowering and that Jews in Poland would be granted the same cultural autonomy as they had received from the Ukrainian government (Ravich 2008, 8). Here, and wherever the members of the Kyiv Kultur-Lige moved, they promoted their dream of a modern but archetypically Jewish culture, a national sensibility that was modern (even avant-gardist), secular, progressive, and global.

The artistic section perhaps provided the clearest expression of national modernist theory and style. Several artists had been involved in the search for cultural roots in pre-revolutionary years. Nathan Altman had in 1913 copied ancient tombstones on Jewish cemeteries in Shepetivka; Issakhar-Ber Rybak and El Lissitsky had in 1915 made drawings of the interiors of ancient synagogues in Right-Bank Ukraine; Solomon Yudovkin had taken over 1,500 photographs of pinkas (Jewish community books); Chaikov, Elman and Kratko had studied Jewish embossed silver. The motivation in each case was the development of an art that drew on tradition in order to rework archetypal forms. In the Kultur-Lige period these same artists attempted to translate the traditional into an avant-garde idiom with the idea of abstract form as the purest expression of the national. The approach was defended by Boris Aronson and Issakhar-Ber Rybak in an influential article published in 1919 in the Kyiv journal *Oyfgang* (Dawn), which criticized the idea of an art focused on recognizably Jewish themes. Instead, the authors argued, the national could best be explored by examining formal qualities, such as the use of color and rhythm, and traditional ornamental patterns. The ensuing discussion on this subject evolved into an entire discourse in which Jewish journals in Berlin, Moscow, Lodz, and Vilnius participated.

Aronson developed this view in *Sovremennaia evreiskaia grafika* (Contemporary Jewish Graphic Art, 1924), which he published in Berlin. He elaborated the concept of a Jewish art based on specifically Jewish forms of ornamentation, compositional qualities, and archetypal imagery, all of which, he felt, could already be found "in the distant sources of ethnography and in the first manuscript publications of sacred books" (Aronson 1924, 24). A Jewish art, in his opinion, could be distilled from the entire range of objects that were used in rituals and daily life. However, the distillation could not be mere copying or stylization; it had to be a new individualization, as practiced by artists such as Altman and Chagall, who had shown how popular elements could be transformed into unique and original combinations. By the time the book appeared, Aronson already felt that the search for a new national style had failed. Not only had the Kyiv Kultur-Lige's great experiment been cut short, but a different artistic sensibility was in the ascendant—one that stressed dynamism, mechanics and fragmentation, and seemed to deny the possibility of stable, recurring forms. However, he still claimed "one priceless achievement" for the earlier inspiration: "it enlivened a whole range of historical materials, blew the dust from the living face of grave stones, animated with warmth the relations between tradition and craft" (Aronson, 104). The traditional and ethnographic, he still maintained, could be reworked into a modernist idiom. In fact this combination was now in vogue, since primitivism had been widely embraced as a programmatic feature of modernism.

John Bowlt has emphasized the contradiction between loyalty to the community and commitment to the international art world, arguing that the attempt to create an international style in architecture and the plastic arts had to win out. According to him, these artists sympathized "with the sincere attempts of their linguistic colleagues to accelerate the application of Esperanto. In the immediate context of Jewish art and the Russian avant-garde, this argument held a particular logic: few modern Jewish artists derived all their artistic inspiration from the patriarchal traditions of Jewish culture observed in the tortured environment of the shtetl, although, certainly, Chagall, Ryback, and Yudovkin did. In many cases, they attempted to interweave these traditions with the aesthetic systems of Cubism, Futurism, Suprematism, etc." (Bowlt 1988, 45). This line of argumentation misses a crucial point: for many of these artists the road to an international style or abstraction passed through the national. After all, they suggested, why should this route be any less acceptable than the exploration of "exotic" African or Polynesian art?

In the early Kultur-Lige years Aronson felt that Jewish folk traditions could be fused with contemporary art "to create a modern Jewish plastic art which seeks its own organic national form, color and rhythm" (*Kultur-Lige Zamlung*, Kyiv, November 1919, 38; quoted in Wolitz 1988, 35). This suggested a Jewish path to abstraction. Rybak and Aronson in the above-mentioned article of 1919 argued that even if the artist's work was successful internationally, it would still reveal the specific, spiritual construction and emotions of the creator`s milieu and the national element in its style, structure, and organization. However, at the same time, these leaders of Kultur-Lige believed that "traditional shtetl life was atrophied and a modern, secular, national culture should replace it. The role of art was to give aesthetic definition to new national and cultural longings" (Wolitz 1988, 36). Under the impact of bolshevik pressure, the emphasis on national specificity was gradually removed. Abstraction came to mean not the refinement of a particular tradition, but the erasure of recognizable traditions and the embracing instead of a universalism that masked or denied national specificity.

The practical application of Aronson's theoretical premises can be seen in the work of many artists. Mark Epstein's cubist compositions, such as *The Cello-Player* (1920) and *Family Group* (1919–20), or Yosyf Chaikov's *The Seamstress* (1922), *Soyfer* (*The Scribe*, 1922), and *The Violin-Player* (1922) treat traditional themes in a cubist manner. Rybak's decorative forms, such as his *Sketch for the Almanac Eygns* (Native, 1920) give a modern graphic interpretation to the forms he had copied from synagogue murals and carved tombstones. And the now famous book illustrations from 1917–24 by El Lissitsky, Rybak and Sara Shor represent an avant-garde graphic art inspired by Jewish folk arts. These did not present a clash between the old and new, but the achievement of a new aesthetic consciousness created by the mingling of tradition and modernism. There were, of course, works in which the tension between the old and new worlds was emphasized. Joseph Chaikov's image for the cover of the magazine *Baginen* (Beginnings, 1919) captures this tension. It depicts the artist with one eye open to the future and a second closed to the past, blind to the rural world he has left behind.[4]

The theorizing of a Ukrainian "renaissance" and Jewish "revival" throw light on both movements. The literature and art produced in one find analogous works in the other. This is to be expected, since there were often strong connections between individuals in both groups, and both movements were inspired by the international avant-garde. Many artists had spent time abroad (especially in Paris, Munich and Berlin) in pre-revolutionary years. They had often come through the same art schools, in particular the Kyiv Art School, Murashko Art School, Exter's studio, and Boichuk's studio of monumental art in the Ukrainian Academy of Arts. They exhibited together in the earliest avant-garde exhibitions within the Russian Empire (in Kyiv, Moscow and Petrograd) and continued to work together, both in the years 1917–24 when the Kultur-Lige was most active, and later.

As a literary and artistic current, national modernism was strongly in evidence in the twenties. It was most forcefully articulated by Khvylovyi on behalf of *VAPLITE* and by Aronson on behalf of Kultur-Lige. The Ukrainian and Jewish modernists associated with these groups saw the new literature and art as an expression of national identity, and attempted to theorize it accordingly. Their rhetoric and imagery were often aggressive. They left no doubt that the past was to be dismissed: it bore responsibility for the catastrophic present. However, they simultaneously argued that, because the tsarist past had oppressed, denied or marginalized national culture, the repressed energies and unexplored potential of the national culture could

4 For reproductions of works by these and other artists of the Kultur-Lige see Kazovsky, 2003, 2007 and 2011.

be used to create new, popular and progressive artistic forms. Utopianism and a faith in the future were, of course, a part of this modernism, but it is also clear that these groups saw the local as the vehicle for reaching this desired future.

In the twentieth century's early decades the explosion of modernity simultaneously transformed millions of Ukrainians and Jews in analogous ways. In response to modernity's pressures, both national revivals aimed at developing secular cultures that accepted European genres and modes of discourse, but simultaneously infused them with elements of their own tradition. A key to understanding the semiotics of this art lies in the cultural discourse out of which it grew.

Artists in the Maelstrom: Five Case Studies

David Burliuk and Steppe as Avant-Garde Identity[1]

The literary myth of the steppe has played a fundamental role in defining Ukraine, its historical origins and cultural characteristics. Depictions of the country as a wild, beautiful and dangerous borderland already made their appearance in Polish literature in the seventeenth and eighteenth centuries. They were particularly prominent in Polish and Ukrainian romanticism. In the 1830s and 1840s Ukrainians who wrote in Russian, such as Nikolai Gogol (Mykola Hohol in Ukrainian) and Evgenii Grebenka (Yevhen Hrebinka in Ukrainian), reshaped the image of the steppe into an icon of vitality—a frontier land settled by a vigorous, colorful and courageous people. Shortly afterwards several classics of Ukrainian literature, notably Taras Shevchenko and Panteleimon Kulish, refashioned the literary steppe into a foundation myth for a people who were attempting to escape subjugation and colonization. In the "Cultural Renaissance" of the 1920s writers such as Khvylovyi, Vynnychenko, Valerian Pidmohylnyi, Yohansen, Yanovskyi, Yevhen Kosynka, and Geo Shkurupii reinterpreted the steppe either as an anarchic zone of conflict, or a fertile and mysterious realm that incubated strong, rebellious natures. These constructs were also reflected in nineteenth-century paintings, notably by Shevchenko, Ilia Repin, Arkhyp Kuindzhi, Serhii Vasylkivskyi, and Fotii Krasytskyi. Their iconic images, reproduced countless times, became deeply ingrained in contemporary popular consciousness.

It is less well recognized, however, that before the First World War the futurists grouped around David Burliuk also aligned themselves with a Ukrainophilic "myth" of the steppe. They counterposed a positive image of wildness to the negative one represented in works such as Anton Chekhov's

1 This chapter adapts sections from my article "The Steppe as Inspiration in David Burliuk's Art," *Journal of Ukrainian Studies* 30.2 (2005): 51–67.

Step (Steppe, 1888) or Ivan Bunin's *Derevnia* (Countryside, 1910). Burliuk's literary and artistic mythologizing of the steppe played a key role in defining pre-revolutionary futurism and challenging the symbolist aesthetic.

Hylaea and Chornianka (Chernianka)

There is almost universal agreement that Burliuk was the crucial figure in the creation of futurism within the Russian Empire. He was its tireless promoter, the stimulus behind its first exhibitions and publications, a participant in all the performances and public interventions that scandalized polite society and brought notoriety to the group. Vladimir Markov thought that without Burliuk there would have been no futurism in the empire (1968b, 9) and drew attention to the crucial importance of the early cohort who called themselves Hylaea (Gileia in Russian) in 1907–13, asserting that the "history of Russian futurism is actually the history of the Gileya group" (1968a, 8).

In the early years of the twentieth century Burliuk's father, an estate supervisor, found work managing the property of Count Sviatopolk Mirskii at Zolota Balka, by the Dnipro River. David began painting at the time. He decorated the walls of old Zaporozhian homesteads and in the summer of 1902 painted portraits of villagers and hundreds of canvases of Zaporozhian *mazanki* (cottages of daubed wood), along with "azure horizons and willows, black poplars and steppe burial mounds" (Burliuk 1994, 113). After spending time in Munich as the student of Anton Azhbe and Willi Dietz, he returned to the estate and continued to paint intensively. In 1904 he traveled to Paris, but was soon back in Ukraine again, first in Kherson and then at an estate near Konstantynohrad in Poltava gubernia, where he painted landscapes and portraits of villagers. In 1906 he spent time on an estate in Romen county, Poltava gubernia, and then in the Ekaterinoslav gubernia (now Dnipro oblast). By 1907, when his father began managing Chornianka (Chernianka in Russian), the huge estate of Count Aleksandr Mordvinov near Kherson that bordered on the Askania Nova reservation, Burliuk had already produced hundreds of impressionist steppe landscapes and village portraits.

Between 1907 and 1913 many noted artists, writers, and cultural figures stayed at Chornianka, including Aleksei Kruchenykh, Velimir Khlebnikov, Benedikt Livshits, Vladimir Maiakovsky, Vasilii Kamenskii, Wassily Kandinsky, Vladimir Izdebskii, Aristarkh Lentulov, and Mikhail Larionov. The Hylaea group, which formed in 1910–11, consisted of the three Burliuk brothers (David, Vladimir and Nikolai), Livshits, Kamenskii, Khlebnikov, Elena Guro (whose St. Petersburg home they often visited and which became a second base for the Hylaeans), Maiakovsky, and Kruchenykh. Sojourns in Chornianka, were often long. Khlebnikov and Kruchenykh stayed several months each year. A number of exhibitions were conceived there, to be realized later in St. Petersburg, Kyiv, Moscow, and Odesa. Boris Lavrentev has noted that several books were also organized there and later published in Kherson or Kachovnia (Lavrentev 1959, 62–3).

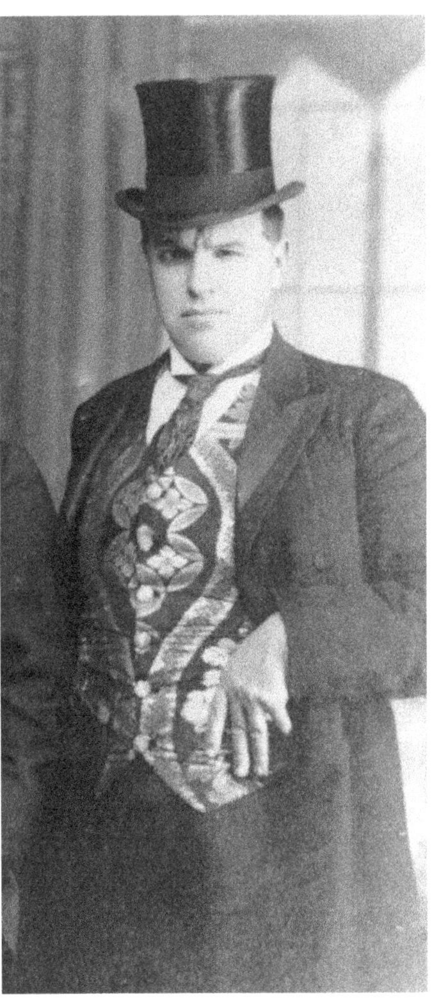

David Burliuk in the 1910s. Photographer unknown.

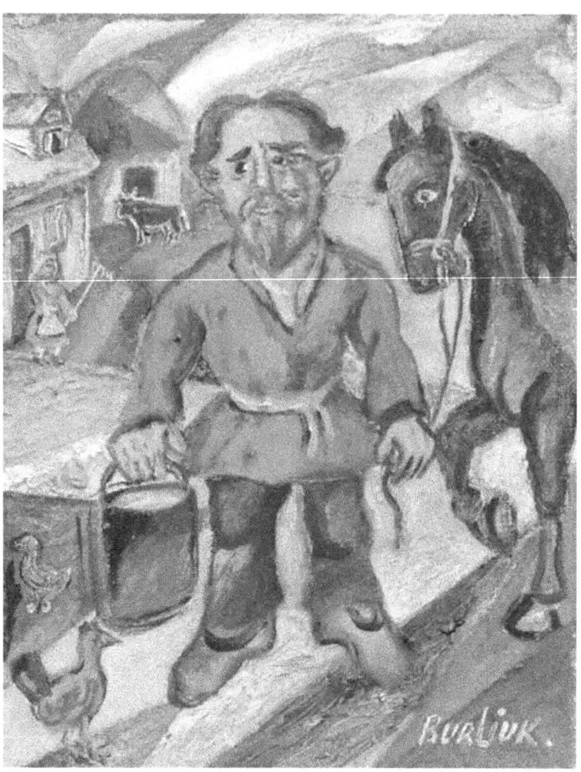

David Burliuk. *Man with Two Faces*, 1912.

The word "Hylaea" was derived from the Greek term for the Scythian territories by the Dnipro's outlet into the Black Sea. Hylaea and the Scythians are described in Herodotus' *Histories* in connection with the feats of Hercules. The idea of calling the group by this name may have been inspired by drawings on old maps in the estate's library, which showed Hercules resting by the Dnipro after his victories. The Burliuk family, who were all tall and physically powerful, would have identified with this figure. Volodymyr, for example, was jokingly advised by Aleksei Remizov to go about naked except for a tiger skin around his loins and carrying a club, a remark that David, in his memoirs, took as a supercilious reference to the "simple and savage life, so inimical to the lords and the effeminate tsarist gentry" (Burliuk 1994, 25).

This area of southern Ukraine had in the 1880s been described in popular Russian-language novels written by Grigorii Danilevskii (whose Ukrainian name was Hryhorii Danylevskyi) as a land of dramatic clashes between escaped serfs and ruthless landlords. The writer presented it as a frontier where enormous fortunes could be made, and where old, conservative traditions were being supplanted by a new ambitious and enterprising farming class. Both Herodotus' account of Hercules and Danilevskii's vision of a self-confident entrepreneurial class contributed to Burliuk's image of the southern Ukrainian steppe as the incubator of a new world. A sense of vital energy and creativity is captured in the description of Chornianka and Hylaea in Livshits' *One and a Half-Eyed Archer* (Livshits 1977, 35–68). His image of a bucolic paradise, set among vast fields and worked by giants with insatiable appetites, is superimposed upon heroic ancient tales associated with Hesiod and Homer.

Burliuk appropriated the idea of barbarian vitality and strength for the Hylaeans, who, after 1913, began calling themselves futurists. A Hellenized Black Sea littoral incorporating imagery from Hesiod, Homer and Herodotus served as a foil to the identification with Greek culture among Russian symbolists such as Viacheslav Ivanov. His Hafiz salon of 1906–7, a meeting-place for the erudite and cultivated, discussed Platonic love, homosexuality, Dionysian ecstasy, and art. Visitors assumed pseudonyms, wore classical attire, and reclined on couches while drinking wine, as though imitating characters from Plato's *Symposium*. This world of the St. Petersburg symbolists was viewed by Hylaeans as over-refined and artificial, and its metaphysical and religious concerns were treated with suspicion. By contrast, Burliuk's coterie identified with the image of a robust Greek civilization that constantly interacted with the war-like Scythians. Moreover, they felt connected to this world in an immediate and direct manner. In the years 1907–12 the Burliuk brothers conducted archaeological research in Crimea, excavating about fifty burial mounds, in which they found Scythian artifacts which were later delivered either to the Kherson Museum, to their "family museum" in Chornianka, or to their house in Mikhaleve, near Moscow. They also brought back stone sculptures (*kamiani baby* in Ukrainian), ancient fertility symbols, that can be found throughout the steppe. Scythian forms, such as the symbolic depictions of horses, appeared in the art of both David and Vladimir, and *kamiani baby* influenced David's depictions of nudes. The archaeological excavation of the ancient world continued during the First World War. Volodymyr, for example, in 1917 was conducting a dig in Salonica before the attack in which he died. In his last letter he described a hundred marble antique pieces he was sending to the old house their mother had bought in Mikhaleve. This was the family museum while the family lived there from 1914 until 1918. When the house had to be evacuated after the 1917 Revolution, it contained two hundred and fifty icons, paintings by Kandinsky, Goncharova, Javlensky,

Franz Marc, Lentulov, Exter, and others, as well as the contents of Scythian tombs, including seventy skeletons and two hundred sculls.

Although most studies consider St. Petersburg and Moscow in the years 1910–12 to be the birthplaces of futurism in the Russian Empire, the 1908 Link Exhibition in Kyiv and the Chornianka period can also make that claim. Livshits, for example, in his wonderful chapter on Hylaea, states that the Link Exhibition held in Kyiv from November 2 to 20, 1908, to which David, Liudmyla and Volodymyr Burliuk, Exter, Bohomazov, Prybylska, Goncharova, Larionov, and others contributed, may be regarded as the first futurist exhibition in the Russian Empire, especially since the participants issued a collective manifesto (Livshits 1977, 65).

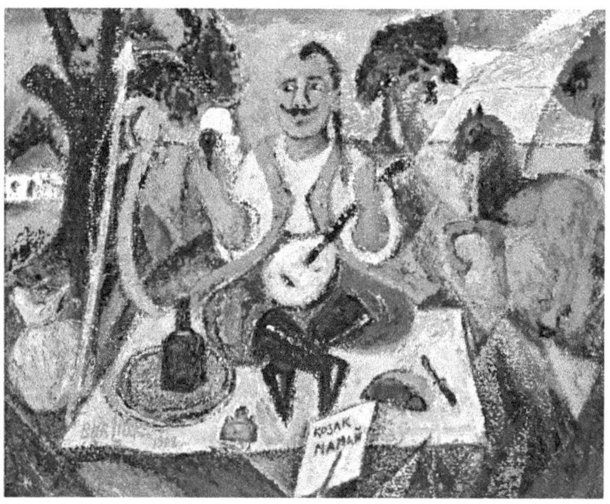

David Burliuk. *Cossack Mamai*, 1908.

Zaporozhians

Burliuk's imaginary steppe also drew heavily on family history. He was proud of his Zaporozhian ancestry, as his son Nicholas has related:

> In his youth, my father was very fond of visiting the little cemetery near Riabushki [the family estate near Sumy, where he was born and grew up]. Surrounded by the solitude of the steppes, under massive oak crosses, his beloved ancestors rested. The aroma of wild flowers added to the melancholy beauty of the sacred place. He would stand and listen to the sighing of the wind in the pines and willows.

> "There they lie," he would say. "From them I received the spark of life to carry to the world and be, myself, a living connecting link between the past and the future" (Nicholas Burliuk n.d., 18).

At every opportunity he emphasized his family connection to the land and its history:

> Ukraine was and remains my homeland, because I was born in Ukraine, [...] the bones of my ancestors, free Cossacks, who fought in the name of glory, power and freedom are buried there [...] What unites them into one general type? Determination, character, the desire to obtain a set goal. All my life I have felt these traits within me [...] However, my determination was aimed at overcoming an old, outdated taste and at introducing a new art, a wild beauty into life [...]
>
> In 1915, I painted the picture *Sviatoslav* in the style of ancient Ukrainian painting. As far as the dominance of one or another color scheme in my work, I have to say, that in my person Ukraine has its most faithful son. My color schemes are deeply national. Orange, greenish-yellow, red, and blue tones gush like Niagaras from beneath my brush [...] A child of the Ukrainian steppes, I have always been most partial to horizontal formats [...] It would be a good idea to transfer a part of my paintings to Ukraine, my beloved homeland. (Horbachov 1996, 373–4)

On their expeditions to archaeological sites in Crimea, the Burliuk brothers would listen to the stories of local people and meet bandura players. David's habit of wearing one earring in the right ear was, according to his son, "in the style of a Ukrainian Cossack" (Horbachov 1996, 87, 111).

Throughout his life Burliuk identified himself as Ukrainian and attached importance to this self-definition. Three documents written by him and one by his sister indicate that his ancestors served as secretaries in the Zaporozhian Sich prior to 1775, and that oil paintings of them hung on the walls of his great grandfather's home.[2] Moreover, Burliuk's father was described in family lore as the model for the enormous, shirtless Cossack sitting on a barrel in Repin's famous painting *Zaporozhians Writing a Letter*

---

2 Two of these documents are attached to Evdaev 2002. They are "Lestnitsa moikh let" by David Burliuk (297–304) and "Fragmenty semeinoi khroniki" by Liudmila Kuznetsova-Burliuk (305–313). The latter appeared as "Fragmenty khronologii roda Burliukov" in *Color and Rhyme* 48 (1961–62): 43–7. Two further documents can be found in Horbachov, 1996. They are "Predky moi" (373–74) and "Frahmenty zi spohadiv futurysta, Za sorok rokiv 1890–1930 (373). The originals are in the State Public Library in Saint Petersburg, Manuscript Section, f. 552, no. 1.

to the Sultan of Turkey. David attributed his own character and view of life to his Ukrainian Cossack background.[3]

The Zaporozhian imagery was associated by Burliuk with elemental force. In one poem he compared the Zaporozhian Cossacks to the powerful flow of the Dnipro, suggesting that, like water passing through turbines, they provided the "electrical power" of revolutions (Burliuk 1928, 14). A similar sense of the elemental is also attached to the descriptions of Taras Shevchenko and Petro Sahaidachnyi, the seventeenth-century Cossack leader, which occur in Burliuk's poetry.

His memoirs continually juxtapose Zaporozhian "freedoms" [*volnosti*] with contempt for the city dweller [*meshchanin*]. In an essay entitled "My Ancestors" he speaks with admiration of his forerunners, making the point that the Cossack settlers and pioneers lived in freedom and prosperity, enjoyed good harvests, and were surrounded by apiaries and windmills on clear streams: "Serfdom […] had not put down as deep roots in Ukraine and was not as evident to the eye, and did not reduced the people to misery. There were many descendants in Ukraine of the recently free Zaporozhians, whose families had avoided the wretched fate of serfdom" (Burliuk 1994, 101–2). David was particularly proud of the endurance, stubbornness and industriousness of his forerunners, qualities which, he felt, he had inherited, and which nurtured his own determination to inject into contemporary culture "a new art, a wild beauty" (Horbachov 1996, 104).

Khlebnikov, whose mother was Ukrainian, in his poem "Burliuk" (1919) describes the impression made by David's self-identification as a Cossack type. After mentioning the fact that in Munich Azhbe had called him "the wild mare of Russia's black earth," a definition that Burliuk accepted proudly and repeated often, Khlebnikov goes on:

> Russia enlarged the continent of Europe
> And greatly amplified the voice of the West,
> Like the voice of a monster amplified a thousand times,
> You plump giant, your laughter rang through all Russia.
> And the stem of the Dnieper's mouth
> Constricted you into a fist,
> Fighter for the right of the people in an art of titans,
> You gave Russia's soul an outlet to the sea.
> A strange break-up of painterly worlds

3 In Burliuk's archive in Syracuse University there is a family tree drawn by his brother-in-law, the Czech artist Vaclav Fiala, which shows his Cossack ancestry (Syracuse University, Burliuk collection, box 6).

Was the forerunner of freedom, a liberation from chains…
…………………………
And the mouth of the Dnieper like an ear of grain,
People like lumps of earth
Were obedient to you.
With the heartbeat of a giant
You moved the deep waters of cast iron
With your fat laughter alone.
Songs of revenge and sadness
Were heard in your voice,
Across the burial mound of iron wealth
And a Hercules you came out of the burial mound
Of your ancient native land.[4]

David's continued interest in Cossack history was expressed in his later reading of authors who had described the Zaporozhians, such as Gogol and Shevchenko (Nicholai Burliuk n.d., 26, 51). His archive at Syracuse University reveals that he spoke at various functions on Shevchenko, and

---

4 Rosiia—razshirennyi materik Evropy
I golos zapada gromadno uvelichila,
Kak budto by donessia krik
Chudovishcha, chto bolshe v tysiachi raz,
Ty zhirnyi velikan, tvoi khokhot prozvuchal po vsei Rossii.
I stebel dneprovskogo ustia, im ty zazhat byl v kulake,
Borets za pravo naroda v iskusstve titanov,
Dushe Rossii dal morskie berega.
Strannaia lomka mirov zhivopysnykh
Byla predtecheiu svobod; osvobozhdeniem ot tsepei…
………………………………………………………………
I kolos ustia Dnepra,
Komia gliny liudei
Byli poslushny tebe.
S velikanskim serdtsa udarom
Dvigal ty glyby voli chuguna
Odnim svoim zhirnymi [sic] khokhotom.
Pesni mesti I pechali
V tvoem golose zvuchali,
Cherez kurgan chugunnogo bogatstva
I, bogatyr ty vyshel iz kurgana
Rodiny drevnei tvoei. (Khlebnikov 30)

tried to obtain the works of the Ukrainian émigré writer Yurii Kosach, who had written on the Cossacks.[5]

He also painted several versions of the Cossack Mamai figure, a popular Ukrainian folk painting. Mamai is always portrayed as a Zaporozhian, seated, with his horse and sword nearby, food and drink in front of him. The figure represents independence, self-sufficiency and rugged individualism. The artist also incorporated the medieval, or princely era of Kyivan Rus into his art. For example, the painting *Sviatoslav Drinking His Own Blood* (1915), conceived as a protest against the horrors of the First World War, was described by him as done "in the style of ancient Ukrainian painting" (Burliuk 1994, 124–5).

The positive idea of the steppe's "wildness" was communicated to other Hylaeans, notably Khlebnikov, whose poetry contains images of *kamiani baby*, Kyivan Rus, and Cossack rebels such as Ostrianytsia and Morozenko, as well as numerous Ukrainianisms.

Primitivism

Another aspect of the myth was primitivism, which Burliuk associated with biological and psychological health. He frequently used the terms "simple," "laconic," "coarse" [*gruboe*] and perhaps described his artistic ideal most memorably as "a wild beauty" (Burliuk 1994, 104). Wildness was aligned with intensity, vitality, joie de vivre, and eroticism. Primitivist qualities appeared in his art as clear outlines, bright colors, and a deliberate coarseness in texture and imagery. These features were counterposed to what he considered effete and decadent in symbolism. David even saw the juxtaposition of colors as a kind of erotically charged primitivism: "When I paint, it seems to me, that I am a savage rubbing the stick of one color against another in order to obtain a certain color effect. The effect of burning. The effect of passion, the sexual arousal of one color's characteristic features and peculiarities by another" (Burliuk 1994, 142).

These ideas, along with Burliuk's personality, had a strong effect on contemporaries, as Viktor Shklovsky has testified:

> He had been abroad. His drawings were powerful and he knew anatomy to perfection [...] Skill had deprived academic drawing of any authority for him.

5 Burliuk's interest in Ukrainian literature appears to have been deeper than most commentators suspect. In the early thirties he and his wife read Vasyl Stefanyk, Ivan Mykytenko, Arkadii Liubchenko, and Ostap Vyshnia (Burliuk, Marussia 1961–62, 23).

> He could draw better than any professor and, now, had become indifferent to academic drawing [...] David Burliuk had grown up in the Steppe [...] They even had their own sculpture gallery: a Scythian idol, found in a burial mound. When David's father subsequently lost his position, the family took this idol to Moscow [...] This Scythian idol, which had traveled to Moscow by mistake, somehow came to rest [...] near a barn where students of the art school gathered. (Shklovsky 1972, 19–21)

David's impact on Moscow's art world was like an elemental force: "In springtime, when the water is going down and the rafts are running aground, the willow branches that tie the logs together are cut apart. Loose tree trunks, racing after one another, jostling one another, drenched by the waves, take off from the sandbanks and float toward the sea. One-eyed Burliuk had set everything in his pictures adrift long ago. This is what he brought to Moscow" (Shklovsky, 22–23). When Burliuk initiated Maiakovsky into art, his impact was immediately magnified. Shklovsky sees the latter's poetry, which employed "declarations, and fragmentary, dislocated and distorted images," thrusting "image into image," as analogous to "the methods of contemporary painting" which had been learned from Burliuk (Shklovsky, 35). The primitive and elemental were employed in an assault on established taste. New forms, Burliuk mused later, "appear absurd," and therefore it took courage to defend them "against critics from around the whole world, who know and love only the old, already dried-out, mummified" (Burliuk 1994, 152).

In his view primitivism was an expression of the forceful, simple and direct in popular art, something that he associated with the ancient past, folklore, Scythian artifacts, and peasant art. Markov has described some of these influences: meandering ornamental patterns on houses, Scythian arrows discovered in mounds, and ancient stone sculptures that can be found throughout the steppe (Markov 1968b, 33, 35). The Scythian forms he appropriated included symbolic depictions of animals, especially horses, and the integration of multiple possible viewing points, a device that was used in Scythian art to depict movement. It reveals new subjects as it is rotated and viewed from various sides. The Burliuk brothers employed "a similar lack of fixed orientation: animals and other figures are depicted upside down, at ninety-degree rotations, and running in various directions along the borders of an image [...] David Burliuk combines the principle of rotation with the Scythians' tendency to place disparate images in dense arrangement" (Ash 2002, 37). Like his repeated painting of the Cossack

Mamai, these features can be seen as part of the turn to a "primitive" art of local provenance.

Burliuk showed an enormous respect for folk, naïve and children's art. Among other things he collected hand-painted signboards. Linked to this inspiration was his democratic attitude to artistic creativity. It was expressed in his attempts to kindle creativity in those around him, often by drawing attention to the artistic power in surrounding objects and popular creativity, and in his praise for the work of folk artists, children, friends, and family members—all of whom he encouraged to paint. His mother participated in the Link Exhibition (1908) under her maiden name Mikhnevych (Evdaev 2002, 32). A painting by his five-year-old son was shown in the First Exhibition of Russian Paintings in Japan in 1920. Livshits reports:

> Among the many inhabitants of Chernianka who used to come and stare at the "boss's little ones" was a man who was much enticed by the Burliuk's painting and saw it as his own vocation.
>
> He was a bearded man, not young, either a merchant or a carpenter, who served in one of the estates. His surname was Kovalenko. The Burliuks furnished him with canvas, brushes and paints and made him into a second Rousseau, exhibiting his paintings alongside theirs. (Livshits 1977, 53)

Like much folk art, Burliuk's paintings demonstrate a fascination with surface texture. Painting was for him a "tactile, sensuous experience" (Bowlt 1986, 31). Livshits has famously described the Burliuks dragging a new canvas outside and flinging it into the liquid dirt, then painting over the bits of clay and sand, so that the landscape would "become the flesh and blood of the Hylaean land" (Livshits 1977, 51). This deliberate cultivation of coarseness was no doubt a way of challenging symbolist refinement, but it was also served Burliuk's attraction to the immediate and close-up, which he saw as a way of being true-to-life. In opposition to the World of Art group, Andre Benois and the salon public in the capital cities, he embraced the roughly textured, disproportional and asymmetrical.

In his memoirs David describes nature as a vast archive of marvelous forms that can be read in details seen close up as much as in panoramas. Every puddle, he says, contains the scent of the ocean, every stone the breath of the desert: "In painting the simple can express the infinitely complex" (Burliuk 1994, 151). He provides the following examples: the flat surfaces of sand-banks with drawings on them left by the tides, the surface patterns of trees and lichen, the white walls of daubed cottages covered with the shadows of leaves and branches, the frosting on window-panes" (Burliuk

1994, 154). By studying these forms, the artist can grasp the macrocosm encoded in microcosms.

The tactile, textural quality of painting was related to Burliuk's blindness in one eye, the result of a childhood accident, his insights often came through studying close up details. He once wrote:

> Let your eyes rest upon the surfaces, faces of my pictures [...] I throw pigments with brushes, with palette knife, smear them on my fingers, and squeeze and splash the colors from the tubes [...] Visual topography is the appreciation of paintings from the point of view of the characteristics of their surfaces. The surfaces of my paintings are laminated, soft, glossy, glassy, tender as the female breast, slick as the lips of a maiden or the petals of a rose, flat and dusty, flat and dull, smooth, even and mossy, dead, sand, hairy, deeply shelled, shallow shelled, shell-like, roughly hewn, faintly cratered, grained, splintery, mountainous, rocky, crater-like, thorny, prickly, camel-backed, etc. In my works you will find every kind of a surface one is able to imagine or to meet in the life's labyrinths. (Burliuk 1949, 8)

Nature's coarse, ruffled, unpolished character attracted him. It also provided a model for personal deportment and appearance. He, for example, wrote rather favorably of Khlebnikov's unkemptness and honesty, and altogether negatively of Igor Severianin's affectation and controlled acting (Burliuk 1994, 58, 64–73). We learn from Burliuk's memoirs that Khlebnikov visited a number of prominent writers, among them Dmitrii Merezhkovskii, Aleksei Remizov and Viacheslav Ivanov, but, according to Burliuk, was met with condescension: "the symbolists found him 'inaccurate' [*nechetkim*], ungroomed [...] No one could groom Vitia; he was grandly tousled by nature." Khlebnikov is described rather admiringly as a "wild, phenomenal organism continually creating words [...] with all the voraciousness of fecundity" (Burliuk 1994, 57–8).

Burliuk's primitivism was also related to his understanding of the emotional, subconscious and mystical. He believed, for example, in invisible realms outside the normal sphere of human perception, realms that could be sensed by artists, but did not submit to rational analysis. This faith appears to have originated from encounters with soothsayers, miracle-workers and gypsies during his archaeological expeditions (Nicholas Burliuk n.d., 86–93). As a youth he asked to be allowed to spend the night in a haunted house (ibid., 93–5).

He was fascinated by hidden processes taking place outside the normal sphere of human perception. In the 1910–12 he painted a series of abstract works showing the movement of parts of the atom, and in the 1920s he painted radio waves and energy forces, perhaps convinced that they could be at least sensed. Most notably, his impressionistic paintings of the steppe completed before 1917 attempt to capture things invisible to the naked eye. These works pulsate with energy that seems to be generated by the interaction of millions of living particles. The canvases typically depict a summer scene under the bright sun. In the earliest works he uses a pointillistic technique; later paintings are reminiscent of Van Gogh's intense juxtaposition of colors. In all cases, the impression produced is of a shimmering surface teeming with activity and displaying a myriad of intricate patterns. The viewer is offered a vision of an endlessly productive, bountiful and mysterious natural world. He later reproduced the same impressionistic patterning in the landscape paintings completed in Japan during the years 1920–22, and then again in paintings done at various times in the United States.

Burliuk also revealed a desire to see the world holistically, something that expressed itself as an ecological consciousness. What has been described as his Naturphilosophie did not appealed to Soviet critics, who only mentioned it to expressed displeasure with what they described mystical tendencies (Postupalskii 1932, 15).

As with other artists, primitivism allowed Burliuk to avoid following the beaten path, and to articulate an authentic, personal view of life. Sometimes he deliberately included the ugly, "brutal" detail, or simultaneously showed several sides of an image in order to break down accepted patterns of thinking and to construct a more "dynamic" and personal model of perception. But his primitivism is perhaps best grasped as an almost mystical union with the earth and the vitality of common people. His works celebrate psychological, cultural and biological health. Even the last paintings of flowers and summer landscapes are full of brilliant sunshine and bursting energy, a final tribute to nature's beauty and power.

His character and sensibility was referred to by contemporaries as Ukrainian. Gollerbakh mentions his "*khokhol* goodnaturedness" and "stubbornness" (Gollerbakh 1930, 16). Lentulov and Livshits saw the optimism and hospitality in Chornianka as evidence of a Ukrainian background. These qualities they associated with his love of the prolific and irrepressible. Burliuk was proud of his own artistic productivity, and lauded it in others. He commented favorably that Khlebnikov "wrote ceaselessly. He was a great graphomaniac [...] Every external impulse stirred him to a stream of words" (Burliuk 1994, 44). Like natural phenomena, both Burliuk and

Khlebnikov produced innumerable works that have been lost, forgotten, or were destroyed. However, their sheer abundance has guaranteed that many would survive.

These qualities are all related to the overarching myth of Arcadia, of steppe Ukraine as an unspoiled, fertile land overflowing with powerful energies.

Critical reception in the United States

Burliuk entered the United States in 1924, after spending two years in Japan and two years before that traveling throughout Siberia. By the late thirties, when he began to paint Long Island fishing ports, village and town scenes, his focus was on relaxed, cheerful interaction between people. From 1949, as he traveled through the United States, Mexico and Europe, painting scenes in these countries. This turn to ethnographic naturalism, as it has been called, occurred at the same time that he began to paint reminiscences of his early life in Ukraine. American critics, who began to take a closer look at Burliuk during the Second World War, greeted these works favorably. In 1942 George Baer voiced his protest that the American art world had neglected Burliuk. Baer praised the vitality and humanism of his "folk art" paintings and the fact that Burliuk had "never given up his identity with the folk art of his native land." Most dear to the hearts of true Burliuk enthusiasts, he wrote, "are the small pictures of farm life with animals—the gnome-like peasants with blue, yellow, green or red cows and horses. The sensuous textures of the lavish pigments are in remarkable harmony with the luxury and joy of these segments of folk fantasy" (Baer 1942).

Herman Baron wrote at this time: "Burliuk is a folk painter fundamentally. His native ability glows very bright whenever he touches any subject that is related to the soil" (Baron 1944, 2). Even Michael Gold, a leading communist-party member and a firm proponent of revolutionary art, expressed the view that the "best of Burliuk" were his peasant paintings: "Here he returns to the green fields and whitewashed thatch-roof villages of his Ukrainian childhood. This is the deepest core of the man" (Gold 1944, 8). Gold felt that these works, full of bright colors and a profound sense of tranquility, showed Burliuk tapping into his earliest sources of inspiration.

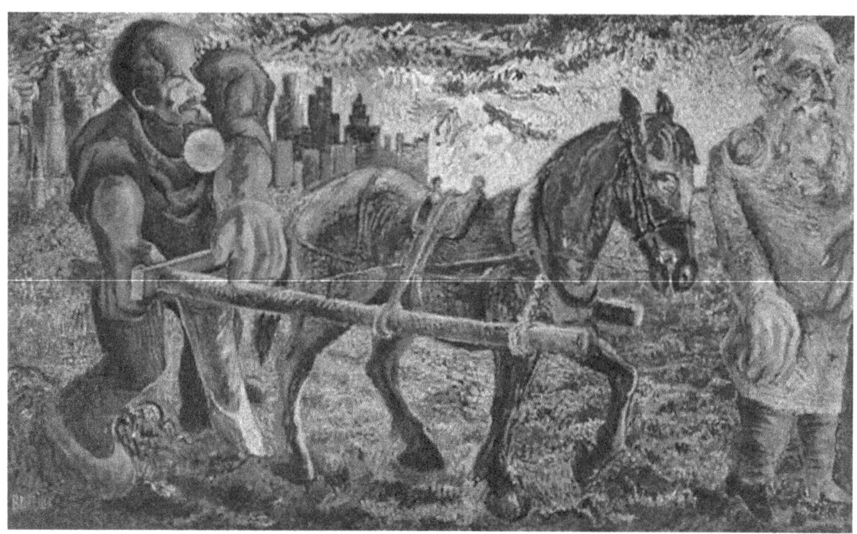

David Burliuk. *Lenin and Tolstoy*, 1925–30 (repainted in 1943).

In the 1920s and 1930s Burliuk worked for the pro-communist *Russkii golos* (Russian Voice) as a proof-reader and art editor. Although he occasional produced propagandistic painting, his revolutionary enthusiasm sat rather uncomfortably alongside a reverence for the land and agricultural labor. *Lenin and Tolstoy* can serve as an example. The painting exists in two versions (1925–40, 1944). The first was exhibited in New York in 1930 and then, renamed *Unconquerable Russia* by Katherine Dreier, was displayed in New York's ACA Gallery in 1943, at a time when the USA and the USSR were wartime allies. The allegorical meaning, even after a reading of Burliuk's explanation, remains obscure. He interpreted the painting as follows: Russia in the first two decades of the twentieth century found its best expression in two names, Tolstoy and Lenin. Tolstoy was the "symbol and mirror" of old, pre-revolutionary Russia, while Lenin was the "plowman" of the new era. The figure of Tolstoy, the "titan of the past," is bathed in the light of the moon, which symbolizes the reflected light of the past, of romanticism, religion and goodness. Lenin, the "titan of the future," has the sun in his trousers. This is the light of the approaching, as yet unknown day. The new government is merciless and cruel.

If this is indeed the meaning, it raises the problem of Lenin's ambiguous characterization. Tolstoy, whose anarchism and pro-peasant stance Burliuk admired, and whose pacifism and belief in equality inspired many followers, seems in the painting to have been demoted to a beast of burden. He pulls the plow, while Lenin directs it. The painting could equally well be interpreted as suggesting that Lenin and Tolstoy represent very different ideas. Burliuk's own sympathies seem to have been closer to Tolstoy's. In his memoirs he describes his early enthusiasm for "the simplicity" of Tolstoy and Thoreau (Burliuk 1994, 107). Among Burliuk's many jottings in his Syracuse archive can be found Tolstoy's words on the powerful urge to happiness, one that moves outside known rules and desires to capture everything around itself in threads of love, like a spider. This message was, in the end, far more congenial to Burliuk than Lenin's bolshevism. The attempt to conjoin the two figures in this painting therefore appears incoherent in ideological terms. The persistent fascination with Tolstoy is all the more interesting because in 1912, when the futurists had scandalized Petersburg society during their performances at the Brodiachaia Sobaka (Wandering Dog) restaurant in which they denounced all the art of the past, Burliuk had described Tolstoy as a "society gossip" (*svetskaia spletnitsa*), a comment that caused an uproar and caused an elderly lady to be carried out after fainting (Krusanov 2003, 105).

In 1929 Burliuk published a long poem entitled "Velikii krotkii bolshevik" (The Great Gentle Bolshevik). Here Tolstoy emerges as a "shepherd" concerned with the fate of the poor and the values of a simple life. Burliuk sees in the writer an early expression of the "bolshevik nature" and refers to him as "the most gentle bolshevik" (Burliuk 1928–29, 12–13).

In general, Burliuk's attempts to describe his intuitions were not helpful. A bemused reporter for the New York's *Sun* from 25 March 1929 has recreated a conversation with the artist, who is described as wearing a "twelve-color waistcoat" and sporting a "five-legged, chicken-headed bull" painted in bright red upon his left cheek. He is reported as discussing an art which will express the soul, not gross, material things. It is the soul that counts, always. This is the very heart of Mr. Burliuk's credo:

> Like the Hindu yogis he has been able, by contemplation, to throw himself into such an ineffable state of mind that he can perceive the imperceptible, vision the invisible, behold the unseeable and put down upon canvas that which not only does not exist but never did exist. This is the fourth dimensional idea in the new art, and it takes a rattling good man to get away with that stuff.
>
> [...] "Man's organism embraces the world through his senses," Mr. Burliuk continued, "but the hypothesis of five senses is incorrect. There are more. There are physical and metaphysical objects. Between two 'real' physical skyscrapers there exists a third created at the intersection of the mentally prolonged surfaces of the 'real' structures. Between two living beings there is always a third—the abstract and metaphysical." (Hill 1929)

In a more lucid explanation he denies the idea that art copies nature, advancing instead the idea that it is analogous to musical expression, and goes on to highlight the elements of rhythm, movement, color, special construction, and texture (Burliuk 1994, 131). Art, he assures us, requires a special sensitivity and can only be revolutionary in the novelty of its forms. He categorically rejects the rationalist and utilitarian views of Nikolai Chernyshevskii, Dmitrii Pisarev and of Russia's critical realists, in this way indirectly criticizing socialist realism (Burliuk 1994, 136). In opposition to these utilitarian approaches to art he defends modernism and the vision of the individual artist. The fact that in making these points he immediately turns to a discussion of Tolstoy suggests a link between his impressionistic paintings of the living, breathing steppe and a Tolstoyan sense of awe before the infinite complexity and intricacy of nature's designs.

Most frequently Burliuk preferred to describe the process of creating new forms as the product of intuition guided by the observation of nature. In the end, therefore, he did not bring a "wild beauty" into art simply in order to scandalize accepted taste, but was also an artist who had at an early age been enchanted by the earth's abundance and beauty. This second Burliuk was perhaps the deeper one.

One of his nature poems is called "Nezabvennaia vesna" (Unforgettable Spring):

I dreamed of silent steppes
Away from the railway lines
Where we wandered in those golden years
Of our excitement in youthful word praise
[.....................................]
I remember the ancient home that sheltered us,
The shadow of the green lampshade,
A picture dear to my heart:
Peaceful daily life and the labor of the countryside
....
I shall never forget how you said
Quiet! Listen how the grass grows!
This is the urge for vital ideals,
This is the head of a new life![6]

6 Mne prigrezilis stepi glukhie,
V storone ot zheleznykh dorog,
Gde bluzhdali my v gody zlatye,
Svoi mladoi slavoslovia vostorg.
[.....................................]

Like Antaeus who needed to touch the earth in order to regain strength, the artist kept returning to the mysterious powers he had first sensed in the steppe. The memory always rejuvenated him. Even towards the end of his life, on 22 June 1959, he wrote:

> I have reached seventy-eight today.
> And I stand at the threshold of discoveries.
> The stubbornest of Cossacks ever ready to campaign
> For the sake of another pole Achievement![7]

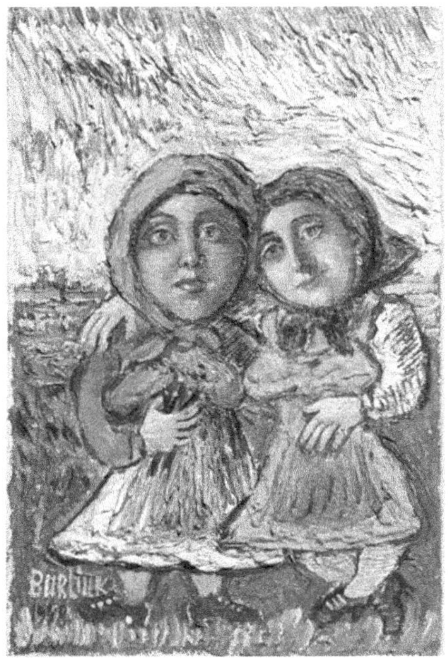

David Burliuk. *Two Ukrainian Girls*, 1948.

Pomniu dom, nas iutivshii, starinnyi,
Abazhura zelenogo ten,—
Doroguiu dlia serdtsa kartinu:
Byt pokoinyi i trud dereven.
....
Ne zabudu kak ty mne skazala
Tishe! Slushai rastet kak trava!
Zdes stremlene k zhivym idealam,
Zdes—noveishaia zhizn glava! (Syracuse University, box 7)

7 Mne semdesiat vosmoi poshel segodnia god.
I ia stoiu na grani otkrovenii.
Uporneishii kazak, vsegda gotov pokhod
Vo imia poliusa inogo dostizhenia! ("Stikhi" 6)

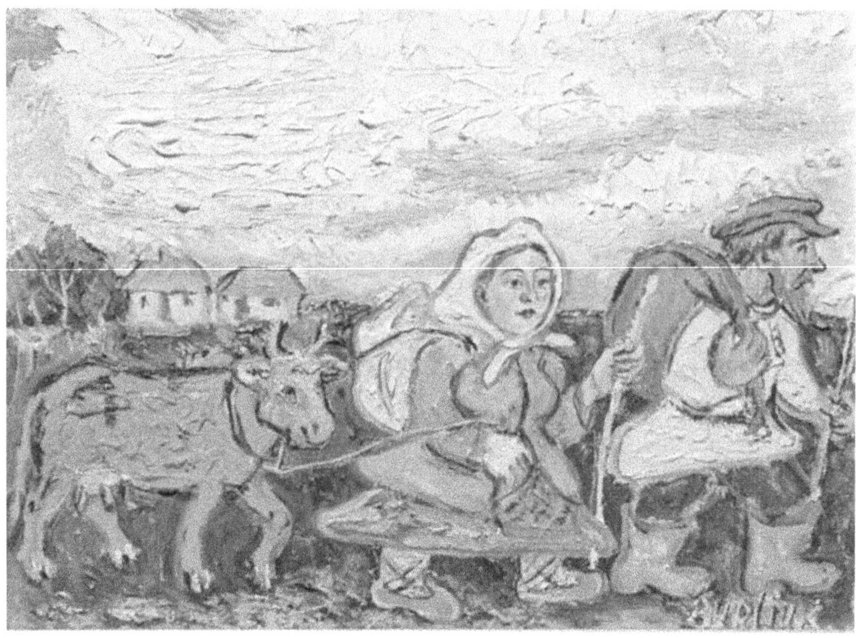

David Burliuk. *Uncle and His Niece*, 1950s.

Even when dealing with urban themes, Burliuk's art and poetry maintain an anti-urban stance and draws on the outsider's viewpoint. Postupalskii has explained the artist's turn to the archaic and appeals to "nature" as the result of drawing on subconscious impressions formed during childhood (Postupalskii 1932, 7). The ability to constantly stand in wonder at the world gave his art a freshness and vigor that appealed to many. Henry Miller was an admirer. He wrote to Burliuk on 15 November 1954 from Big Sur, California, that he had "often stood enraptured" before the artist's canvases, particularly his "Southern scenes" which "were orgiastic in color and rhythm" (Syracuse University, Correspondence, Miller). In fact, Burliuk's ability to capture nature had been noticed by his earliest critics. In 1909, Andre Benois had written: "His pictures [...] are full of a great feeling for nature and portray with originality the august despondency of the steppe expanse" (Benois 1909; quoted in Basner 1995, 24).

These considerations lead one to think that the interpretation of Burliuk's art has been too narrowly focused on an aesthetic of rupture, a "futurist" desire to surprise or shock. This feature of his work has deflected attention from the cult of vitality that sustained him through a long career. Not only do his early paintings of the steppe delight in a universe alive with countless life forms, so do his pictures of Japanese landscapes,

Mexican street scenes, and Long Island villages. Significantly, people in these pictures melt into the landscape, becoming part of nature's universe. Individuality is deemphasized, seemingly humbled and dwarfed against the vastness of the sky and the open plain. Perhaps the original inspiration for this art, and the key to understanding his evolution, lies in his feeling for the steppe as an Arcadia, an unspoiled, fertile land with links to ancient cultures. Contemplating the steppe provided Burliuk with a repertoire of ways to make art new, and to stimulate intense creative excitement in himself. Although the turn to primitivism first appeared in the Hylaean period, it remained an inspiration throughout his life. He took elements of the steppe "myth" that already existed in Polish, Russian and Ukrainian cultures, and refashioned them with an eye to both affronting and enlightening the contemporary public.

Kazimir Malevich's Autobiography and Art

In 1988–91 retrospective exhibitions of Malevich's work were held in St. Petersburg (then still named Leningrad), Moscow, Amsterdam, Los Angeles, Washington, and New York. They signaled belated recognition in the West of the artist as a major force in the avant-garde, and were the first significant presentations of his art since the retrospective in Kyiv in 1930, which was also the last to be held during Malevich's lifetime.[1] His life and work have continued to attract interest. He is now sometimes called the central figure in the Russian avant-garde (Vakar and Mikhienko 2004, vol. 1, 5). At the same time, however, the continued appearance of new materials culled from recently opened archives and the publication of a substantial memoir literature on the artist have not clarified many puzzling questions. The impressive two-volume collection of writings, letters and memoirs published in 2004 by Irina Vakar and Tatiana Mikhienko brought to light previously unknown facts about the artist's life and his relations with other figures in the art world. Tetiana Filevska's volume published in 2016 made available Malevich's Ukrainian-language articles, minutes of meetings, exhibition catalogue, four previously unpublished articles, and notes taken during Malevich's seminars. The materials were found in 2015 in the personal archive of Marian Kropyvnytskyi, Malevich's assistant during the time he worked in Kyiv. These discoveries, however, have not produced a consensus among scholars concerning key issues in the artist's biography and work. In fact, to some degree they have highlighted the conflicting judgements and polarizing viewpoints that have characterized discussions for more than a century.

1 Two exhibition catalogues were produced, both entitled *Kazimir Malevich 1878–1935*. The first, edited by W.A.L. Beeren and J.M. Joosten, at the Amsterdam: Stedelijk Museum in 1988, and the second, edited by Jeanne D'Andrea, in Los Angeles at the Armand Hammer Museum of Art and Cultural Center in 1990.

Over the last three decades art critics in the West have frequently described Malevich as "an enigmatic figure" (Golding 1991, 16). Although hopeful comments have occasionally been made that the meaning of his paintings are "beginning to be adequately understood" (Crone and Moos 1991, 8), in the 2004 Irina Vakar noted that enormous challenges still face those who try to interpret the artist's work: readers often find Malevich's own attempts to explain his art impenetrable, and at a deep level his belief system continues to mystify (Vakar 2004, 577). According to Vakar, Malevich realized that he was unable to explain his insights. He was "a foreigner in every social milieu" and his devotion to an art that was "in the highest degree elitist [elitarnomy] made him inaccessible to most people surrounding him." As a result, he became convinced that society and the "new art" were incompatible (Vakar, 578).

The new materials have, however, allowed Malevich to be viewed as a figure not formed exclusively by the atmosphere of Moscow and St. Petersburg (named Petrograd in 1914, Leningrad in 1924, and again St. Petersburg in 1991), or by the years immediate preceding and following 1917.[2] Even so, his youth, family life and existence prior to the move to Moscow in August 1904 at the age of twenty-six are still under researched. In Vakar's words they have remained "an almost complete blank spot" (Vakar, 578).

In this situation his autobiographies represent an important key to understanding his work and provide reference points for many events in his life. Since the longer of the two was written near the end of his life, it was conceived with the purpose of presenting a final retrospective and guide to his entire development. These writings focus heavily on his early life in Ukrainian villages and small towns, and explain his debt to the icon and folk arts. One of the crucial and most puzzling issue they raise is the artist's continual focus on the rural-urban divide, which appears to confound any narrative that concentrates on Malevich as a defender of a revolutionary, urban, machine art. Instead, the first commissar of the Bolshevik Revolution and theorist of the visionary new emerges in these autobiographies as an artist inspired by peasant primitivism.

Two autobiographies

The evidence offered by his autobiographical essays deserves closer attention than it has received. The shorter one from 1923–25, and especially

2 This has often been the case. See, for example, John E. Bowlt 1990.

the second, much longer account from 1933 represent Malevich's attempt to explain his evolution up to the moment when suprematism's appearance was announced at the "0-10" exhibition, the so-called "Last Futurist Exhibition" held in Petrograd in 1915. It was the first to included a large number of suprematist paintings.[3]

Malevich's celebration of the village and aversion to factory life might come as a shock to readers more familiar with his Moscow and Petersburg periods. This validation of his early life presents some difficulties for biographers and critics alike. In the 1933 text Malevich describes his earliest memories of sugar-beet plantations in Ukraine, where his father worked as an assistant director and a sort of technical engineer. Because Seweryn Malevich found work in different places during the 1880s and 1890s, Kazimir's entire childhood and youth were spent traveling with his family throughout the length and breadth of Ukraine.[4] He lived in the town of Yampil (Yampol in Russian) near Kamianets-Podilsk until the age of twelve, then in Avdiivka (Avdeevka) and Koriukivka (Koriukovka) near Chernihiv, in Maivka (Maevka) near the border with Bessarabia, in Parkhomivka (Parkhomovka) and Vovchok (Volchok) near Kharkiv, and then, until he was about seventeen, in Konotop and Bilopillia (Belopole), towns situated between Chernihiv and Sumy.

The autobiography describes his earliest impressions, which are of young women in colorful dress working enormous fields. Thousands of acres required cultivation by thousands of people in order to supply the sugar refineries. He contrasts the beauty of the land and peasant life with the ugliness and oppressive nature of factory existence. The young Malevich perceives machines as predatory creatures, the most dangerous of which must be caged like dogs to prevent them from injuring a person (Vakar and Mikhienko, vol. 1, 18). The food eaten by peasants is far superior to the buckwheat and stinking cabbage soup that is the daily fare of factory workers. He describes the diet of peasants as consisting of pure fatback with garlic; Ukrainian borshch made with fresh beans, potato and turnip; bread (palianytsi), knyshes with onions, mamalyga (corn meal) with milk, butter

---

3 A translation into English of the first autobiography, made by Xenia Glowacki-Prus and Arnold McMillin, appeared in Andersen 1968, vol. 2, 147–54 as "IZ 1/42: Avtobiograficheskie zametki, 1923–1925." The second autobiography was first published in Khardzhiev 1976, 85–127. An English translation, made by Alan Upchurch, appeared in Malevich 1985. Abridged and revised translations were published in Malevich 1990, 169–75. The two autobiographies are republished in full in Vakar and Mikhienko, vol. 1, 17–45.

4 Seweryn is the Polish spelling. It is Severin in Russian, Severyn in Ukrainian.

and sour cream. The life of the peasantry fills him with wonder: "In the winter, while the factory laborers work day and night, the peasants weave amazing materials, sew clothes; the girls sew and embroider, sing songs and dance; the boys play violins" (Vakar and Mikhienko, 19). Factory workers have none of this. Even their sugar is inferior to the honey produced by the villagers. This sets him to thinking that apiaries should replace sugar beet fields, making unnecessary the production of sugar in dismal, regimented factories. If that were to occur he would be able to listen to the endless stories of old men "who know everything about bees" (Vakar and Mikhienko, 19). His preference for village children over those of factory workers is so strong that he organizes a pitched battle, leading the village youth in heroic and victorious combat.

In this way Malevich describes his childhood as a psychological transformation, a "going native" that results in an almost complete identification with the peasantry. He spends half the narrative describing how this process occurred: "I imitated the entire life of the peasants. I rubbed the bread crust with garlic, ate fat back while holding it in my fingers, ran barefoot and refused to wear shoes" (Vakar and Mikhienko, 20). He marvels at the way the peasants make their own clothes, dress up "in colorful patterns" for special occasions, engage in dignified ceremonies and rituals, such as the custom for a bride and bridesmaids to travel through the village solemnly inviting families to the planned wedding.

However, it was not simply the food, dress and customs that thrilled the young Malevich. The autobiography makes clear that his contact with the peasantry imprinted him with an aesthetic. He thought of village people as "clean and well dressed" (*chistymi i nariadnymi*), two adjectives that become shorthand for his description of the qualities he admired in art (Vakar and Mikhienko, 20). At the end of his description of life in the countryside, he emphasizes that his sympathies for the village lies above all in the way the people practiced art: "I watched with great excitement how the peasants made wall paintings, and would help them cover the floors of their huts with clay and make designs on the stove. The peasant women were excellent at drawing roosters, horses and flowers. The paints were all prepared on the spot from various clays and dyes. I tried to transfer this culture onto the stoves in my own house, but it didn't work. They told me I was making a mess, so I worked on fences, barn walls, etc." This, concludes the author, "was the background against which the feeling for art and artistry [*khudozhestvu*] developed within me" (Vakar and Mikhienko, 20).

The Malevich family led a liminal existence, situated between town and village, urban and rural life. The autobiography demonstrates that the young artist loved the countryside, but it also shows that the modern, urban world provided employment. Kazimir and his brother worked on the railway. His father Seweryn, as a factory supervisor, would visit Kyiv annually to sign contracts for the sugar refineries, or would converse with engineers in Konotop and other towns. The family led a liminal life in other ways also. On Seweryn's side it could trace its descent from sixteenth-century Polish gentry (Vakar and Mikhienko, 372–73). Nonetheless, Seweryn's working life was spent in factories, where he often put in twelve-hours shifts, frequently at night. The rest of his life included interaction with the rural intelligentsia, mainly with Ukrainian doctors, priests, agronomists, and teachers. Seweryn was a skeptical man who attended both Orthodox and Catholic church services and, to amuse himself, occasionally invited a priest from both churches to his house at the same time. Kazimir's mother, Ludwika, kept a record of neighboring Polish families. She wrote poems in Polish and sang songs in the language. Although the family was Catholic, at least in outward form in the case of Seweryn and Kazimir, both his father and the young Malevich appear to have spoken ironically about religion. The language of communication in the family was Polish, but Kazimir grew up also speaking Ukrainian, which he knew well, as his sister has attested (Naiden and Horbachov 1993, 221). This, of course, was only natural given his surroundings. At one point he describes his impressions as a child when icon painters from Russia arrived to work in Bilopillia. Significantly, he remembers clearly the fact that they spoke Russian, a detail that his mind retained as memorable and unusual (Naiden and Horbachov, 23).

Awareness of the city's art came gradually, first through pictures seen in shop windows in Kyiv, then through a meeting with the painter Mykola (Nikolai) Pymonenko, whose works made a powerful impression on him. On many of the easels he saw in Pymonenko's studio, he informs, "stood pictures representing life in Ukraine" (Naiden and Horbachov, 25). Pymonenko taught in the Kyiv School of Drawing, to which Malevich applied and which he may have visited in 1894–96 (Naiden and Horbachov, 25). It was at this time that he decided to become a painter. Charlotte Douglas has noted that Pymonenko's subjects, "drawn from rural life—villagers at work, haying scenes, and full-length portraits of peasants—later became Malevich's own" (Douglas 1994, 8). One of Malevich's most famous late paintings from 1930, *The Flower Girl,* recalls the eponymous work by Pymonenko and was conceived, no doubt, as a way of paying homage to the older painter.

In 1896 the family moved to Kursk, where the young Malevich was influenced by Shishkin, Repin and other Wanderers (Peredvizhniki), whom he studied from reproductions. His intensive contacts with Ukrainians, however, continued. It is worth noting that this Russian province neighboring Ukraine had a mixed Russian-Ukrainian population at the time. In 1926 over half a million people, or 19.1 percent of the oblast, identified as Ukrainian. Ethnographically, some areas were, in fact, entirely Ukrainian, and were considered such by contemporaries.[5] It is not surprising, therefore, that the painter's closest friends in Kursk were often Ukrainians. The list included the artist Lev Kvachevskyi, with whom Malevich continued to correspond in future years, Valentyn Loboda, who had studied art with the great Ukrainian modernist Oleksandr Murashko, and Mykola (Nikolai Roslavets), the avant-garde composer and conductor who later moved to Kharkiv. Malevich underlines Kvachevskyi's Ukrainian background: "Lev Kvachevskyi was my very best friend. We couldn't live without each another [...] Every day in summer, spring and winter we'd walk thirty versts for our sketching sessions [...] While we ate we'd discuss various matters, or reminisce about Ukraine. We were both Ukrainians" (Vakar and Mikhienko, vol. 1, 26). In 1904 at the age of twenty-six Malevich moved to Moscow. Even then he spent his summers in Kursk, only making the complete move with his family in 1907.

Kursk did, however, produce a change in his views. Vakar has suggested that during his time there he underwent a radicalization, which was expressed in his atheism (he apparently refused to baptize his children) and in his anger over the police supervision of his two brothers, Anton and Mechislav, and Mechislav's wife Maria (whose maiden name was Zgleits). It is likely that the stay in Kursk transformed Malevich from a "respectable young man into a rebel and nihilist" (Vakar 2004, 582).

However, it was in Moscow, where he attended the studio of Fedor Rerberg and visited local galleries, that an even more radical transformation took place. He discovered that icons had an unexpectedly strong impact on him: "I felt something familiar and wonderful in them" (Vakar and Mikhienko 2004, 28). At that moment he recalled his childhood, "the horses, flowers and roosters of the primitive murals and wood carvings," and sensed a bond between peasant art and the icon. The emotional and spiritual elements in icon art suddenly revealed to him the "high-cultural form of peasant art" (Vakar and Mikhienko, 28). His autobiography continues: "I came to understand the peasants through the icon, saw in the

5 The region of Ostrogozhsk, for example, had been settled by Ukrainian Cossacks, who after 1783 had mostly been enserfed by Catherine the Great. The 1897 census revealed that this area was still over ninety percent Ukrainian. This is why after 1917 the Central Rada wanted to include it within the borders of the Ukrainian People's Republic as province to be named Podon. See Zhyvotko 1943, 10.

faces not saints, but ordinary people. And [I understood] the colors and the painter's attitude" (Vakar and Mikhienko, 28).

Moscow was therefore a further stage in his development. Through the art of the icon, he tells us, he was able to grasp the emotional art of the peasantry, which he had loved earlier but had been incapable of explaining to himself. As a result, Malevich rejected perspective, anatomy and the entire realist-naturalist approach that he had cultivated while studying the Wanderers. He decided that icon painters had achieved a high degree of technical mastery, and had succeeded in conveying content in an anti-anatomical way, outside the laws of perspective. They created color and form through a purely emotional way of approaching a theme.

It was then, he tells us, that he realized there was a direct artistic connection between the icon, on the one hand, and the little horses and roosters on peasant walls, along with peasant costumes and domestic tools, on the other. He informs the reader that he decided not to follow the classical art of antiquity, nor its revival in the Renaissance, which he now viewed as an art for beauty (*dlia krasoty*). Nor did he follow the realist art of the Wanderers (Peredvizhniki), which he now characterized as propaganda art. Instead, he decided to remain "on the side of peasant art" and "began painting pictures in the primitive spirit" (Vakar and Mikhienko, 29). In 1910–13 he first imitated icons, then painted peasants at work, people in suburbs and small town, and finally explored the world of town signs.

This narrative in large part contradicts the idea of Malevich's artistic life as beginning with his move to Moscow, where he supposedly embraced the new art of the city and the machine. In critical literature there has been a tendency to focus heavily on the exhibitions in Moscow and St. Petersburg/Leningrad, and to ignore his previous life. This is to some degree understandable given the amount of information available about the artist's life during the latter periods. Naturally, he was keen to escape provincial surroundings and to gain artistic enlightenment, and his artistic projects in both Moscow and St. Petersburg succeeded in placing him indisputably in the forefront of artistic innovation. One can agree that these two cities "were places that spoke of reform and revolution" and that they represented for Malevich centers both of "thought" and "intrigue" (Crone and Moos 1991, 51–52). However, Vakar describes the Moscow period as still one of the least studied and most interesting in the artist's life: "In ten years, from a completely unknown self-taught provincial he was transformed into the leader of the newest artistic movement, one summoned to complete the development of contemporary painting" (Vakar 2004, 583). A reader who takes seriously the description of his evolution presented in the autobiography must deal with an inescapable irony: he rejected the established, long respected art of the city's academies and galleries, and rediscovered the art of the rural folk from whom he had recently departed.

It is sometimes overlooked that radical experimentation can be inspired and conducted outside "centers," and that the latter frequently serve as bastions of reactionary, imperialist or authoritarian thinking. Young people who journey to capitals can and often do make the trip with a view to overthrowing dominant intellectual and artistic trends, and to introducing a radical perspective that they have incubated elsewhere. This kind of oppositional stance toward the imperial capitals has frequently appeared in Ukrainian cultural history as an anti-colonial reflex. It can be read clearly, for example, in the work of Taras Shevchenko, who elevated Ukrainian history and culture as part of a romantic rediscovery of native traditions. Both tsarist officials and metropolitan intellectuals quickly rejected this poet's construction of what they considered a highly problematic identity and assessed his writings as an anti-colonial "writing back" against imperial civilization.

To be sure, Malevich's autobiographical sketches might have been conceived as part of a longer, never completed account, one that that would probably have given more space to his life in Moscow and Petersburg/Leningrad. This, however, is doubtful. Malevich wrote a great deal about his life in the two Russian capitals elsewhere. In his Ukrainian essays published in 1928–30 he described, for example, his own evolution in the Russian cities against the background of modern art's development.[6] The point of the autobiographical essays is to underline the importance of peasant traditions as wellsprings of inspiration throughout the artist's life. It is telling that when translations of the 1933 autobiography were first published, the sections dealing with the painter's early life and his Ukrainian connections were sometimes omitted.[7] This part of Malevich's narrative wrenches attention away from his life in the two capitals, and offers in place of the city, technology and machine a startlingly different interpretive matrix. His "apologia of the peasantry," as Vakar has noted, began as a rejection of positivism. Although in his cubo-futurist years, 1910–13, the artist demonstrated a typically futurist attraction to the machine and dynamism, the autobiography suggests that all along he was steadily working toward

6 These appeared mostly in the journal *Nova generatsiia* and have been republished in Horbachov 2006, 28–161, and Filevska 2016, 29–120.

7 This is the case, for example, both in the Upchurch translation (Malevich 1985) and in the version published in *Kazimir Malevich* 1990.

solving other issues. Vakar argues that Malevich found constraining the antithesis between village and city, nature and civilization: "His imagination reached for the limitless, in which earthly antinomies would be overcome" (Vakar 2004, 580). According to this interpretation, his early life and experiences must be seen as crucial. They continually inspired his visionary work and stimulated his insights into the power and nature of art.

As will be seen, suprematism's links to peasant crafts can be traced throughout the post-1915 period. Its designs were introduced to folk peasant artists by Exter (Birnie Danzker 1993, 15, 104–5).[8] Along with two other Ukrainian women artists, Yevheniia Prybylska and Natalia Davydova, she facilitated joint projects between avant-gardists like Malevich and "peasant-futurists," by whom she meant folk artists from the cooperatives of Skoptsi near Poltava and Verbivka near Kyiv. In 1915–16 embroideries on scarves and pillows, and patterns on kilims—all based on suprematist designs—were produced in these village cooperatives and sold in Kyiv, Poltava, Moscow, and Berlin as examples of folk production (Naiden and Horbachov 1993, 221). However, the influences also flowed continually in the other direction. Exter introduced traditional folk elements into avant-garde art, and Malevich himself painted stoves in the traditional Ukrainian manner (Zhdanova 1982, 34).

In this context the clash with ideas expressed by Malevich in his *Non-Objective World*, published in German translation in 1927, is arresting. He made the following claim:

> The pictorial culture of the provinces is incensed at the art of the big city (Futurism, etc.) and seeks to combat it, because it is not objective-representational and consequently seems unsound. If the viewpoint that Cubism, Futurism, and Suprematism are abnormal were correct, one would necessarily have to conclude that the city itself, the dynamic center is an unwholesome phenomenon because it is largely responsible for the "morbid alteration" in art and the creators of art.
>
> The new art movements can exist only in a society that has absorbed the tempo of the big city, the metallic quality of industry. No Futurism can exist where society still maintains an idyllic, rural way of life (Chipp 1971, 339).[9]

8 For Exter's comments on Sobachko-Shostak, see "On the Works of Evgenia Pribilska and Ganna Sobachko," in Ukrajinska Avangarda, 1990.

9 The work was originally published in a German translation from the original Russian in Kasimir Malevich, *Die Gegenstandslose Welt, Bauhaus Book II* (Munich: Langen, 1927). For an English translation, see Malevich, *The Non-Objective World* (1959).

How should one explain Malevich's fulminations in the 1920s against the dominance of "provincial" art in the cities. A number of comments can be offered. Firstly, by "provincial" Malevich did not mean folk primitivism, but realist and representational art. He says precisely this in his autobiography when he argues that, although the futurists rejected Renaissance classics and the authority of the ancients, along with artists who subordinated themselves to societal demands, "we never rejected [*ne borolis protiv*] folk art or icon painters, or talented sign painters [*vyvesochnikov*]" (Vakar and Mikhienko 2004, vol. 1, 37).

Secondly, he opposed the idea of "reviving" the icon or the fresco in the sense of providing a stylization, a copy of old examples. The key thing, he argues in his autobiography, is the emotional power encoded in a work by a peasant artist, sign or icon painter. Therefore, the primitivists he was close to—Mikhail Larionov, Natalia Goncharova and David Burliuk—"belonged to a style [that represented] the peasant attitude toward phenomena, worked with the same emotional forms" (Vakar and Mikhienko, 37). They merely added to them elements learned in the city schools.

Thirdly, Malevich's outlook probably changed after 1927, as his views on urbanism, industrialism and the "metallization" of culture underwent a transformation. As will be argued, his works from the Kyiv period of 1928–30 suggest an implicit rejection of earlier opinions, such as the following passage from *Non-Objective World*:

> The provinces fight for their tranquility. They sense in metallization the expression of a new way of life in which small, primitive establishments and the comforts of country living will come to an end. The provinces therefore protest against everything which comes from the city, everything which seems new and unfamiliar, even when this happens to be new farm machinery (Chipp 1971, 339).

Although it is widely recognized that much modernist and avant-garde art drew inspiration from primitivism, in Malevich's case the connection has been obscured by his image as a bolshevik revolutionary and defender of machine civilization. The autobiography challenges this image and suggests that he was drawing intuitively on the power of ancient, peasant forms in art.

There are, of course, other ways of interpreting his artistic evolution. Charlotte Douglas has pointed to a mixture of aesthetic and intellectual influences contributing to the genesis of the first suprematist paintings in 1915. These include Henri Bergson, Umberto Boccioni and contemporary speculation concerning the fourth dimension (Douglas 1980, 1, 3, 67). Oleksandr

Naiden and Dmytro Horbachov have made a case for the artist's roots in specifically Ukrainian folklore of Yampol county in the Podillia region, where he spent his early years: "Only in 1976 when his autobiography, in which he spoke of his love of the peasantry, appeared in print in Stockholm did it become clear that the closest analogy to his suprematism are the geometrical forms of wall paintings in the homes of Podillia, the *pysanky* [painted Easter eggs] with their astral signs, the patterns of the *plakhta* [woven woman's skirt]—[all of which express] the magical code of universal elements (fire, earth, water). His pictures, in which sharply delineated patterns are scattered on a white background, capture the spirit of folk cosmology. The only difference is that the established order, embodied in the harmony of the peasant ornamental 'tree of life' is disturbed, dramatized and made dynamic in the spirit of the breakneck twentieth century" (Naiden and Horbachov 1993, 221–22).

These two Ukrainian researchers point out that the black square, circle and cross have for many centuries performed a symbolic function in folk beliefs and customs. Their presence is widespread in houses, graveyards and on clothing. The cross, for example, performs decorative, ritualistic and symbolic functions. The Yampil region is known both for its short, stone crosses and its tall, light wooden ones, which are often painted. These abound not only in graveyards but also on roadsides, and crosses as details appear on *pysanky*, kilims and embroideries. They symbolize salvation and protection. In combination with the vase and bird the cross represents the tree of life (Naiden and Horbachov, 216). A simple black cross on the face was also typical of dolls made by peasants from Podillia. This image was used by Malevich in his works from 1928–30.[10]

The years 1928–30 in Kyiv

Recently published memoirs indicate that even when he lived in Moscow and Petrograd/Leningrad Malevich was often in contact with "countrymen" from Ukraine, among whom there was a strong contingent of avant-gardists with an interest in primitivism. These included Tatlin, who was his constant competitor for primacy in the avant-garde, Alexander (Oleksandr) Shevchenko, and David Burliuk.

From 1926, when the government closed the Leningrad State Institute of Artistic Culture (GINKhUK) and merged its staff with the State Institute for Art History (GIII), Malevich was pressured to close his laboratories. In

10 For illustrations see Naiden and Horbachov 1993, 217, 219.

1927 he traveled abroad to exhibit his work in Berlin and Warsaw. In the latter city he described himself as Polish in an effort to obtain a job in that country. He then visited relatives in Kyiv, where Tatlin, who left Leningrad in 1925, was teaching at the Kyiv Art Institute (KKhI). Two other friends, Andrii Taran and Lev Kramarenko, were also lecturing there, along with Oleksandr Bohomazov and Viktor Palmov, who were exploring the use of color. The Institute's ambitious director, Ivan Vrona, hoped that Archipenko would join the faculty in 1929, but the latter, who was in the United States at that time, declined the invitation. Vrona, however, convinced Malevich to lecture at the Kyiv Art Institute in the years 1928–30.

In these two years Malevich published fourteen articles in Ukrainian in the Kharkiv monthly *Nova generatsiia* (New Generation), and the Kyiv *Avanhard-Almanakh* (Avant-garde Almanac, 1930). He planned to develop these articles into a book on the history and theory of the new art. Under the title "Izologia" (Artology) it was rejected by Russian publishers. At this time Matiushin's long essay on the fourth dimension, motion and expanded vision appeared in *Nova generatsiia*.[11] Increasing attacks on the avant-garde made this journal one of very few available publishing outlets for Malevich and Matiushin.

Nova generatsiia promoted itself as an international journal, publishing versions of its articles in English, French, German or Esperanto, and providing abstracts in foreign languages. The editorial board included figures such as László Moholy-Nagy and Johannes Becher, and the journal's cover displayed the names of Russian avant-gardists, including Osip Brik, Aleksei Gan, Sergei Eisenstein, Vladimir Maiakovsky, and Viktor Shklovsky. Like the Kyiv Art Institute it emphasized formal, constructivist concerns, and an international perspective. Malevich found a supportive environment in Kyiv and made a point of identifying himself as a Ukrainian. His younger sister Victoria (married name Zaitseva) recalled that he always recorded his nationality as Ukrainian on official documents, and insisted that other family members should do the same (Naiden and Horbachov 1993, 221).[12]

Mykhailo Boichuk also found a refuge in the Kyiv Art Institute in these years. Boichuk and Malevich met frequently for discussions in 1928–30. Boichuk came from a peasant background in the same Podillia region that Malevich had lived in as a child. While both had been influenced by symbolism and the Nabis artists, Boichuk had actually studied in a Parisian

11 See: M. Matiushyn, "Sproba novoho vidchuttia prostorony" (Attempt at a New Feeling for Space), *Nova generatsiia* 11 (1928): 311–22. For an English translation see Mudrak 1986, 227–43.

12 He did this on all forms. For an example see Vakar and Mikhienko 2004, vol. 1, 549.

studio of the Nabis. Both also had studied the forms and symbolic codes of iconic and primitive art.

Malevich's arguments with his Kyiv colleagues were candidly expressed in lectures, articles and letters.[13] His criticisms of Boichuk's monumentalism were published in 1930 in an article for *Avanhard-Almanakh* (Avant-garde Almanach). In it Malevich opposed the use of a fresco form that he felt had developed out of monastic principles and canons and was inappropriate in a proletarian state (Malevich 2016, 117). However, it has been suggested that the argument between Boichuk and Malevych was between two individuals who began from a common departure point, the icon, and had then moved in different directions (Naiden and Horbachov 1993, 229).

The heavy attacks on Boichuk and his school in these years may have spurred Malevich into rethinking his views of the rural/urban dichotomy. Moreover, his discussions with Boichuk may have inspired him to return to painting the peasantry in the years 1928–30 and then later to rework the genre of Renaissance portraiture, in which Boichuk was intensely interested.

However, it is Malevich's now famous series of peasant paintings from 1928–30 that have attracted most attention. They differ markedly from those done in the serene style of 1911–13 that evokes a stable community living close to nature. These later works with their disturbing blank faces and armless figures floating in space are now often read as a protest against the treatment of villagers who were being collectivized, arrested or deported. The peasants in these portraits appear helpless, isolated and displaced. *Untitled (Man Running)* (1928–30) portrays a figure running from a sword toward a cross. On the back of *A Complex Presentiment (Half-Length Figure in a Yellow Shirt)* (1928–32), Malevich wrote: "The composition is made up of the elements of the sensation of emptiness, loneliness and the hopelessness of life. 1913, Kuntsevo." This picture, like many others, was backdated because such images and sentiments, if they referenced contemporary reality, were punishable with imprisonment. Sarabianov has described the figure in the last picture as follows: "cramped by the expanse, the neck is stretched, the arms extended. Edged to the right, the figure has lost its dominant position on the surface of the canvas and is torn from the center. These devices symbolize the uprooting of mankind, its proximity and muteness, its captivity and doom" (Sarabianov 1991, 146). Today many

13 His discussions with Viktor Palmov and the spectralists were recorded by a student, Marian Kropyvynskyi, and have now been published in Filevska 2016, 298–329. For a selection of his letters to Lev Kramarenko and Iryna Zhdanko see Filevska 2016, 263–79. For minutes of meetings in which Malevich participated while in Kyiv see Filevska 2016, 171–98.

viewers interpret these paintings as Malevich's presentiment of the enormous tragedy that was about to engulf the peasantry.

His drawings from the period show images of a coffin, a hammer and sickle, and an Orthodox cross on the faces of peasants. Malevich may in this way have been recording the widespread sense of an imminent apocalyptic event. In rural areas mass movements had appeared foretelling the end of the world and the coming of the Antichrist. In folk-songs, which have survived from these movements, symbols of death, salvation and the Antichrist were common. They can be linked to the images in Malevich's paintings (Naiden and Horbachov 1993, 220). The artist would have been aware of these movements among the peasantry and likely used symbols familiar to the popular psyche in order to convey his sense of imminent disaster.

In spite of the increasingly threatening tone in public discourse, Malevich was able to hold an exhibition in Moscow at the Tretiakov Gallery in late 1929, one that was given almost no publicity. Then in Kyiv in 1930 he held what would prove to be his last exhibition. It was a retrospective for which he selected forty-five works, although a number had been freshly painted and backdated to avoid the charge that he was commenting on contemporary events. At the start of the 1930–31 academic year he also made plans to take up a permanent teaching post at the Kyiv Art Institute and to transfer all his works to the city. However, a government order dismissed all professors who were not members of the party, and Malevich, Boichuk and Kramarenko, found themselves among those who were fired.

The autobiography was written shortly after this, in 1933, two years before his death. It can be interpreted as evidence that Malevich was setting the record straight concerning the sources of his inspiration, reconsidering some earlier views, and perhaps even expressing a veiled protest against the forced collectivization, grain requisitioning and the famine that occurred in that year. These events, which constituted a war on the Ukrainian countryside and people, led to the death of an estimated four million peasants. Artists and writers of this period found various ways of encoding resistance to the régime's policies and actions. One of the best known is Oleksandr Dovzhenko's film *Earth* (*Zemlia*, 1930), which ostensibly lauds the benefits of collectivization, but in fact derives its power from a depiction of the vitality and beauty of peasant life. Malevich's autobiography, like his art of 1928–30, might be viewed as a similar encryption of an oppositional stance.

Vadym Meller and Sources of Inspiration in Theater Art[1]

Vadym Meller is known as one of the most important Ukrainian theater artists of the twentieth century. Although his contribution to theater design spanned over forty years, from 1919 until 1961, a period in which he made sets and costumes for the most prominent Ukrainian stage directors, it was his work with Bronislava Nijinska's ballets in 1919–21 and for Les Kurbas's Berezil Theater that has come to represent artistic excellence in theater art.

Meller's long career as chief artistic designer for over a hundred productions in several leading theaters has left a rich legacy. His artistic evolution is a complex story. During the twenties, his most creative years, he explored cubo-futurism and constructivism, before introducing satirical and playful features, and finally realist, even grotesque, elements into his costume and set designs. Each phase produced memorable innovative productions and he became widely known for his versatility and skill.[2] It is less well known that in the years after 1917 he collaborated with the suprematist artist Nina Henke and the cottage craft industry. Henke, whom he married on August 11, 1919, was a key link between the avant-garde and cottage workers. She strengthened Meller's interest in folk decorative arts and introduced him to the designs of craft workers.

The ethnic and family roots of both Meller and Henke were not in Ukraine; nor were their origins in any sense proletarian. Meller was born in St. Petersburg on April 13, 1884 (April 26th, according to the Julian Calendar) to Georgii and Elena Meller. Georgii served in the Ministry of Justice and became

1 A Ukrainian-language version of this article appeared as "Henii Vadym Mellera: Tanets ta dekoratyvne mystetstvo v ukrainskomu avanhardi" in *Kurbasivski chytannia* 7 (2012): 122–37. I would like to thank Brigitta Vadymivna Vetrova for providing access to materials and for their advice in the preparation of this article. Many of the ideas expressed here are taken from conversations with her in Kyiv.

2 A noteworthy exhibitions of his work occurred in 2009 at the Museum of Theater, Music and Cinema Art in Kyiv which presented 54 works from the period 1919–33, including posters designed by Meller for the Berezil Theater's productions.

a state counselor (*statskii sovetnik*), the fourth highest rank in the imperial hierarchy. He was granted the status of hereditary noble (*potomstvennyi dvorianin*) and converted from the Lutheran faith to Orthodoxy in order to accept the rank. From the time of Peter the Great all Georgii's relatives had been Lutherans of Swedish origin. He was the first to marry a non-Swede. Vadym's mother Elena was born in Italy of an Italian father and a Greek mother.

Vadym Meller's personal modesty and sense of restraint have often been attributed to his Swedish Lutheran background. However, they might also have been the product of some painful experiences early in life. He was the younger of two sons. When his older brother, the parent's favorite, drowned while swimming in the Dnipro, his mother reportedly turned grey overnight. For the rest of his life Vadym feared water and dreaded the prospect of anyone close to him becoming ill. Always careful and meticulous, he developed a gift for translating every inspiration into harmonious composition.

He entered Kyiv University to study law, but in December 1905 in order to avoid the revolutionary disturbances that had broken out in the city his father sent him to Geneva, where he studied art with Franz Roubaud (Rubo). Upon his return he published his first caricatures in the newspaper *Kievskaia myst* (Kyiv Thought) in 1907, then graduated in law from St. Vladimir's University (now Kyiv State University) in 1908. At the time he was also taking classes at the Kyiv Art School. Upon Roubaud's recommendation he was able to enter Heinrich Knirr's school of drawing in Munich, and then attended the Munich Academy of Arts from 1908–12, where he met Paul Klee and was introduced by the latter to Kandinsky and other Der Blaue Reiter artists. In the years 1912–14 he worked in Paris, first in private studios, then in his own. His work was noted in the press and he was invited to exhibit in the Salon d'Automne.

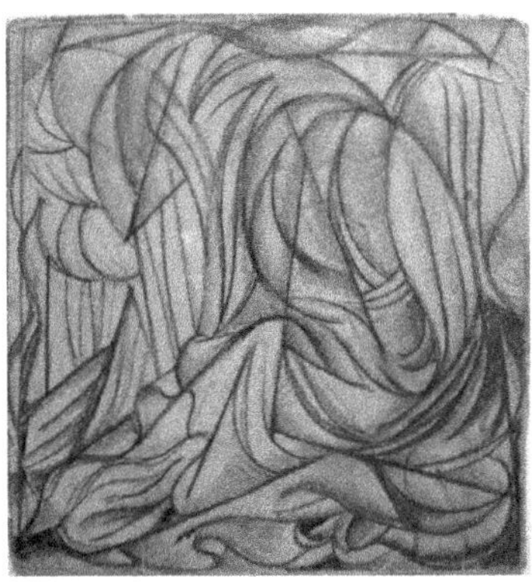

Vadym Meller. *Sketch for a painting in cubo-futurist style*, 1910s.

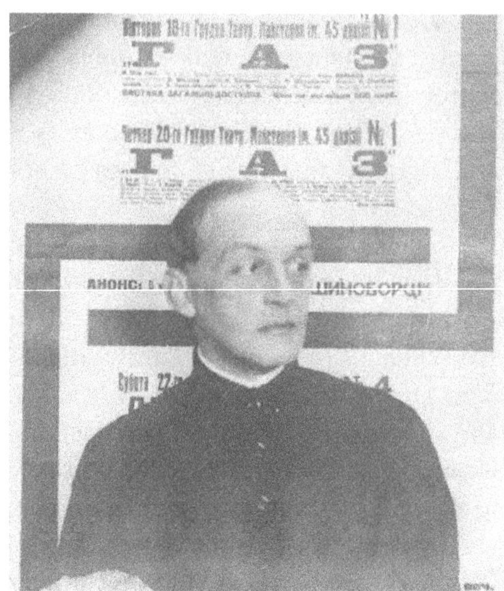

Vadym Meller in the early 1920s. Photographer unknown.

In June 1914, shortly before the First World War broke out, he returned to Kyiv. Although not required to do military service, he joined a support organization attached to the Third Army, which served on the Western front. In the summer of 1918 he returned to Kyiv and in the years 1919–21 worked with Exter and with Bronislava Nijinska's dance studio.

Nina Henke worked as a student assistant to Exter in the latter's Kyiv studio in 1916, where she met Meller.[3] Nina's family on her father's side had emigrated from the Netherlands in the days of the Spanish Empire in order to avoid religious persecution. Her father directed a merchant's office in Moscow; her mother was Russian. Nina completed Kyiv's Levandovska Gymnasium for girls in 1912 and studied at the Hlukhiv Teachers' Institute in 1914. She lost her first job when a teaching supervisor and well-known reactionary called Derevytskyi charged her with "malicious perversion of historical facts" and "contact with the Jewish population." As a result, she was transferred to the village of Skoptsi near Poltava, where she taught history, geography and drawing. It was in this now famous village that she met and began working for Yevheniia Prybylska, a design artist and organizer of the local cottage industry.

3 Meller's first wife, Carmen, whom he met while in Paris, and who was of Spanish origin, returned to France.

From 1916 to 1920 she worked closely with Exter in the latter's Kyiv studio, filling orders from Moscow theaters. She helped Exter make the designs for Alexander (Oleksandr) Tairov's production of *Famira Kifared* in the Kamernyi Theater. Based on the tragedy by Innokentii Annenskii, the production has been described as "a magnificent parade of Cubism" and is credited with making a revolution in theater art (Ratanova 2010, 314). According to Horbachov, Exter presented antiquity as humanity's childhood against an intensely blue background that recalled Sobachko's paintings (Horbachov 2000, 502). From 1915 Henke also worked independently, completing her own costume designs and theater backdrops, and producing decorative work for woven materials.

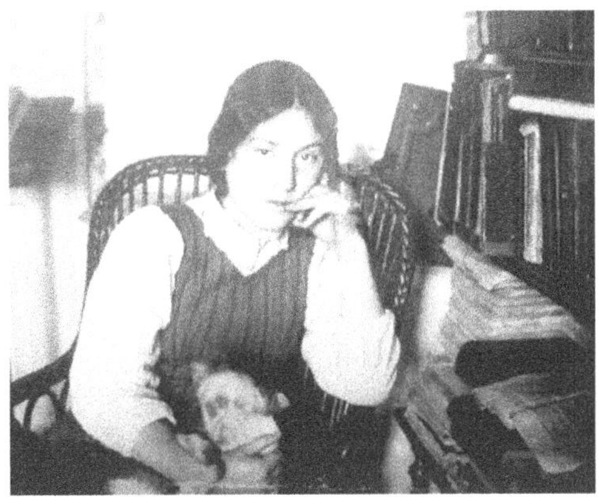

Nina Henke in the 1920s. Photographer unknown.

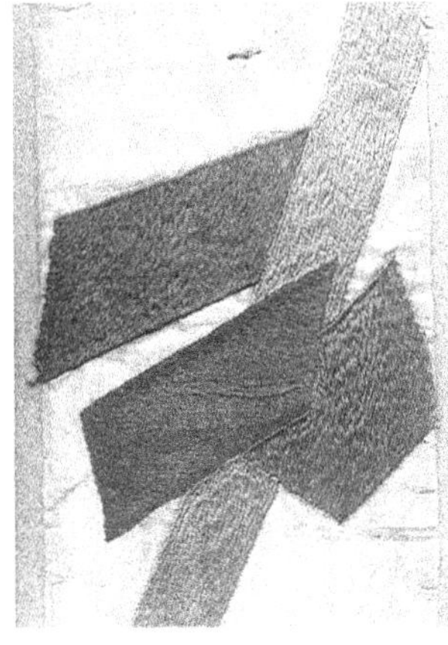

Nina Henke. *Suprematist composition produced by Verbivka folk artists*, 1910s.

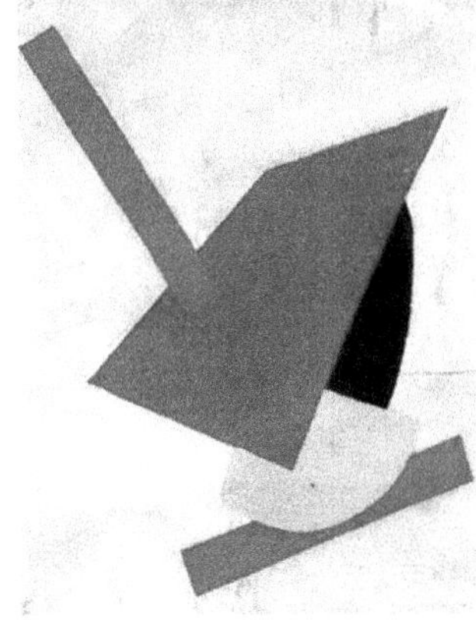

Nina Henke. *Suprematist composition*, 1910s.

Already in 1915 she headed the Verbivka center in the Kyiv region, and in this way became a leader of the Kyiv Cottage Industry Society. Prybylska meanwhile continued to head the center in Skoptsi. These two were in contact with other points of production, such Kaminka (Kamenka in Russian, in the Kherson region) and Zoziv (Zozov in Russian, near Kyiv). In 1917 Henke traveled to Moscow to organize an exhibition of Verbivka's products in the city's Lemercier Gallery. She returning to Kyiv in the autumn of 1918, and worked for the Society until 1922.

Through his contact with Exter, Henke and Prybylska, Meller was drawn into the work of peasant collectives. He became a member of the Cottage Industry Society's directorate in the months before the October Revolution. This interaction with craft workers strengthened his appreciation for the exuberance and vitality of folk creativity.

Dance and movement

Meller's work was shaped initially by the contemporary fascination with the human figure as displayed in dance and movement, which accounts for much of the elegance, gracefulness and poise of his work. In Kyiv, while collaborating with Nijinska's innovative École de Mouvement in the years 1919–21, both he and Exter explored movement. Nijinska, who was the sister of the legendary Vaclav Nijinsky, had come from Paris to St. Petersburg in the summer of 1914. Prevented by the war from returning, in 1915 she staged ballets by the modernist Mikhail Fokine at the Kyiv Opera House. After her return to Paris in 1921 she became known as "one of the greatest ballet innovators of the twentieth century," particularly for her 1923 staging of *Les Noces* to Stravinsky's music (Ratanova 2010, 313–14). During her Kyiv period she worked with Exter, Meller and other artists. Her school, which initially set itself the task of training dancers for her brother's troupe in London, resembled an art studio, in which dancing classes alternated with classes in visual arts and stage design (Ratanova, 314).

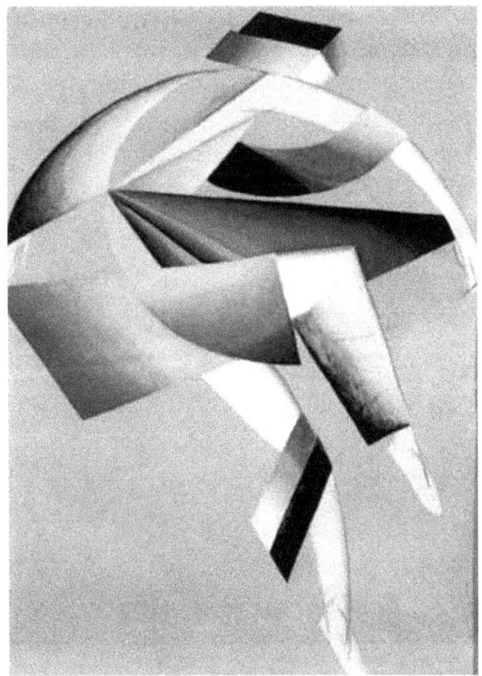

Vadym Meller. *Blue Dancer*, from *Mephisto*, to music of Liszt, 1919–20.

Meller's costume sketches of dancers hung on the school's walls. At that time Exter and Meller were introducing cubo-futurist elements into their designs. Both had attended the Kyiv Art School, and had been friends since meeting in Paris in 1912. Exter was by then an influential creative force in the Kyiv. From 1918 her apartment became a club in which artists, writers, directors, and musicians mixed. Besides Nijinska and Meller, visitors included the stage director Les Kurbas, the theater designers Oleksandr (Alexander) Khvostenko-Khvostov, Aleksandr Tyshler, Isaak Rabinovich, and the artist Nisson Shifrin.

Art deco was another strong influence on Meller. The term was coined following the Paris Exposition Internationale des Arts Décoratifs et Industriels Modernes in 1925, which has been described as "one of the most important artistic events of the twentieth century" (Makaryk 2010, 479). Meller won the gold medal at the exposition for his set model of the Berezil Theater's production of *Sekretar profspilky* (The Trade Union Secretary, 1924). Art deco is associated with a decorative environment that blends the "exotic" with the contemporary, and which often makes use of the sleek, refined figure of a dancer in an elegant pose recalling classical sculptures and vase paintings. Meller's costume sketches for Nijinska's ballets fit this description. Some, such as his figures for *Assyrians*, *Masks*, *Mephisto* and other dances have now become internationally famous. Art deco's geometrical forms and color contrasts, designed to produce a luxurious look, are also evident in Meller's costume sketches, which are composed of unusual surfaces such as silver paper, rich colors such as cherry reds, and unexpected contrasts.

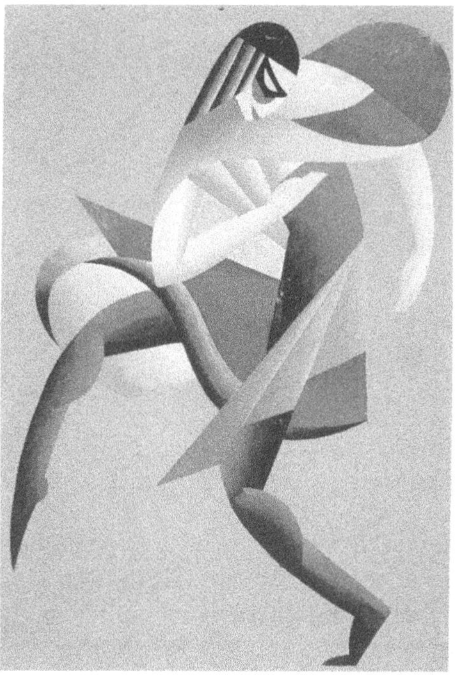

Vadym Meller. *Mask*, to music of Chopin, 1920.

Meller's paintings of figures were broken down into curves, triangular or sharpened forms, and parabolas. He positioned these in ways that create a dynamic tension and sense of movement. In describing Meller's *Mephisto* figure Ihor Dychenko felt it represented the ontology of dance: "It's as if you have a photograph of the 'biology' of dance, its magnetic lines, its elevated simplicity in the curve of the body and the poetically sad positions of the arms." According to Dychenko, what singled out Meller was his "unique spiritualism, the arrangement of forms as if devoid of a spatially objective subtext. It's as if he 'raised' the body, as a plastic material, to the height of movement spiritually rich in content" (quoted in Makaryk 2004, 51).

In 1921–22, when the constructivist infatuation with metal, machine-produced objects, and geometrical patterns began, Meller started designing in this style for the theater. Elements of the satirical and grotesque also first appeared at this time. But his portrayal of character through movement and gesture, his love of elegance, and use of unexpected color contrasts remained constant throughout the decade.

In their set designs both Exter and Meller eschewed naturalistic conventions, experimenting instead with rhythmically organized space. They arrived simultaneously at the idea of balancing mass in space through intersecting planes and verticals. These principles were employed to fill theatrical theater space from top to bottom with bridges, platforms, ladders, and banners. Both artists adapted cubist and then constructivist ideas with elegance and simplicity. However, Exter had been active in Paris since 1910, where she had been strongly influenced by cubism and color experimentation. She showed a fascination with the kilim designs, color clashes and movement for its own sake. The work of Meller, who had been trained in drawing and composition in Geneva and Munich, was more restrained. He concentrated on analyzing the human form, used more subtle color schemes, and admired poise as much as movement. Already in Paris in 1913 his work had been described as dance produced in a decorative manner (in *Le Lynx*, 21 June 1913; quoted in Krasylnikova 2000, 112). This love of the graceful was later communicated to Meller's students, among whom Vasyl Shkliaiev demonstrated a similar fascination with the deco-like figure and luxurious color.

A comparison of perhaps the three greatest Ukrainian theater artists of the twenties is revealing. The costumes sketches of Exter are known for celebrating the wild energy of movement; those of Anatolii Petrytskyi disconcert or shock the viewer; Meller's work, in contrast, always remains a study in balance and harmony.

Folk decorative impulse

The folk decorative arts were the other major influence on Meller in the post-revolutionary years. Many Eastern European avant-gardists were captivated by a discovery of the exotic that had been "hidden in plain view"—namely their own folk art. As previous chapters have shown, artists from Ukraine exploited their native folk arts in remarkably original ways. Part of this attraction to folk creativity was inspired by patriotism. Around the time of the First World War and in the immediate postwar years, folk design and ornamentation in Poland, Czechoslovakia, Hungary, and Ukraine was used in an effort to create uniquely "national" styles. The avant-garde interaction with local, international with national, modern with ancient, gave a particularly exciting, even transgressive tone to artistic experimentation. Exter even claimed in 1919 that color intensity was "typical of young nations, particularly Slavs" (Exter 1990, 209). Meller's artistic development could not remain unaffected by this rediscovery of village culture, particularly after he was drawn into the project, championed by Henke and Prybylska, of connecting local artisans with the art world with a view to changing societal attitudes toward the decorative arts.

Yevheniia Prybylska

Although Prybylska's name is not widely known, she had a profound impact on the story of the Ukrainian avant-garde and its relationship to folk creativity. After graduating from the Kyiv Art School in 1907 she began helping the textile workers in Skoptsi in 1910. At the Second All-Russian Cottage Industry Exhibition in St. Petersburg held in 1913 she was awarded the silver medal for an exhibition of products from this village. This proved to be her first major breakthrough. That autumn she also showed the work of the Skoptsi women in Kyiv, and in the following year in Berlin and Paris in the Salon d'Automne. Exhibitions followed in Moscow's Gallery Lemercier in 1914 and 1915. While in Paris she met the artists Raoul Dufy and Charles Dufresne who worked with woven materials, and who were excited by her collection of peasant drawings.

However, contacts were cut off when the war intervened, isolating the peasant craft industry in Ukraine from Western markets and denying it materials, which were needed at the front. Nonetheless, as part of their contribution to overcoming wartime hardship, an initiative group organized production points in Galicia and Bukovyna, two regions of Western Ukraine that were rich in folk arts. Ten workshops were set up by 1916, and an exhibition of their products took place in the Kyiv Museum in April 1917, and then in August and September in the Moscow's Lemercier Gallery. In May 1919, with the help of Henke and Meller, Prybylska organized an exhibition in Kyiv which displayed work from Skoptsi and the Poltava area.

These exhibitions had a strong influence. Prybylska has written that after viewing the works many individuals changed their opinion about peasant art, which until then they had considered "crude and vulgar" (Pribilska n.d., 8). After moving to Moscow in 1922 she continued to order designs from cottage workers in Ukraine. In 1924, when the overseas market began to grow again, she organized a major exhibition of Ukrainian folk arts in Berlin and Dresden, drawing on her own, by then substantial, collection. In later years she organized exhibitions of Ukrainian art in Russia and continued to write articles for various journals.

The story of how Prybylska became interested in peasant designs and developed an international market for them has rarely been told. When as a student she began exploring the rich collection of decorative folk arts in Kyiv's museums, she was so taken by what she found that she "fell in love with decorative art" and decided to devote herself completely to "the study of Ukrainian folk art and its ancient images" (Pribilska, 9). She made many copies from pieces both in museums and in private collections, and worked on her own decorative compositions. The copies she made from eighteenth-century weavings and embroideries in the Museum of St. Sophia Cathedral (Sofiiskyi Sobor)[4] and the collections belonging to the Monastery of the Caves (Pecherska Lavra) attracted two figures in Kyiv: the art historian Adriian Prakhov and the artist Mykhailo Nesterov, a member of the Kyiv Cottage Society. This led to a request from the Society and the Poltava Gubernia Zemstvo (County Council) for more drawings of embroideries and compositions. Soon afterwards, Prybylska received an invitation to work with Nikolai Vartram in Moscow at the toy museum of the Cottage Industry Technicum, which he directed, and as a researcher in the Academy of Artistic Sciences' peasant art section, which he headed (Pribilska, 10).

A delegation of cottage industry workers had learned of her intention of traveling to Moscow, and approached her with a proposal that she should sell "for money or food products" a large collection of their designs. She immediately realized the value of these, and the fact that when they were put into production for profit the workers would receive only token payment. Therefore, she decided to act as an intermediary and to put the Moscow workshops in direct touch with the designers themselves. As a result, the products of the craft workshops were soon being exhibited and sold internationally.

Like other artists who were then discovering the folk arts, Prybylska was not simply a copyist but made original designs in the spirit of folk traditions. Both as an artist and exhibition curator she tried to promote a wider awareness of the beauty and power of the designs she had discovered. There were many individuals who did not share her enthusiasm. Initially, for example, the Poltava Zemstvo and Kyiv merchants refused to display

---

4 Now the Archive-Museum of Literature and Art.

or sell the work, which they considered too colorful and therefore vulgar. The situation changed after the work of individual peasant artists such as Yevheniia Pshechenko from Skoptsi were greeted with acclaim in the Gallery Lemercier in 1914 and 1915. Exter's enthusiastic endorsement at the opening of the Kyiv exhibition in 1919 also served as legitimization. In her address Exter noted folk art's "two-dimensional solution of vegetal, animal, and architectural pattern" in woven cloth and rugs, embroidery and printing. She argued that color intensity had been replaced by the public's taste for "the muted patina of time, which conveyed an impression of authenticity and the charm of the antique." Such an understanding of popular art "was not based on in-depth research into the roots and laws which dictate the choice of color, of lines and composition" (Exter 1990, 209). Prybylska's drawings, she said, were related to the works of Matisse, who was also "inspired by the East, by its ornaments and colours." In the workshops where the embroidery and weaving was done Prybylska's drawings were treated "both as embroidery patterns and as creative art" (Exter, 210). The exhibition demonstrated that Sobachko had "emerged as a distinct personality, establishing by her choice of color and her composition a style of her own" (Exter, 210).

Henke and suprematism

The public's reassessment of folk art came at a time when avant-garde artists such as Liubov Popova, Alexandra Exter and Olga Rozanova were looking to introduce color and dynamism into their works. Henke and Prybylska were able to recruit them for their project, with the resulting unexpected marriage of high and popular art. The fusion of suprematism with peasant art was largely the result of collaboration between these four talented women artists—Prybylska, Exter, Henke, and Davydova. Through their efforts the villages of Skoptsi, Verbivka and Zoziv (near Kyiv) became laboratories in which "the ultra-modern fused with the ancient" (Papeta 2006, 123).

Henke's role was crucial. Initially she had directed the work at Skoptsi. In 1916, while working with Exter on the designs for *Famira Kifared*, she developed contacts with suprematist artists. In this way she became the link between avant-garde artists in Moscow and St. Petersburg, including Kazimir Malevich's Supremus group, of which she was a member, and the craft workers in Ukraine. She maintained both networks in later years, keeping in regular contact with Rozanova, Popova, Nadezhda Udaltsova,

Ivan Puni, and Ivan Kliun, preparing their sketches for the embroiderers in the craft workshops, and also creating her own suprematist compositions for them (Papeta, 124–25).

Lost works

Many of the works produced by Henke and Meller have been lost, along with them a portion of this period's history. Meller's prewar works were lost in 1914 when he moved back to Kyiv from Paris. The outbreak of the First World War prevented their shipment, and they were never seen again. Only a few photographs now exist of paintings done in cubo-futurist style, produced in Munich and Paris, and shown at the Salon des Indépendants, Salon de Printemps and Salon d'Automne. Another loss occurred during the Second World War, when in 1941 many works were removed from the Kyiv apartment of Meller and Henke by German soldiers. The fate of these works also remains unknown. Most of Henke's works were removed from the Kyiv apartment during this confiscation. As a result, her contribution to suprematism and post-revolutionary graphic art is not well known. Only a few cover designs made for futurist publications in the twenties and a couple of suprematist works hastily packed during the evacuation have survived.[5] Although the full story of the avant-garde's collaboration with the folk arts still requires reconstructing, is clear that Henke and Meller were at the center of an important interaction between innovative art trends, folk designs and commercial production.

In spite of the losses, today Kyiv's Museum of Theater, Music and Cinema Arts, which is located on the grounds of the Monastery of the Caves (Pecherska Lavra), contains 420 works by Meller, including sketches for costumes and decorations for 59 performances. His work can also be found is several private collections and museums.[6] Meller's legacy also includes the students that he trained and his collaborative work with playwrights and directors, such as Vakhtang Beridze, Les Kurbas, Mykola Kulish, and Marian Krushelnytskyi.[7]

---

5 For two examples, see Lahutenko 2007, 10, 27.

6 These include the National Art Museum of Ukraine in Kyiv, the Bakhrushinskii Museum in Moscow, the Shevchenko Theater Museum (formerly the Berezil Theater) in Kharkiv, and the Archive-Museum of Literature and Art in Kyiv.

7 His students included Dmytro Vlasiuk, Yevhen Torbin, Vasyl Shkliaiev, and Mylytsia Symashkevych.

His reputation always remained high, and his work popular with the public. A tribute, of sorts, to Meller's enduring popularity is the fact that his works reputedly provide the largest number of forgeries of Ukrainian art found on the market.[8]

Meller in avant-garde theater

Under the Soviet regime Meller avoided being drafted into the Red Army when on May 30, 1919 his work in the field of art was deemed to be of state importance. In 1921 he helped to organize the Kyiv Art Institute, the major post-revolutionary art school in Ukraine, and lectured there from 1921–25.[9]

Meller designed numerous displays for the Soviet Ukrainian republic. He was in Magdeburg at the German theater exhibition in 1927 and in Cologne for the Press exhibition in 1928, for which he designed the Ukrainian section. Later he organized state exhibitions that took place in England, France and Japan. In the years 1921–26 he worked in the Odesa and Moscow film studios, collaborating with Les Kurbas on *Makdonald* (MacDonald, 1925), *Arsenaltsy* (The Arsenal Workers, 1926) and *Vendetta* (Vendetta, 1926).[10] He also exhibited his own work in various international art exhibitions in Paris, Prague, Cologne, Geneva, and New York, most famously winning the gold medal in 1925 at the World Exhibition in Paris for the set model he made for Berezil's 1924 *Sekretar profspilky* (The Trade Union Secretary).

From 1922–46 he was the leading artist of the Berezil Theater (renamed the Shevchenko Art Theater in 1934), where he collaborated closely with the stage director Kurbas and the playwright Kulish. Known affectionately

8 In 1994 Sotheby's sold his costume sketches for the 1920 production of *Haz*, but attributed them mistakenly to Exter. In the same year, a forgery of his *Blue Dancer*, made for Nijinska's ballet *Mephisto*, was also offered for sale shortly after the original was exhibited in Toulouse, allowing enterprising forgers to made a copy (Kucherenko 1997, 342). The forged works, it might be noted, are sometimes reproduced on websites as originals. They generally lack the graceful balance that the artist always demanded. A perfectionist, he made many variations of a work before settling on a final version and carefully destroyed any remaining versions.

9 A list of his students is available in the Central State Archive of Higher Organs of Power (TsDAVO): f. 166, op. 2, spr. 377, ark. 38 contains a list eleven students for 15 November 1921); f. 166, op. 2, spr. 1553, ark. 21–21 contains an outline of Meller's course for 1922–23.

10 Kurbas was arrested in 1933. The films disappeared and appear to have been lost or destroyed.

as the "three musketeers," they together transformed the Ukrainian stage, making Kharkiv into a leading theatrical innovator. Meller designed the sets for their greatest successes, which included *Narodnii Malakhii* (The People's Malakhii, 1928), *Myna Mazailo* (1930) and *Maklena Grasa* (1933). Unfortunately, detailed records of these productions have not survived. They appear to have been destroyed after Kurbas's arrest in 1933 and his execution in 1937. Although Meller himself was not arrested, for the rest of his life he was deeply pained by the fate of his colleagues. The expressionistic style he employed in *Maklena Grasa* (1933) and other productions at this time conveyed the sense of anxiety he and the public felt during this period of mass arrests.[11]

Already in his early agitational works for Berezil, which included *Haz* (Gas, 1923), *RUR* (Ruhr, 1923), *Jimmy Higgins* (1923), *Mashynobortsi* (The Machine Wreckers, 1923), and *Liudyna masa* (Mass Man, 1924), Meller had introduced elements of constructivism and expressionism. These productions were characterized by asceticism and emphasis on dynamic, quick scene changes. The production of *Macbeth* (1924) was the culmination of this experimental phase and brought him recognition as Ukraine's leading theater artist.[12] He emptied the stage. Instead of traditional decorations, the place of action was designated by enormous screens on which were written: "Hall," "Field," "Gates to the Castle," and so on. Only the most essential furnishing was used and some actors were dressed in contemporary worker's overalls covered with short coats to remind the audience of the medieval setting (Tsybenko 1967, 159). "The characters were the equivalent of cubist geometric forms in new, discontinuous relations with each other and with the world around them. Raised or lowered when needed at the sound of a gong, the screens served as more than background. They gave each scene a particular rhythmic character. [...] Lowered at the same time, they indicated the simultaneity of the action in different parts of Scotland. At other times, they moved in slow, stately rhythm to underscore the emotions of the lead actors, to emphasize tension, the dynamics of the action, or even to interfere in the action—as, for example, in the banquet scene, where they physically blocked off Macbeth's attempt to follow Banquo's ghost—represented by a spotlight" (Makaryk 2004, 84).

The constructivist aesthetic of the early twenties was justified by many commentators in ideological terms as appropriate for the "mechanization"

11 After the Second World War he worked for the Theater of Musical Comedy (1948–51) and the Franko Ukrainian Theater (1952–59), both in Kyiv.

12 For a discussion of this production see Makaryk 2004, 65–112. Meller's art and stage sets are also discussed in several articles in Makaryk and Tkacz 2010.

required by the times. In the years 1921–22 it was common to speak of the rhythms of the factory worker and peasant as completely different from those of the banker or diplomat. The cultural worker was urged to create what were perceived as the new and superior rhythms of industry. For example, the leading Kharkiv journal *Chervonyi shliakh* (Red Path) in 1923 published an article that applauded Meller's artistic studio for preparing new theatrical artists who could work with contemporary directors and theaters ("Maliarska maisternia" 1923, 221). The studio made posters for *Gas* and other shows, and illustrations for the Red Cross. Under the influence of the machine aesthetic, the silk- and velvet-like textures of the early post-revolutionary period gave way to functional black and white forms, while individual characteristics were submerged in depictions of the collective.

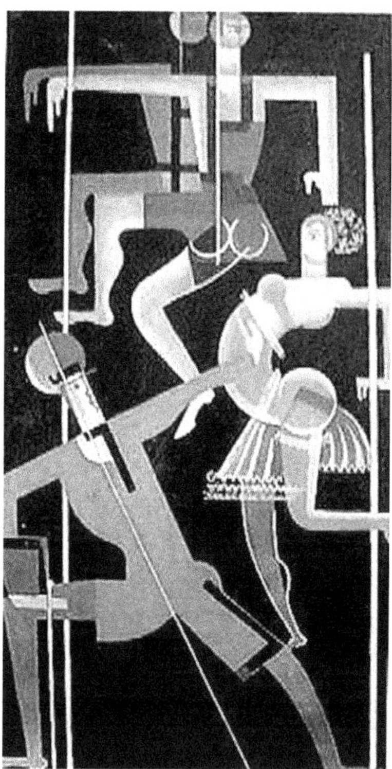

Vadym Meller. *Carnival*, 1923.

In the mid-twenties Meller began exploring the satirical. Productions such as *Sekretar profspilky* (The Trade Union Secretary, 1924) allowed him to introduce local color and indulge his love of the whimsical. Playfulness was already evident in the costume designs for Nijinska's ballets *Marriage of Figaro* and *Metr Patlen* (both, 1919), but they came to the fore in the Berezil productions of *Jimmy Higgins* (1923), and in *Karnaval* (Carnival, 1923), *Zolote cherevo* (Les Tripes d'Or, 1924) and *Sedi* (1926) directed by Kurbas. Meller's costume sketches and paintings from this period reveal an ability to capture essential traits. He had a remarkable ability to mimic. He spoke French, Russian and Ukrainian, and later learned German in Munich, and Spanish from his first wife. On one occasion in a train he imitated the sounds of the English language in a made-up gibberish, pretending to have a discussion with his partner in front of an astonished English couple sitting opposite them. The ability to mimic and reproduce personality traits became useful in the thirties, when Soviet authorities demanded positive heroes and heroic social "types."

During Berezil's heydays of 1927–31 Meller experimented with designs for various genres: the oratorio, the tragicomedy, the operetta, and the revue. His signature productions were *Zhovtnevyi ohliad* (October Survey, 1927), *Narodnii Malakhii* (The People's Malakhii, 1928), and *Allo, na khvyli 477* (Hello on Channel 477, 1929). In the first, Meller fused various scenes into a poetic whole by presenting the action as though taking place around a globe, which lit up from the inside in different places, suggesting that the action was occurring at different spots around the earth. In *Narodnii Malakhii* the use of details added associations to the action. Thus, when Shevchenko's poem was sung (the opening lines are "*Reve ta stohne Dnipr shyrokyi*," The Dnipro roars and groans), the moon, poplars and sunflowers appeared, reenforcing stereotypical images of Ukraine. However, the play's action, which ridicules Malakhii's utopian dreams, worked against these associations. For the review *Allo, na khvyli 477* (Hello on Channel 477) Meller made use of a central cone which would light up different scenes and movable backdrops that continually covered or opened parts of the stage. This allowed for quick kaleidoscopic changes of scenery, and a dynamic production. Viewers were mesmerized.

For both Meller and Kurbas art was about finding the right equivalent, the key gesture, feature or device, which would stimulate intuitive associations in the viewer. Kurbas's system demanded "transformations," or the discovery of condensed images that were symbolic generalizations capable of interpreting an event, condition or phenomenon. Meller's skill in finding these "transformations" was one of the most important reasons for his theater successes in the twenties and early thirties. Even when, after a theatrical performance, ideologically driven critics found fault with a production, Meller's stage and costume designs still garnered enthusiastic reviews. He succeeded in making every play, even those of pedestrian writers, into a delightful visual spectacle, a gift that made him useful to consecutive cultural and artistic commissars.

In later stage productions Meller translated gestures into characteristic mannerisms and essential features, magnifying them until they appeared to fill an entire space. The individual gesture represented a character, and the character harmonized with the entire set design, producing a total effect. Sometimes he would criticize other theater artists precisely for the inability to fill the entire stage or production with this kind of unified conception, to translate a governing idea into what he called "the large form." It was partly for this reason that he loved the classical Greek aesthetic, which represented for him not simply the ideals of harmony, balance and restraint, but above all monumentalism, the ability to capture and reproduce form as a totality and finished product. According to his daughter, the artist perceived a link between the Ukrainian aesthetic and that of classical Greece, seeing grace, poise, restraint, and inner harmony as characteristic of both.[13]

Some critics were offended by Meller's satirical treatment of Soviet life, especially by his ridiculing of low quality consumer goods. For example, the fact that he made fun of the lack of galoshes raised a complaint from a certain M. in *Kharkivska hazeta* (Kharkiv Gazette) on January 11, 1929. During the "anti-cosmopolitan campaign" (a euphemism for an anti-Jewish campaign) that occurred in the last years of Stalin's life, roughly from 1949–53, Meller was accused of encouraging formalism. An antisemitic article entitled "Proty kosmopolitychnykh proiaviv u arkhitekturi" (Against Cosmopolitan Features in Architecture) appeared in *Kyivska pravda* (Kyiv Truth) on April 5, 1949, attacking Jewish architects for embracing modernist and American styles and denouncing Meller as a "confirmed aesthete and formalist" who admired "the decadent art of the West." It accused him of being a "bourgeois cosmopolitan" who found places for Jews in the Institute of Monumental Sculpture and Art, which was part of the Academy of Architecture. Ironically, only a few years earlier, Meller had received the highest citations and had been celebrated as a living link to the earlier Soviet past (one of the few that remained after the mass imprisonments and executions of the thirties).

Meller's best work resulted from a fusion of stylistic influences. In the early twenties his interest in the human figure and the decorative aesthetic blended with the avant-garde's attraction to folk design, constructivism, and his interest in the playful, satirical and grotesque. Although much of

13 Based on personal interviews with Brigitta Vetrova.

the visual evidence associated with his successful productions disappeared in the 1930s during the years of mass arrests, a significant amount has survived, and can today be found in various museums and private collections. The existing sketches for costumes, photographs of set designs, eyewitness accounts, and memoir literature allow for a reconstruction of his legacy and his role in the creative ferment of the twenties.

Appendix

A list of theatrical productions in which Meller was the chief artist from 1918 to 1933

Choreographic Studio of Bronislava Nijinska
Masky (Masks) by Nijinska, music of Frederick Chopin (1918)
Asyriiski tantsi (Assyrian Dances) by Bronislava Nijinska (1919)
Mephisto by Bronislava Nijinska, music of Franz Liszt (1920)
Misto (The City) by Bronislava Nijinska, music of Sergei Prokofiev (1921)

Russian Traveling Theater
Marriage of Figaro by P. Beaumarchais, directed by O. Smirnov (1919)
Metr Patlen, directed by Faust Lopatynskyi (1919)

Shevchenko First State Theater
Mazepa by Juliusz Slowacki, directed by K. Berezhnyi (1921)

H. Mykhailychenko Theater of Mass Action
Nebo horyt (The Sky Is Burning), directed by Marko Tereshchenko and Vadym Meller (1921)
Universalnyi nekropol, after Ilia Ehrenburg, directed by Marko Tereshchenko (1922)
Karnaval (Carnival), after Romain Rolland, directed by Marko Tereshchenko (1923)

Berezil Theater (1922–26 in Kyiv, 1926–34 in Kharkiv; renamed Shevchenko Academic Ukrainian Drama Theater in 1934)
Zhovten (October), directed by Les Kurbas (1922)
RUR (Ruhr), directed by Les Kurbas (1923)
Haz (Gas) by Georg Kaiser, directed by Les Kurbas (1923)

Jimmy Higgins, after Upton Sinclair, directed by Les Kurbas (1923)
Mashynobortsi (The Machine Wreckers) by Ernst Toller, directed by Faust Lopatynskyi (1924)
Liudyna masa (Mass Man) by Ernst Toller, directed by Hnat Ihnatovych (1924)
Protyhazy (Gas Masks) by Sergei Tretiakov, directed by Les Kurbas and Borys Tiahno (1924)
Sekretar profspilky (The Trade Union Secretary), directed by Borys Tiahno (1924)
Zolote cherevo (Les Tripes d'Or) by Fernand Crommelnyck, directed by Les Kurbas (1926)
Sedi (Sadie) by Somerset Maughan and D. Coulton, directed by Valerii Inkizhunov (1926)
Mikado, after Gilbert and Sullivan (reinterpreted by Maik Yohansen and Ostap Vyshnia), directed by Valerii Inkizhunov (1927)
Zhovtnevyi ohliad (October Survey), directed by Les Kurbas and Borys Tiahno (1927)
Narodnii Malakhii (The People's Malakhii) by Mykola Kulish, directed by Les Kurbas (1928)
Allo, na khvyli 477 (Hello on Channel 477), directed by V. Skliarenko (1929)
Myna Mazailo by Mykola Kulish, directed by Les Kurbas (1929)
97 by Mykola Kulish, directed by Les Dubovyk (1930)
Dyktatura (Dictatorship) by Ivan Mykytenko, directed by Les Kurbas (1930)
1905 rik na KhPZ (The Year 1905 at the Kharkiv Train-building Factory), directed by Les Kurbas and Les Dubovyk (1931)
Chotyry Chemberleny (Four Chamberlains), directed by Artem Baloban (1931)
Narodzhennia veletnia (Birth of a Giant), directed by Les Kurbas (1931)
Tetnuld by Sh. Dagiani, directed by Volodymyr Skliarenko (1932)
Khaziain (The Landlord) by Ivan Karpenko Karyi, directed by V. Skliarenko (1932)
Chotyry Chemberleny (Four Chamberlains), directed by V. Skliarenko (1933)
Maklena Grasa by Mykola Kulish, directed by Les Kurbas (1933)
Zahybel eskadry (Death of a Squadron) by Oleksandr Korniichuk, directed by Borys Tiahno (1933)

Ivan Kavaleridze's Contested Identity

The Ukrainian avant-garde has long presented interpreters with puzzles and problems. One need only consider the ambiguities and contradictions attached to the identities and the work of artists such as David Burliuk, Kazimir Malevich, Volodymyr (Vladimir) Tatlin, Oleksandr Dovzhenko, and Dziga Vertov. These ambiguities are nowhere more salient than in the life and work of Ivan Kavaleridze (1897–1978). He has long been recognized as one of the great twentieth-century avant-gardists; an early influence on cubist sculpture—along with Alexander (Oleksandr) Archipenko—and a founder, of Soviet Ukrainian cinema—along with Dovzhenko and Vertov—he is one of the least analyzed of the great avant-gardist of the 1920s. In recent articles he has been described as a "forgotten outsider," part of the "national museum of cultural mummies," an artist who has been "canonized without being understood" (Menzelevskyi 2017, 11–12).

Moreover, his work and identity have been appropriated by both nationalists and communists, traditionalists and innovators. The interpretation of Kavaleridze's achievement has always found itself in the crossfire of incompatible narratives. Both the sculptures and films were initially praised, then strongly criticized. A number were destroyed only to be reproduced and gain iconic stature in later years.[1] The present struggle to juggle these narratives and redefine his legacy provides insights into how

1 Kavaleridze's most important sculptures are *Princess Olga*, Kyiv, 1911, partially destroyed in 1919 and 1923, restored in 1996; *Shevchenko*, Romny, 1918; *Yaroslav Mudryi*, grounds of St. Sophia Cathedral and grounds of the Golden Gates, 1997; *Hryhorii Skovoroda*, Kyiv, 1977, Lohvyn, 1922, bronze version, 1972; *Artem*, Artemivsk, 1924; *Artem*, Slavianohirst, Sviatohirsk, 1927; *Shevchenko*, Poltava, 1926. His most important films are *Zlyva*, 1926; *Perekop*, 1930; *Shturmovi nochi*, 1931; *Koliivshchyna*, 1933; *Prometei*, 1936; *Natalka Poltavka*, 1936; *Zaporozhets za Dunaiem*, 1937; *Hryhorii Skovoroda*, 1959; *Poviia* (*Huliashcha*), 1961.

Ukraine's national identity and cultural memory are being constructed. It is instructive to examine how his work has been repeatedly reinterpreted, and why it has been both celebrated and condemned.

When Kavaleridze died in 1978 at the age of ninety-one his career in art had spanned seven decades. The building in which he worked on 21 Andriivskyi uzviz was opened in 1993 as a museum of his work. It was here (incidentally a few doors from the Mikhail Bulgakov museum and childhood home) that Kavaleridze worked on his monument to *Princess Olga* (Synko 2002, 5). Although the UNESCO calendar recognizes the centenary of his birth, his life and legacy remain poorly understood. In particular, many biographical episodes have never been adequately explained. They are glossed or passed over in silence in his autobiographical writings, extracts of which were published in 1978 and 1988. Only after the original manuscript was retrieved from the archives and published in 2017 could readers access the full version.[2]

Biography

Born into a mixed Georgian-Ukrainian family in Ladanskyi Khutir, Sumska oblast, Kavaleridze moved to Kyiv in 1899, where he lived with his uncle Serhii Mazaraki, an artist and archeologist who worked in the Scythian section of the Kyiv Archaeological Museum and whose friends included the painters Ilia Repin, Arkhyp Kuindzhi, Serhii Svitoslavskyi, Fotii Krasytskyi, Ivan Trush, and many artists who worked in the Lyiv Opera, such as Porfyrii Martynovych, Opanas Slaston, Ivan Seleznov, and Serhii Vasylkivskyi. Ivan's studies in the private gymnasium (high school) were interrupted by the 1905 revolution. Suspected by the police of "conducting agitation against the existing order," he was forced to quit the school (Nimenko 1967, 6). In 1906 he enrolled in the Kyiv Art School and worked during the evenings as a statistician in the Kyiv Opera Theater. His early sculptures from 1908 were of theater artists. In 1909 he made a bust of the great opera star Fedor Shaliapin (Chaliapin) while the latter was performing in the city. Kavaleridze then attended the St. Petersburg Academy of Arts in 1909, before moving in 1910 to the Paris studio of the sculptor Naum (Naoum) Aronson. Here he reconnected with his friend Alexander Archipenko, met Auguste Rodin, Claude Debussy, the Jewish poet Hayim Bialik, and numerous other prominent figures (Kozlenko and Menzelevskyi, 112).

2 For the full version, see Kozlenko and Menzelevskyi, 81–230.

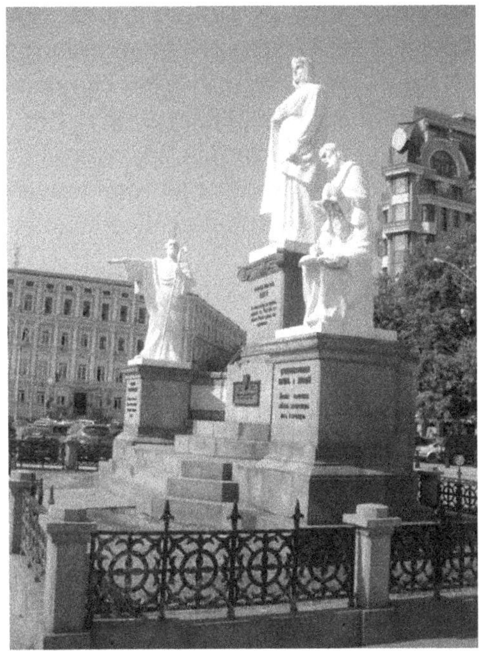

Ivan Kavaleridze. *Princess Olga*, original 1911, restored 1996. Square of St. Michael's, Kyiv.

Princess Olga (1911)

In 1910 a competition was announced for sculptures of ancient Kyiv. It resulted in Kavaleridze's first big commission. He and a fellow student, P. Snytkin, submitted a project for four sculptures: *Princess Olga*, *Cyril and Methodius* and the *Apostle Andrew*. It was accepted, and commentators celebrated the unveiling of Kavaleridze's *Princess Olga* in August 1911 as marking the arrival of a promising new talent. The sculptures were destroyed in 1923 in circumstances that remain poorly documented. In 1996, five years after Ukraine gained its independence, they were restored in accordance with the original designs and placed in their original location outside St. Michael's Cathedral (Mykhailivskyi Sobor), which was also rebuilt at that time.

The destruction of *Princess Olga* in 1923 occurred at a time when many of the sculptor's students and coworkers were being arrested under bolshevik rule. Kavaleridze has written that the sculpture was buried in the ground (Kavaleridze 1988, 5). However, even before its construction, the original project for *Princess Olga* had been criticized and revisions required. Metropolitan Flavian in 1911 had demanded that Olga lose her sword and have a cross placed around her neck, a demand to which the sculptor agreed. A mother superior complained that the author had given the sculpture breasts that were too large. It is not clear whether Kavaleridze made this particular adjustment to the final version (Kavaleridze 2017a, 119).

In 1915 he was mobilized into the imperial army and assigned to the Winter Palace, where he commanded soldiers guarding Tsar Nicholas II. After the February Revolution he was sent by the Provision Government of Alexander Kerensky to attend the All-Ukrainian Army Congress called by the Central Rada in Kyiv. Here he met Petliura, who advised him to stay out of politics and concentrate on art. He then traveled to Romny, where the revolutionary chaos overtook him. He was assigned by the bolsheviks to work in popular education and was reportedly mobilized to build a Shevchenko monument in Romny, in what is today the Sumska oblast. This part of his biography is particularly unreliable. In 1918 the bolsheviks had been driven out of the country by the government of Pavlo Skoropadsky, which was installed by the German army from April 29 until it was ousted in November by a popular uprising led by Petliura. The artist may have been assigned the task of building the Shevchenko monument under the first bolshevik occupation during February and March, but the unveiling of the monument on October 27 must have taken place under the rule of the Hetmanate. A moment of great national pride, it was attended by many important figures in Ukraine's cultural life. These facts have until recently been suppressed, or, as in the autobiography, presented in a confused way. The inspiration behind the two Romny monuments produced in 1918, *Shevchenko* and *Heroes of the Revolution*, has never been clearly explained. Kavaleridze's autobiographies are also evasive when he describes his wounding on a bolshevik agitational train during the revolutionary years, and his near death from typhoid.

Avant-gardism

What remains evident is the link between Kavaleridze's avant-gardism and the earlier pre-revolutionary period. He has long been recognized as a seminal influence in avant-garde sculpture. His works of the early 1920s in particular have been praised for their "geometric generalizations" (Pevnyi 1992, 11). The early films have also been admired for their monumental quality, "carved" screen images, and their epic-like plots taken from crucial episodes in the nation's life (Kapelhorodskyi et al. 2007, 7). However, only in the post-independence period have his links to pre-revolutionary dramatic artists attracted attention. As a child he met the great dramatic actors and directors Marko Kropyvnytskyi, Maria Zankovetska, Mykola Sadovskyi, Panas Saksahanskyi and developed an interest in the art of capturing expressions and gestures. It is also now widely acknowledged that, like Archipenko, his classmate in his Kyiv Art Institute, he introduced cubism into sculpture. The inspiration for this innovation was, as with Archipenko, a fascinated with ancient times.

It is also now recognized that the great architectural designer Vladyslav Horodetskyi, who produced stunningly innovative work in concrete prior to the revolution of 1917, introduced Kavaleridze to the Orlenko brothers. The latter were able to make concrete sculptures resemble marble. They first met Kavaleridze in 1911, when he was working on the *Olga* monument, but their collaboration continued into the 1920s, when they helped make the *Artem* sculptures.

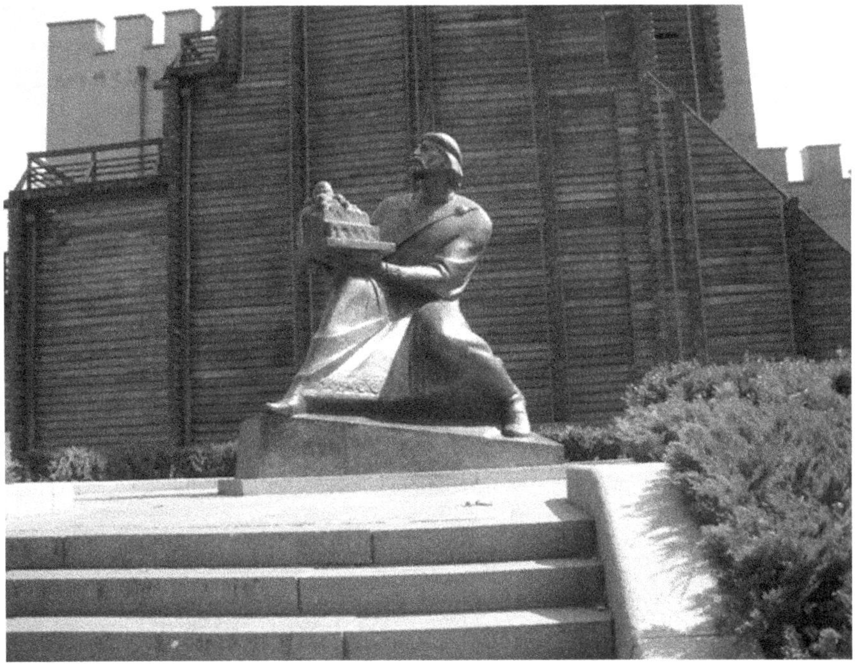

Ivan Kavaleridze. *Yaroslav the Wise*, 1997, after a model made by the artist in the 1960s. Golden Gates, Kyiv.

On December 23, 1922 Kavaleridze's sculpture of *Skovoroda* was unveiled in Lohvyn. He later produced sculptures of Shevchenko in Poltava in 1925, and Sumy in 1926. The sculptor's interest in Shevchenko and Skovoroda continued throughout his career, as viewers of the many projects and smaller works on display in his museum in Kyiv can attest. So did his fascination with the age of Kyivan Rus. A sculpture of *Yaroslav the Wise*, which Kavaleridze wanted to be placed on the grounds of St. Sophia Cathedral, was erected there only after his death. The same project became the basis for a statue erected in 1997 outside the Golden Gates of Kyiv. This focus on national heroes sat somewhat uncomfortably with his glorification of bolshevik leaders, whose models are also on display in the Kyiv museum.

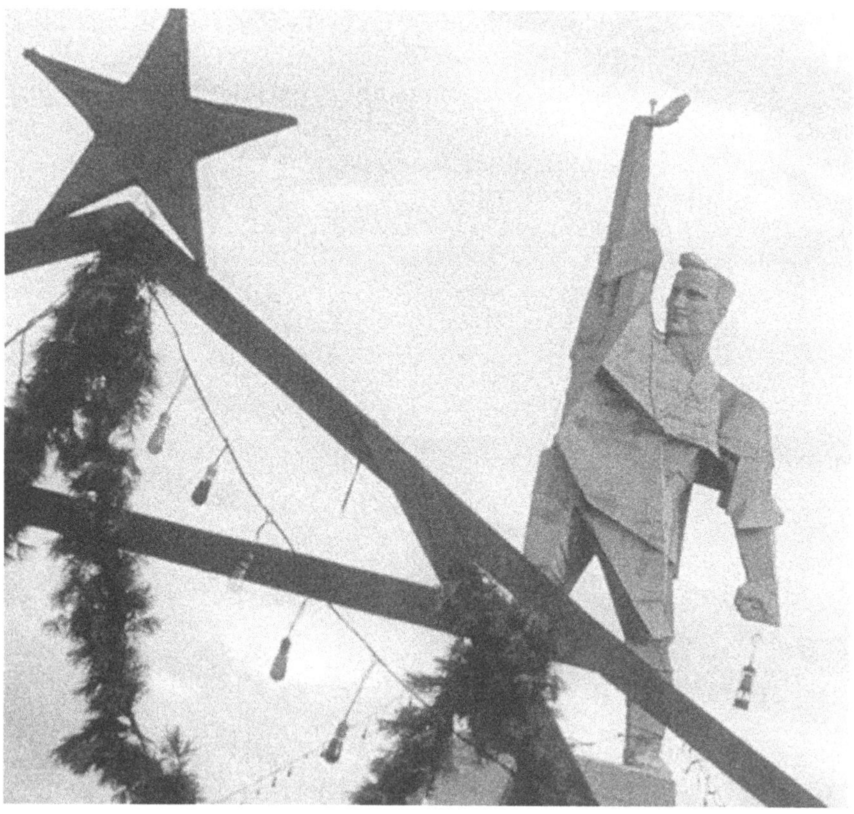

Ivan Kavaleridze. *Artem*, 1924. A still from Dziga Vertov's *Enthusiasm*, 1930.

However, the avant-garde period is best captured by his two *Artem* statues. His most famous avant-garde monument, the *Artem* of 1924, was named after the first head of the Soviet (or Council) of People's Commissars (Radnarkom) of the Ukrainian Soviet Socialist Republic. Unveiled in Bakhmut in the Donetsk oblast on July 27, 1924, it immediately became a symbol of the new proletarian and constructivist age. It figured prominently in various posters and publications, and in Dziga Vertov's film *Entuziazm* (Enthusiasm, 1930). Made of reinforced concrete, a material that itself symbolized power and endurance, the statue produced an overpowering effect on viewers. Much of the construction work was done in a synagogue commandeered by the regime (Nimenko 1967, 21).

There has been resistance to telling the full story about the decision to destroy this monument. Although it had been damaged during the Second World War, the details were saved, and it could have been restored. After all, it was described in the twenties as embodying the epoch, symbolizing the whole liberated working class (Kapelhorodskyi et al. 2007, 21). Nonetheless, in the postwar period the city administration decided upon a traditional image and a naturalistic depiction, which replaced the statue in 1959 (Kapelhorodskyi et al., 21).

Kavaleridze then produced a sculpture of Lenin in Shostka in 1926 and a second avant-garde *Artem* monument in Sviatohirsk in 1927. Almost thirty meters high, this colossus still dominates the skyline. Kavaleridze set it on a high bluff overlooking the Pivnichnyi Donets (Dinets) River. Like the earlier *Artem*, it has a geometrical quality. Produced in layers, it resembles a multi-story building. One observer commented: "Artem rose up as a severe and hard monument against the background of shapeless [rozplyvchatykh] mountain lines, like organized, materialized will dominating the soggy river and soft surfaces of distant fields" (Gorev 1927). The Central Executive Committee of the Communist Party (bolsheviks) of Ukraine insisted that Kavaleridze carve into the sculpture Artem's phrase: "I find the sight of unorganized masses insufferable" (Nimenko 1967, 27).

Over time the work gained enormous popularity. It also proved impregnable. Although the first *Artem* sculpture was destroyed along with several of other Kavaleridze sculptures, this second *Artem* survived not only plans by Soviet authorities to take it down (by the thirties they no longer tolerated the avant-garde), but also German attempts to destroy it during the war (they viewed it as an example of degenerate modernism). Its pock-marked surface testifies to its being fired upon by guns and cannons (Kavaleridze 1977, 122).

This surviving monument, like Kavaleridze's posthumously erected sculptures, have now acquired a new symbolic meaning. The statue in Sviatohirsk (known until 1964 as Bannovskoe and in 1964–2003 as Slavianohirsk) now finds itself on the boundary of the Donetsk, Luhansk and Kharkiv oblasts. Situated not far from Kramatorsk, the center of Ukrainian-ruled Donetsk oblast, the statue is now interpreted as representing the strength of the local worker—today, of course, the Ukrainian rather than the communist or pro-Moscow worker. Originally described as a monument to Artem and the working class, from 2007 it has been described as symbolizing the "young industrial Donbas," and, because Sviatohirsk is on the Ukrainian side in the war, in the ongoing conflict the sculpture now represents national, rather than communist, endurance.

Of course, the historical and cultural context has radically changed since the twenties. In 1922, under Soviet rule, a monastery located in Sviatohirsk was closed down and a rest home created on the premises. The monastery was reopened in 1992 and in 2004 obtained the status of a Lavra. The mineral waters of the town that made it a health resort in pre-Soviet days are being restored, and the city is proud of its location in a national park called Sviati Hory (Sacred Hills). Today, like the statue, the new context presents a rebuke to Soviet history.

Critics have not found disentangling this layered symbolism an easy task, the more so since throughout his career the sculptor continued to produce works depicting leading figures in both Russian and Ukrainian cultural history, and bolshevik political leaders. For example, alongside sculptures of figures such as Pushkin, Gogol, Mussorgskii, and Shevchenko, in the postwar period he made many models for sculptures of party leaders.

Film

A similar identity contest surrounds his films. In 1911–15 Kavaleridze worked as a sculptor and artistic director for "P. Timan and F. Reinhardt" films, and in both Moscow and Kyiv with the film directors Yakov Protazanov and Vladimir Gardin. In the 1920s he became a founder of Ukrainian film. He was initially richly praised for his *Zlyva* (The Downpour, 1929), *Perekop* (1930), *Shturmovi nochi* (Storm Nights, 1931), one of the first sound films *Koliivshchyna* (The Koliivshchyna Rebellion, 1933), *Prometei* (Prometheus, 1936), the first Ukrainian opera put to film *Natalka Poltavka* (1936), and *Zaporozhets za Dunaiem* (The Cossack beyond the Danube, 1938).

The early avant-garde films in particular reveal a sculptural and monumental quality. However, their fate parallels that of his sculptures. *Zlyva* was criticized, destroyed and lost. Today it is described as "one of the most sought after lost films" (Kozlenko 2017, 64). The others films, particularly *Koliivshchyna*, *Prometei* and *Poviia*, came under attack and were removed from circulation. They remain difficult to find and are rarely analyzed by scholars.

The cinema criticism has now been republished by Kozlenko and Menzelevskyi in their 2017 volume. It demonstrates that the attack on Kavaleridze in 1936 for his *Prometei* was an important turning point in Soviet cinema and art history, paralleling the attack at the time on Shostakovich for the latter's *Lady Macbeth of Mtsensk*. Kavaleridze is described by Menzelevskyi as resisting the main trends of socialist realism, including the rehabilitation of great leaders and Russian imperial history, which was occurring at the time (Mendzelevskyi 2017, 37–38).

Already in the 1930s Kavaleridze had a reputation for being unruly and a "dissident." This explains why a number of his films, such as *Koliivshchyna* and *Prometei*, were not allowed distribution and why in that decade several of his statues were destroyed, something that Soviet-era articles on Kavaleridze failed to admit. The topic of their destruction was either avoided or blamed on the Second World War (Nimenko 1967, 44–45).

Moreover, several projects proposed by the artist were never built. For example, a postwar monument to Shevchenko was first proposed for Kyiv, then Leningrad, then Moscow, but was turned aside each time. The monument that actually went up in Moscow resembles Kavaleridze's project of 1944. In fact, he worked on it with the sculptor who received the commission. However, Kavaleridze's name could not be associated with the finished work (Synko 2002, 19–20).[3] Nikita Khrushchev complained publicly of the sculptor's work. Kavaleridze had spoken positively about modernism in private conversations. His words were conveyed to Khrushchev, who on March 8, 1963, while polemicizing with Evgenii Evtushenko over realism and formalism, said: "After the civil war in the town of Artemivk in Ukraine

3 When Kavaleridze offered his model for the postwar Shevchenko monument to St. Petersburg, it was originally accepted and only later rejected. The Canadian sculptor Leo Mol (Leonid Molodozhanyn) proposed his own sculpture at this time to the city's mayor Anatolii Sobchak. In the early sixties Mol also received the commission for the Shevchenko monument in Washington. As a result, the two most innovative and famous Ukrainian sculptors of the twentieth century, Arkhipenko and Kavaleridze, who had both studied together in the Kyiv Art School, had their projects for the Shevchenko statues in St. Petersburg and Washington rejected at approximately the same time. Mol's Shevchenko statue was erected in Washington in 1964.

a monstrous formalist monument was erected [a reference to the *Artem* monument of 1924], whose author was the cubist sculptor Kavaleridze. Its appearance was horrible, but the cubists loved it. The author of this formalist monument, when he was on the territory occupied by the fascists, behaved in an undignified manner" (Kavaleridze 1988, 6). Following these remarks the sculptor's *Shevchenko* in Sumy was destroyed. In response Kavaleridze wrote a telegram to Khrushchev. He received no answer but was eventually called to the offices of the city council, where he was informed that there had been a misunderstanding and those who had prepared the leader's text had been punished (Kavaleridze 1988, 6). After that, no other existing monuments created by him were touched.

Another iconic statue by Kavaleridze, the *Skovoroda* that now stands in Podol, also had a difficult fate. It was to be unveiled in 1971, but the event was delayed until 1977, shortly before the artist's death, because of complaints from a party authority named Malanchuk, who was concerned that Skovoroda was portrayed barefoot. Malanchuk demanded that the figure be given shoes, and therefore cheap bast shoes appeared in the final version (Kavaleridze 1988, 5).

In his memoirs, the sculptor complained about similar intrusions into the production of his films. For example, when working on his *Poviia* (Harlot, 1961), which was based on Panas Myrnyi's nineteenth-century realist novel, he was told that the heroine, a prostitute, had to act modestly in every scene. No embraces, kisses or sex could be shown. By then what Kavaleridze describes as a "lacquered, primitivized" style had come to dominate art and film making (Kavaleridze 1988, 6).

The puzzle of the wartime years

Although the sculptor was already treated with suspicion during the "revolutionary" twenties and even more so during the Stalinist thirties, he fell into complete disfavor after the Second World War mainly because he had been behind enemy lines during the German occupation. Shortly before the war he had received permission to travel (from May 19 to July 2, 1941) to Lviv to work on a film about Oleksa Dovbush, the Ukrainian equivalent of Robin Hood. On his way to the Carpathians to begin filming, he found himself stranded behind German lines and was forced to walk back to Kyiv, where he lived throughout 1943–46 in the film studios of Kinostudia. Kavaleridze has described how he was approached to do a bust of Hitler but refused, saying that he was already working on another statue, that of Apollo. After the war, it turned out that the German officer who had approached him had been a Soviet spy (Kavaleridze 1988, 5). Nonetheless, anyone who had not been evacuated could be viewed by Soviet authorities as a traitor, and in 1944 Kavaleridze was included in a blacklist of artists who had "spent time under occupation." Although in the postwar period he was allowed back into the Union of Artists, the classification "spent time under occupation" disqualified him from most commissions. Therefore, after the restoration of Soviet rule his theater work remained under an unannounced boycott in Kyiv (even though some plays were produced in other cities), and his films were not shown.

It is entirely possible that his negative experience in Stalin's Soviet Union prompted him to work during the war years in the Kyiv city administration under German occupation. From 1941 he headed the City of Kyiv's Department of Culture and Art, where he tried to renew the Kyiv Cinema Studios as a private enterprise (Samchuk 1990, 24, 28). He is described as having big plans for developing film studies in Kyiv and other cities (Kozlenko 2017, 61). Many people in the administration of German-occupied Kyiv were in touch with him until February 1942, when the arrests and executions of Ukrainians associated with Andrii Melnyk's wing of the Organization of Ukrainian Nationalists began. It was this wing that had set up in Kyiv the local administration with which Kavaleridze worked. The artist continued to be an influential figure until September 1944 (Kozlenko, 62). It appears that when Soviet troops approached Kyiv he simulated injury to avoid evacuation to the West. Kavaleridze puts a pro-Soviet spin on these events in his writings, particularly in his play *Votaniv mech* (Wotan's Sword, 1965–70), which was an attempt to "rehabilitate" his reputation before Soviet authorities. It describes life in Kyiv under occupation, portraying those who expect positive change from the Germans, nationalists who try to defend the population from the ruthlessness of occupying forces, members of the "Soviet" underground who work under cover (their leader is disguised as a priest), and even a Soviet spy in German uniform.

Ulas Samchuk and Dokia Humenna, who knew him at the time and later emigrated to the West, tell a different story. Samchuk met him in 1941, first in Rivne and then in Kyiv. This leading interwar writer, who represented the nationalist viewpoint and was close to members of the OUN's Melnyk wing, stayed with Kavaleridze when in Kyiv. They developed a close relationship, as is clear from Samchuk's wartime memoir, *Na koni voronomu* (On a Dark Horse, 1990), in which he provides a description of Kavaleridze's apartment, a guided tour of Kyiv given by their host, and discussions in Kavaleridze's home with the city's mayor Danylo Bahazii (Samchuk 1990, 6–7, 8, 14, 16–18). These discussions often centered on how to make culture less socialist realist and more national in both style and content (Samchuk 1990, 17–18). The memoirs show that Samchuk was enthralled by his host, whom he calls a great artist. The film *Zlyva*, made in the Odesa film studio, is described as "etchings for a history of the *haidamakas* [peasant revolutionaries]." Samchuk makes it clear that it was singled out for having a dangerous ideological subtext—an incorrect interpretation of Russian imperialism. Soviet officials, reports Samchuk, saw the film as "an artificial amalgamation" of the *haidamakas* of late eighteenth century with "the *haidamakas*" of the twentieth, an approach that in their view did not "take account of the concrete historical circumstances" (Samchuk 1990, 20). The director, according to the critic I. S. Kornienko, "failed to show the strivings of the Ukrainian people to unite with the brotherly Russian people" (Samchuk 1990, 21). Kavaleridze constantly had to face similar criticism. His film *Perekop* did not restore him to official favor, even though it showed the defeat of Wrangel, the seeding of the conquered land by peasants, and the taking apart of houses for blast furnaces. This "melodrama," according to Samchuk, convinced no one (Samchuk 1990, 21).

Kavaleridze appears to have been equally attracted to Samchuk. He read the latter's *Volyn* (Volhynia), which so impressed him that he apparently proposed making a film based on it (Samchuk 1990, 41). Dokia Humenna's portrayal of Kavaleridze in her novel *Khreshchatyi iar*, which was based on a diary she kept during the occupation, is much more critical of Kavaleridze. Herself a product of the Soviet period, she had been expelled from the Union of Writers. Humenna detected a cautiousness and craftiness in Kavaleridze's behavior, something she felt that émigrés from abroad like Samchuk failed to see.[4]

Nonetheless, both depictions of Kavaleridze are decidedly at odds with the image of a loyal Soviet citizen, which was painted by the artist himself and his early biographer Nimenko. The artist's life in wartime Kyiv has therefore remained a mystery. He was elected to his post on the city council. When Bahazii, the mayor, was executed by the Germans, the council was liquidated, and the OUN members who helped to create it were arrested and shot. Kavaleridze somehow survived.

4 See Humenna 1956. The protagonist in the book who resembles Kavaleridze is called Viktor Prudyus.

Post-independence ambiguities in cultural memory

Kavaleridze has had many faces, all of which are reflected in contemporary cultural memory: a persona non grata under the tsarist regime, a Ukrainian patriot during the years of national state building in 1917–20, a celebrated Soviet avant-gardist, a condemned Ukrainian nationalist and formalist, and finally, after independence, a forgotten founder of the Ukrainian avant-garde in art and cinema. Unsurprisingly, ambiguities persist.

In the current "decommunization" period, the image of a "Soviet" Kavaleridze is for some a source of embarrassment. After completing the *Artem* statue of 1924, he moved to Kharkiv, the capital of Soviet Ukraine at the time, and worked as an artist and sculptor with the publishing house Komunist (Communist), where he produced a series of sculptures of Soviet leaders, including Vlas Chubar and Hryhorii Petrovskyi, and met with the writer Yurii Yanovskyi and the film director Oleksandr Dovzhenko. However, in spite of these credentials, his monument to Lenin in Sumy was taken down in 1957 and replaced with a naturalistic one. Moreover, although he was continually described as "one of the most significant directors of Soviet cinema," in Ukraine his films remained under a boycott and were never serious studied (Kozlenko and Menzelevskyi 2017, 19). His *Zlyva* was based on Shevchenko's poem, *Haidamaky*. When it premiered in Moscow and Kyiv in April 1919 it was accepted as a courageous experiment but destroyed soon afterward as formalist. *Perekop* premiered on November 21, 1930 in Moscow. His *Koliivshchyna* (1933), an early Ukrainian sound film, was sent back to the director seventeen times by party authorities with orders to make changes. *Prometei* (1936) was immediately criticized. Kavaleridze's relations with Soviet film authorities still require exploration.

Finally, there is the unknown Kavaleridze. As a writer he remains practically unexamined. Although banned in Kyiv, several of his plays were staged in the 1960s outside the capital. Nonetheless, they were never published and could not be read by contemporaries. They are now available in the 2017 volume edited by Kozlenko and Menzelevskyi.

The many puzzles in his creative and personal history pose problems for contemporary researchers. A recent attempt to investigate his autobiography cautiously describes the author as trying to "leave a picture of his age," breaking with the Soviet canon but never becoming a dissident, "uncritically maneuvering between discourses and critical canons" (Papash 2017, 29–30). It is clear, however, that at different times Kavaleridze's various profiles as an avant-gardist, national patriot and Soviet artist have been either embraced or rejected, depending on the political sympathies and aesthetic tastes of commentators. Only recently has a sifting through the evidence become possible. As a result, a new composite and still contentious image of the artist's identity is still emerging.

Dziga Vertov: *Enthusiasm*, Kharkiv and Cultural Revolution

Literary Kharkiv in the minds of most contemporary Ukrainians is probably composed of several layered images, including a picture of the early settlement in the steppe founded by the legendary Kharko, the world described in the 1830s by Hryhorii Kvitka-Osnovianenko, and the one depicted in the 1860s by the humorist Oleksa Storozhenko. These representations convey an ebullient natural vitality and an optimistic faith in the future. However, the city became most closely identified with the idea of transformative cultural energy during the "Cultural Renaissance" of the 1920s, when it was the capital of the newly created Soviet Ukrainian republic. At this time Kharkiv's writers and artists set themselves the ambitious project of creating a radically new identity. It soon became clear that there were different views of what this identity should be. At least three distinct cultural visions lay behind the "enthusiasms" that motivated writers and artists in the 1920s and early 1930s, each of which can be linked to particular aesthetic and formal-artistic concerns.

The first current emphasized the idea of cultural revolution as a national transformation: the creation of a reconfigured, modern literature and art devoted to Ukrainian culture, history and identity. A Ukrainization policy was embraced with fervor by many after 1923; the Ukrainian language was standardized in the so-called Kharkiv orthography of 1928; and different literary and artistic groups each promoted their own version of an innovative, intellectual, modern, and urban creativity. The result was experimental work often of a high-quality in literature and the arts. Enthusiasts of the national transformation (today frequently referred to as the "Cultural Renaissance") frequently relied on the resources of Ukraine's past, even when they broke from tradition, and explicitly refused to subordinate cultural development to trends in Russia. The resulting cultural élan generated a burst of energy that produced remarkable achievements in literature, art, theater, and film.

A second current heralded the creation of a proletarian culture, perceived as something entirely new, even on a global scale. Kharkiv's mission was, according to this project, to break decisively with the rural, bourgeois and individual, and become a center of working-class creativity. The image of newness for those closest to this current was associated with internationalization, machinery, speed, technique, technical innovation, and collective work. Like the "national-cultural," the "proletarian" dimension of the Renaissance demanded a new language, new forms in literature and art. Writers, for example, often introduced acronyms and technical terms. In the arts technical experimentation was often modeled on the use of the camera and montage in films: it exploited quick transitions, fragmentation, unexpected recombinations, and views ("shots") from surprising angles. The search for the "modern" and "industrial" led to a revolt against established genres. Attempts were made to write texts collectively, to mix media (such as poetry and art), and to create entirely new genres (such as a "literature of facts," and a "cinema vérité" in documentary filmmaking). Much daring experimentation occurred in the late twenties, with the year 1928, for example, produced an entire spate of works in literature driven by formal innovations and new processes of creation, while the late twenties and early thirties produced some of the boldest new ideas in filmmaking, as evidenced by the work of Oleksandr Dovzhenko and Dziga Vertov.

The enthusiasm released by this second, "proletarian," project sometimes contradicted or clashed with the vision underpinning the first. In the cultural debates of the mid-1920s some asked: Was the Ukrainian language an apt vehicle for the proletarian reworking of culture? Should Ukraine's cultural past be discarded as predominantly peasant, or was it, on the contrary, Russia's past that first needed to be jettisoned as imperial and reactionary? Where, in any case, were the sources of the new culture, and who was responsible for creating it? In this way questions of politics, organization and ideology quickly became entangled with creative endeavors. This led to discord. Only a few years later, in the early thirties, many Ukrainian writers and artists who formed part of the "Cultural Renaissance" were arrested, imprisoned, exiled, or shot.

Of course, neither the "national" nor the "proletarian" current stood outside the political and ideological commitments of the day. In both cases how the new manifest itself in terms of aesthetic sensibility and form varied from creator to creator and group to group. A simple juxtaposition of opposites, as some have proposed, in terms of "modernists" versus "massists," "aesthetics" versus "ethics," pro-Ukrainian versus pro-Russian, or sophisticated versus primitive, fails to capture the complex manner in which competing visions interacted (Movchan 2008, 204). The term "modernist," after all, also encompasses the experiments of those who felt they were creating a radically "proletarian" culture. Attempts to set up an interpretive matrix marked by such stark contrasts has more often than not been guided by political or ideological considerations, and is usually undermined by a closer examination of the creative works themselves.

The entire "Cultural Renaissance" and the avant-garde creativity that accompanied it were ultimately crushed during the period of the First Five-Year Plan, 1928–33. This turning point, described by some as Stalin's "second revolution," saw the collectivization of agriculture and rapid forced industrialization, the Great Famine (Holodomor), and the first curtailment of the Ukrainization policy. However, at least in some circles, this "Stalinist" revolution initially also produced its own upsurge of enthusiasm. It claimed to be making a rupture with the past that was more complete than envisioned by the "national" or "proletarian" revolutions. It viewed collective work in uncompromising terms—not simply as a collaboration between willing participants but as a collectivism whose hallmarks were the cult of discipline and uniformity, the militarization of society, and complete subordination to central authority, which included Kharkiv's acquiescence to Moscow. Emphasis in the Stalinist revolution shifted away from elevating the worker and toward glorifying the state. This third "enthusiasm" demanded its own forms of expression in literature and the arts, along with a new, monolithic organizational order and a new ideology. In terms of artistic expression it moved away from celebrating human ingenuity to admiring gigantism in state-sponsored projects, such as hydro-electric dams, factory complexes and smokestacks. It turned away from exploiting natural rhythms to breaking them. Because Ukrainian scholarship has not paid much attention to the aesthetics of this third, Stalinist "enthusiasm," it has often failed to identify it as a distinct phenomenon. Few scholars have suggested that there might even be an aesthetic here worth exploring.

In short, when examined more closely, the creative energy of the twenties and early thirties reveals different sources of inspiration: the quest for sophistication and the romanticization of national cultural development; the thrill of creating a new proletarian world; and the excitement of belonging to a strong unified industrial state. Each source produced a different aesthetic current, its own appreciation of the beautiful, and generated its own forms of expression. Of course, because today's researchers look back on the twenties with an awareness of what came later—the Holodomor, the waves of arrests and purges, the Great Terror, and the crushing of an entire generation of creative people—there is a tendency to overlook or deny the enthusiasms of the day. However ambiguous, contradictory and often confused, they were in many cases real. They motivated millions and drove much of the creativity during this period.

Yurii Sherekh captured some of the excitement felt by participants in the "Cultural Renaissance" in his marvelous essays and sketches. His "Khvylovyi bez polityky" (Khvylovyi without Politics) today reads like a manifesto of the national-cultural project. Yurii Lavrinenko's classic text *Rozstriliane vidrodzhennia* (The Executed Renaissance) similarly brims with the passionate commitment and thrilling sense of discovery felt by this generation. And, of course, Mykola Khvylovyi's pamphlets and the Literary Discussion of 1925–28 bear witness to the bold aspirations of writers and artists associated with this current.

In his essay, Sherekh indicates several features that can be seen as the artistic platform of the Khvylovyi group: a love of and playful delight in language; a desire for the full, unedited and uncensored human experience; a life-affirming joy that brings with it a kind of wise optimism. He writes: "Khvylovyi's circle—of word-lovers, life-lovers, people-lovers—was nonetheless unsentimental. At least in the sense that they did not fear the tortures and pains of life, struggle and death" (Sherekh 1964, 56). When discussing their delight in language he quotes a passage from Khvylovyi in which the narrator says: "Maria! You are being naïve. Nothing of the kind happened. All I wanted was to bring you the fragrance of the word."[1] Sherekh comments that this word-fragrance can be ironic, mystical or sacred. Unfortunately, he says, literature in the twenty years that followed "almost completely lost the ability to sense and recreate the fragrance of words" (54).

On love of life and people he quotes several now well-known passages. Among them Pavlo Tychyna's "Aeroplanes and all the achievement of technology—what are they worth if people do not look one another in the eye?"[2] He also cites a passage from Ivan Senchenko: "I am a citizen who

1 The original is: "Маріє! Ти наївнічаєш. Нічого подібного не було. Я тільки приніс тобі запах слова."

2 In the original: "Аероплани й усе довершенство техніки—до чого ж це, коли люди одне одному в вічі не дивляться?"

cares about the full-blooded health of his contemporaries—I have to call out: down with skepticism, with sarcasms and ironies."[3]

Sherekh says that this generation's optimism was not built on ignoring "the monstrous in the world and the human being." It included "not only the smile but also tears, not only life but also death" (58). This generation of optimists "felt the tragedy and fatedness [pryrechenist] of life…" (58).

On the desire for a full, unedited experience Sherekh quotes Yurii Yanovskyi's words: "we know all the harmfulness and falseness of simplified emotions" (60). These writers explored taboo topics in the realm of the erotic, the psychological and philosophical. In Sherekh's words, their ultimate goal was to model a rich image of the "fully developed Ukrainian individual," and to express the complex "music in the human soul" (67).[4] Openness to new experiences and interest in exploring trends in recent Western literature led them to formal explorations, which have variously been defined as neo-romanticism, impressionism, expressionism, and symbolism (Movchan 2008, 207).

At the same time Sherekh describes in highly negative terms those who opposed the national-cultural revolution, who denied the creation of what he called the "Third" Kharkiv (Sherekh 1978, 204). In his estimation the "First" had been formed by the declining Ukrainian gentry in the 1830s (Kvitka-Osnovianenko's age), and the "Second" was represented by the sleepy Russian provincialism of the late nineteenth century (Chekhov's age). Sherekh's anger at people he considers compromisers and collaborators is boundless. The "other" Soviet literature, he says, talked nonsense "about Stakhanovites, life being better and happier, about flowering cities in a flowering Ukraine" (Sherekh 1978, 208). Such compromisers belonged to a system that created "ersatz feelings," manufactured "a false happiness," one that had to be uniform for everyone. He recalls being proudly told in one restaurant: "We have the same menu for everyone" (Sherekh 1978, 212–13).

The enthusiasm of the first current, the national-cultural renaissance, with which Sherekh identifies was crushed. But here is the difficult part: What are we to do with the other two forms of enthusiasm? How do we integrate them into a narrative of the period? It is not enough to say that they broke with tradition. The plans and projects of the "proletarian revolution" and the second "Stalinist" revolution lashed out at the old, but so did the national-cultural revolution associated with Khvylovyi and the *vidrodzhentsi* (people of the Renaissance), who also demanded radical

3 Original: "Я громадянини, якому дороге повнокровне здоров'я своїх сучасників—я мушу гукати: геть із скептичизмом, із сарказмами й іроніями."

4 In the original: "за чи проти існування повноцінної української люлини."

change. We can argue that the vision of the *vidrodzhentsi* was different: they saw national liberation as coinciding with social and personal liberation. In their minds the new beginning was to be built upon old foundations. The image of Urbino is perhaps a good way of capturing this. It was the name of a group Khvylovyi tried to form out of the organization Hart (Tempering) in the early 1920s. The name "Urbino" not only stood for the urbanization of culture, but also referred to the town in Italy that in the fifteenth century became a center of Renaissance humanism. On orders of the Duke of Urbino, artists made use of pre-existing structures to construct a unique city in the form of an asymmetrical palace, an edifice of symphonic complexity and grandeur.[5] The palace may be seen as a metaphor for what the *vidrodzhentsi* were trying to accomplish—their "new" was to be European and sophisticated; it was to break with the outdated and backward, but to maintain links with the Ukrainian past.

This message is embedded in the literature and art of many avant-garde groups in the twenties. It is manifest, for example, in Dovzhenko's great silent films, where the old and new are contrasted but linked, revealing deep continuities at the philosophical and spiritual level. By contrast, the "proletarian" and the "Stalinist" revolutions often viewed any depiction that found elements in the Ukrainian past that were admirable, or worthy of sophisticated artistic treatment, as suspicious, or, worse still, as retrograde and counter-revolutionary.

All three forms of enthusiasm had common features, many of which were associated with avant-gardism. The idea of change, modernity and urbanization captured the imaginations of those who thought that the artist ought to be a visionary, even a fanatic. Exceptional talent, recognition of the ability to break through to new forms of consciousness, to "dare" [*derzat'*], to use Khvylovyi's word, were celebrated. This, incidentally, was true not only of writing within Soviet Ukraine, but also of the so-called "nationalist" writings produced in the interwar emigration and in Galicia. Oleh Olzhych, the OUN's spokesperson on cultural affairs, Yevhen Malaniuk, Yurii Lypa, and other leading figures in emigration glorified the demiurge, the artist ahead of his time, and they particularly admired the drive and radicalism of the literature produced in Kharkiv in the twenties.

Avant-gardism, the pursuit of the new and visionary, was therefore something that all three revolutionary enthusiasms shared. This is evident in the attraction to the dynamic and vital, which expressed itself in various forms, one of which was the cult of health, strength and endurance.

---

5 See Shkandrij 1992, 40–41.

It can be found in writers such as Yurii Yanovskyi, Oleksa Vlyzko, Arkadii Liubchenko, Maik Yohansen, and Mykola Khvylovyi. It was also picked up by Olzhych, Lypa, Olena Teliha, and many other Ukrainian writers living in Central Europe and Western Ukraine. The human body, its psychological and physical powers (Yanovskyi, Khvylovyi), animalistic urges (Liubchenko), even the energy contained in landscapes (Yohansen) revealed an optimistic faith in human and physical nature, the ability to overcome obstacles and to create the new. The individual artist who had the courage to explore new horizons, "colonize" new territory, was celebrated.

In the "proletarian" current the avant-garde attraction to vitality was translated into a glorification of the working class's drive and accomplishments. We are perhaps most familiar today with the powerful, bronze-like figures of laborers, whose bodies are admiringly captured in films. This current elevated the innocent, childlike, unspoiled, naïve, even primitive, in opposition to the excessively sophisticated, Westernized and bourgeois. The worker in the writings of many authors. including, for example, Petro Panch and Andrii Holovko, is portrayed as direct, untutored and hence trustworthy. This fascination with the proletarian also manifest itself as an enthusiasm for technique, technical innovation and experimentation, linking these qualities to the ingenuity of the worker-creator.

In the third, Stalinist enthusiasm, the idea of the avant-garde and vitality is reworked into something more robotic, sometimes infantile. The worker becomes all muscle and no reflection, all marching rhythms and nursery rhymes. Unabashed propaganda replaces critical thought. For many readers, Pavlo Tychyna's strange, doggerel-like verse from the late twenties and early thirties—of which "*Partiia vede*" ("The Party Leads") of 1933 is an example—falls into this category, along with many of the panegyrics to the leader, party, plan, army, and state that soon became typical of socialist realism.

We are now most familiar with this kind of cultural production in the works that have been categorized as socialist realism and that were produced in the thirties and ensuing two decades. However, the seeds of this thinking were already present in the twenties. In 1927 Mykola Skrypnyk wrote: "The issue is not to discover and correctly build the link between cultural work and the economy, but to now view cultural-educational work as the industrialization of man's brain, the industrialization of qualified human material" (Skrypnyk 1927, 124).[6] The ambition of this third revolutionary enthusiasm was not to release the genius within the

6 The phrasing in the original is: "Справа стоїть не в тому, щоб знайти і правильно збудувати звязок між культурною роботою і господаркою, а в тому, щоб тепер

individual, but to glorify utilitarianism and functionalism. Brilliance was not attached to the individual or even the group creator, but to the plan, which had sprung from the mind of the great leader. The idea of completely transforming people in this way was already evident in 1927, when Mikhail Semenko spoke of forming a new psyche, a new person, even "a new race" (Semenko 1927, 43).

These three enthusiasms appear to have stimulated many creative individuals and numerous formal experiments. Writers and artists were, of course, not free even in the twenties. All were watched in one way or another by state authorities and instructed by the party, but there was still in the mid-twenties a greater degree of freedom of expression and a greater capacity for resisting party pressures. As the national renaissance morphed into the proletarian revolution and then the Stalinist second revolution, the degree of freedom became progressively circumscribed.

This can be illustrated in a number of ways. Theater gradually moved from the national romanticism of Mykola Kulish's plays to the Stalinist vision of Ivan Mykytenko's *Dyktatura* (Dictatorship, 1930). Film moved from the depiction of national transformation in Dovzhenko's *Zvenyhora* (1927), *Arsenal* (1929) and *Zemlia* (Earth, 1930), to the glorification of proletarian vigor and construction in his *Ivan* (1932). In each case the movement was from celebrating natural rhythms to subduing and channeling these rhythms by the proletarian strongman, and finally to the triumph of the impersonal Plan. A similar shift is evident in Dziga Vertov's films. Whereas *Cholovik z kinoaparatom* (Man with the Movie Camera, 1930) admires personal ingenuity and creativity, in this way suggesting the ideal of the individual's liberation from an outdated, false consciousness, his *Entuziazm* (Enthusiasm, 1931) is dominated by scenes of proletarian masses and individual workers who pledge to work harder for the benefit of the state. These films move from celebrating human creativity to praising the Plan and the great planner. Exploring links to the country's history is replaced by celebrating the erasure of links to history—perhaps most clearly suggested by images of vast dams that submerge the countryside and scenes recording the destruction of churches and their conversion into Komsomol clubs.

Nonetheless, both Vertov films were remarkable artistic experiments and much lauded achievements. The aesthetic that underpins them, especially the less frequently analyzed *Enthusiasm*, deserves closer investigation. Filmed in 1930, *Enthusiasm* was the first sound film produced by

---

культурно-освітню роботу розглядати як індустріялізацію чоловічого мозку, індустріялізацію кваліфікованого людського матеріялу)."

Ukrainian film studios. It was based on footage made mostly in Kharkiv, Odesa and the Donbas. The director took his crew to Kharkiv to film the Eleventh All-Ukrainian Congress of Soviets and then to the factories and coal-mines of Donetsk. The film, subtitled "Symphony of the Donbas," promotes itself as both a documentation of how the new culture is being created and a representation of this new culture. Like *Man with the Movie Camera*, this was an experimental production—only this time in the new genre of sound film. It incorporated a musical montage of voice recordings, industrial sounds (trains, factories and machines), and music from Dmitri Shostakovich's Symphony no. 1. Vertov's crew designed and redesigned their recording apparatus while filming. Much of the original sound was lost or proved unusable, and therefore to make the final product the film had to be changed on the cutting board. The crew had little transportation and were often obliged to carry equipment into locations themselves. The recording devices were taken onto the roofs of trains and deep into mine shafts. Lacking playback possibilities the crew was unable to listen to the footage produced or to check devices. The resulting trembling of sound made some recordings unusable. The final editing was done in a frantic fifty days and nights. Nonetheless, the resulting soundtrack is a fascinating montage that combines clanging iron, roaring fires, shuddering sounds on the factory floor, rushing trains, radio addresses, speeches, marching bands, and crowds. Charlie Chaplin found it stunning and commented on the "beauty of mechanical sounds."

The film, in fact, can be interpreted as combining all three enthusiasms mentioned. There are references to the national dimension and Ukrainization; to the glorification of proletarian culture; and to the Stalinist drive for standardization, mechanization and militarization, even of the human body. Uniting them all is the avant-garde cult of natural and physical vitality. Moreover, today's viewer can read into the film an unresolved tension between these three currents or dimensions.

The national dimension is present in the images of Ukrainization. Throughout the film the viewer is exposed to the use of Ukrainian in street signs, the film's headings and subtitles. Ukrainian identity markers can be found in the chronicling of specific events, such as the All-Ukrainian Congress of Soviets held in Kharkiv in 1931 and in the behavior of the people, which the camera attempts to capture as "life unawares," a manner that would later in the 1960s be dubbed cinema vérité. There are no professional actors. Instead, ordinary people are shown going about their business; many scenes are clearly not staged. This allows footage to reveal, for example, the widespread use of Ukrainian in publications, institutions, and parades. Although Jeremy Hicks sees in the film an attempt to erase Ukraine as a place "in favor of a universal, international, Communist space, "this is debatable, because the spectator would have been attuned to local specifics in geography, personal appearance and culture" (Hicks 2007, 74).

The proletarian dimension is present in the glorification of workers, factory life and solidarity. Speaking of Vertov's *The Eleventh Year*, Hicks writes: "Superimpositions show apparently giant workers hammering flat huge rocky outcroppings. The incredible energy of the bolsheviks transforms the physical properties of earth, so that by the end of the film it is not static but seething with activity above and below ground" (Hicks 2007, 59). Vertov's next two films also serve up similar metaphors for renewal and transformation, with electricity and hydro-electric power dams symbolizing change (Hicks, 59). They thematize movement and energy (in hostile opposition to the stasis associated with the past). Rushing water, for example, becomes a metaphor for the unstoppable force of history. However, the focus of *Enthusiasm* is on the awakening of an invigorated and active spectator to the new, particularly to the sounds of a new civilization, and to the images of working class life, which is presented with much greater frankness than would later be allowed. The viewer sees laborers trudging to and from the factory with their lunch boxes, as well as dangerous factory conditions and industrial sites.

The Stalinist dimension is also everywhere to be seen in these films, especially in the serried masses of marching columns, the choral singing, the mechanized and almost robotic movements of workers, the marching music and military metaphors. *Man with the Movie Camera* also contains within it the dominant idea of "total surveillance" by the camera eye, which the film suggests, like the state and secret police, has a right to be everywhere (Hicks, 70).

The opening sections of *Enthusiasm* are about overcoming false consciousness, symbolized by a church being turned into a workers' club. However, the later sections focus on the need for the entire society to work harder, to produce more coal and fulfill the Plan. They attempt to show workers' faces radiating "joy, health and vitality," but this is not entirely successful (Hicks, 74). In fact, the film received a hostile reception, partly because the audience had difficulty understanding it, but also because it reveals the way workers are manipulated, and the poverty of their circumstances. In fact, from the party's point of views some scenes were considered too candid. These included shots of the population's religiosity, of alcoholics and destitute people living on the streets ten years after the revolution, and the reactions of bystanders to the destruction of their church.

In this sense the film was a propaganda failure, which led to its being attacked for the "fetishization of fact," a charge essentially aimed at its excessive honesty in portraying Soviet life. "Life caught unawares," a motto of Vertov, brought his art too close to reality. By the early thirties staged reality was promoted as a superior way of showing mass enthusiasm. Articles appeared criticizing documentalism, now dubbed formalist (Hicks, 84). "Dispassionate objectivism" had now become an obstacle to party propaganda and Vertov was forced to reorient toward scripted, staged documentaries. Instead of filming "life caught unawares," meetings and speeches were reenacted in the studio or in public. As one commentator put it in 1933: "We are not against moments of staging. Just because we shoot this or that real shock-worker in more convenient circumstances for recording, the essence of the shock-worker will not change" (Hicks, 87). Clearly, political persuasion was too important a goal "to be potentially sacrificed to the niceties of recording unprovoked events" (Hicks, 88). Hicks has pointed out that by staging events it was easier for the filmmaker to show what should be occurring rather than what actually was occurring (Hicks, 88).

In the end *Enthusiasm*'s "life caught unawares" produced a more honest picture than Stalin's cultural commissars were prepared to allow, and this led to the film's quick removal from circulation. An attentive viewer could detect an enthusiasm that is manufactured and at times forced. Some in the marching columns and gathered crowds appear to be distinctly unenthusiastic, as they cast furtive glances and self-conscious smiles. An Orwellian tone dominates much of the film: the dominant image is of masses being driven to listen and obey, while anonymous radio voices or speeches delivered for the camera by shock workers urge overfulfillment of production norms. The towering smokestacks and factories make less of an impression on today's viewer than an awareness of the appalling working conditions, management's bombast, the browbeating of workers during mass meetings, and the demands for ever-greater sacrifices to maintain the forced pace of industrialization. The commissar gives his speech, the stakhanovites (record setters) announce their commitments, but the effects of these calls to discipline are shown in the actual lives of workers—in their training and the conditions on the factory floor. It takes little imagination to grasp the punitive work regime and the lack of attention to safety and health.

Although the film attempts to intertwine and mix the three enthusiasms, almost in the form of three "motifs," the result is dissonance rather than harmony, cacophony and incongruity rather than unified composition.

The viewer is left wondering what lies behind the surface expression of this enthusiasm.

Their final impression is that the political message (the narrative of transition from degeneration to the onward-and-upward of Stalinist industrialization) lacks conviction. In fact, for the contemporary spectator, this film is a demonstration of how propaganda can be used to distort or hide reality. Ironically, the final scenes of happy peasants dancing in the fields during harvesting cannot help but draw the attention of today's viewer to the Great Famine that gripped the country in the wake of collectivization just two years after the film premiered.

As with other outstanding films made at this time, such as Dovzhenko's *Arsenal* (1929) and *Earth* (1930), and Vertov's *Man with the Movie Camera* (1929), party authorities expected a clear message contrasting a degenerate past with a radiant future. However, the audience inevitably would have noticed the military metaphor with which *Enthusiasm* ends ("With song into battle"), the Orwellian Big Brother voice, and the message that the individual is nothing while the state is everything. The idea that individual lives have to be mechanized, industrialized and forced to produce more at a faster pace evokes resistance in today's viewer, and would probably have done the same for most viewers in the thirties. It is a message that serves to condemn the system more than celebrate it. This may be an indication that Vertov's failure to produce what the party leadership considered a convincing film was, in fact, due to his own inner resistance to the required message. His faith in individual creativity and in the cinema vérité method were at odds with the new propaganda strictures.

The hopes and dreams of writers and artists who witnessed the cultural revolutions of the twenties and early thirties were intermingled with varying degrees of cynicism and political apprehension. Ukraine had, after all, been ravaged by wars fought against the Red Army, which had largely been recruited in and sent from Russia in three separate attempts (1918, 1919, and 1920) to establish bolshevik rule. Nonetheless, the enthusiasm of some local people for economic and cultural reconstruction was genuine, widely noted, and often reported by Western visitors, many of whom were prepared to embrace what they interpreted as a civilizational breakthrough. These Western enthusiasts came in many varieties. Not all were, or remained for long "useful idiots" in the manner of the duped George Bernard Shaw and Edouard Herriot, or the deceitful Walter Duranty. In fact, most journalists who spent more than a few days time in Russia and Ukraine also reported critically on the economic and political situation, and noted the presence of dissent.

In 1926 René Fueloep-Miller spoke of the old world that had ceased to exist and the potential beginning of a "new humanity" (Fueloep-Miller 1965, x). However, this German visitor cautioned that Soviet Russians believed excessively in "naïve magic formulas" and attached "almost religious ecstatic emphasis" to the notion "scientific" (Fueloep-Miller, 18). Ukrainian writers, with Viktor Domontovych (pseudonym of Viktor Petrov) perhaps the most salient example, warned at the time against precisely such an irrational faith in science and technology. Domontovych's great works from the twenties are *Divchynka z vedmedykom* (Girl with a Teddy Bear, 1928), *Doktor Serafikus* (Doctor Seraphicus, 1947) and *Bez gruntu* (Rootless, 1948). The last two were published in emigration after the war, but were written earlier. They portray the experimenters and enthusiasts of the twenties with a detached amusement and in a jaded tone that recalls Khvylovyi's stories from the same period.

An amusing portrait of visiting Western enthusiasts is provided in E. M. Delafield's *I Visit the Soviets* (1937). While most of her Western companions declare that they never want to return, some, such as the Englishwoman Mrs. Pansy Baker, are gushing: "How splendid it all is, they cry, and how fine to see everybody busy, happy and cared for. As for the institutions—the crèches, the schools, the public parks and the prisons—all, without any qualification whatsoever, are perfect. Russia has nothing left to learn" (Delafield 1937, 316).

Even many Western visitors who were critical of their surroundings admired the collective spirit and the perceived strength of Stalin. Sherwood Eddy, who wrote in 1934 of Russia: "All life is focused in a central purpose. It is directed to a single high end and energized by such powerful and glowing motivation that life seems to have supreme significance. It releases a flood of joyous and strenuous activity" (Eddy 1934, 177). Much of the enthusiasm, however, was a throwback, an attempt to re-galvanize the military fervor that characterized the early years of bolshevik rule. Extravagant forecasts by bolshevik leaders in the years 1918–21 had set the tone, but the distance between "imagination and creativity and the demands of Bolshevik creativity rapidly widened" and that it was not long before "the excitement of the early period vanished, along with most of its participants" (Rosenberg 1990, 11). By the late twenties, as the earlier dreamers lost faith, the youngest generation entered the work force for the first time. Many accepted the promise of a transformed life and devoted their vigor and (often naïve) optimism to its realization.

On the other hand, many Westerners, like many Soviet citizens, saw through the bombast. By the late twenties Ukrainians were witnessing the repression of their national leaders, restrictions placed on their language and cultural identity, and they were aware of the treatment of the peasantry. Consequently, they were less likely to be duped by party propaganda. This fact was also noted by Western visitors who spent time in Ukraine and made attempts to examine the devastation caused by collectivization and the Great Famine of 1932–33. Here is Louis Fischer writing in 1935:

> The Bolsheviks were carrying out a major policy on which the strength and character of their regime depended. The peasants were reacting as normal human beings would. Let no one minimize the sadness of the phenomenon. But from the larger point of view the effect was the final entrenchment of collectivization. The peasantry will never again undertake passive resistance. And the Bolsheviks—one hopes—have learned that they must not compel the peasantry to attempt such resistance." (Fischer 1973, 171–72)

To his credit, Fischer changed his views. He soon dropped his apologias for collectivization and the mass violence and starvation that accompanied it. In 1949 he published *Thirteen Who Fled*, in which former Soviet citizens from all walks of life recount their experiences under Stalin's rule. A similar path of apologism followed by disillusionment was traveled by Arthur Koestler, Alexander Weissburg and a host of Soviet sympathizers, who eventually saw through the mendacity and grasped "the larger point of view" in an entirely different manner. Many Soviet citizens experienced a similar change of attitude.

The picture of local enthusiasm is therefore a complex one in which degrees of hope and commitment mingled with disenchantment and fear of repression. Nonetheless, during the years it served as the capital of the Ukrainian Soviet republic, Kharkiv acted as the symbolic center, generating in Ukraine the three currents of "enthusiasm" outlined above, which today color our understanding of literature, film, and art produced in these years. The achievements of the period might be fruitfully examined by locating tensions within and between the different imagined projects, as well as the aesthetic that underpinned them, the forms of expression they generated, and, finally, the disillusionment that eventually overcame enthusiasts.

The Avant-Garde in Today's Cultural Memory

Remembering the Avant-Garde

In the early decades of the twentieth century, scores of young people from Ukraine made their way to France and Germany, where they completed their education and then made major contributions to the international avant-garde, including in its French, German, Russian, and Jewish dimensions. Since Ukraine's independence in 1991 there has been an effort by the country's curators and scholars to return these sometimes long-neglected figures to the country's cultural history.

Numerous exhibitions around the world have been devoted to members of the École de Paris, the epicenter of the artistic revolution that swept through Europe during the first three decades of the century. Various retrospective displays have focused on members who were Russians (Paris, 1961), Italians (Milan, 1971), Jews (New York, 1975), émigrés in Montparnasse (Paris, 1992), Spaniards (Madrid, 1993), and Poles (Warsaw, 1996). The Ukrainian contribution to modernism and the avant-garde has been the subject of exhibitions in Zagreb (1990–91), Munich (1993), Toulouse (1993–94), Winnipeg (2001), Hamilton (2002), and New York (2006). In Paris UNESCO organized an exhibition of artists of Ukrainian descent who contributed to modern French art in the years 1900–60 (2000).[1]

In Ukraine itself the Lviv Art Gallery has held exhibitions devoted to Ukrainian, Polish and Russian artists who worked in Paris in the first half of the century under the title "Nerozhadanyi rebus 'Paryzh'" (The Unexplained Rebus 'Paris') (2000), while Kyiv's National Art Museum of Ukraine has devoted numerous exhibitions to avant-gardists of the 1920s, to those who

---

1 For the best recent volume on Ukrainian artists in Paris, see Susak 2010. For earlier references to Ukrainian artists in Paris, see Ladzhynskyi 1973, and Popovych 1968, 1977, 1983.Exhibition catalogues that have drawn on the works in the National Art Museum of Ukraine include *Phenomenon of the Ukrainian Avant-garde* 2001, and *Ukrainian Modernism* 2006.

worked abroad as well as in Ukraine. This effort of reclamation constitutes part of a wider project aimed at restoring neglected chapters of cultural history. Today, galleries and museums in Ukraine explore not only of the avant-garde and modernism, but also medieval and baroque art, icons, folk traditions, underground and dissident art, and new experimental trends. Narratives are being rewritten to incorporate "native" artists into European history, and European trends into the story of Ukraine's cultural development. There is now a greater public awareness that many figures, such as Archipenko, Burliuk, Malevich, Exter, and Hryshchenko (Gritchenko) were part of both "European" and "Ukrainian" art. The reconstruction of this history has sometimes been contentious, largely because it has coincided with a vigorous debate over cultural memory and identity.

Artistic modernism and avant-gardism in Ukraine have frequently been described as "interrupted projects." The great achievements of 1910–30 were denied recognition and deliberately obscured from public view after the early thirties. Some aspects of the history resurfaced briefly in the 1960s before full disclosure became possible in the 1990s. Since then, public awareness of the "historic" avant-garde has served as an inspiration for many contemporaries. In the decade following independence, many in the artistic and literary communities rejected all forms of realism and populism, as they were considered compromised by association with the Soviet regime. Younger artists and writers embraced various forms of avant-gardism or turned to postmodernism as a "hallmark of high culture and orientation towards European values" (Shumylovych 2006, 87). However, the post-independence years also revealed a significant and growing tension between individuals who aspired to ground their art in the national heritage, however broadly conceived, and those who wanted to deconstruct mythologies or who were interested in artistic experimentation for its own sake.

Today members of the first camp are often conscious of their roles and responsibilities as representatives of the nation. They feel a need to explore their own culture, to examine, for example, the connection between folk and elite values, or continuities between the historical past and the present. Sometimes this leads to the adoption of a more widely comprehensible idiom, a strategy that tends to be popular with the mainstream viewer. Those in the second camp tend to embrace the idea of multiple discourses, different tendencies, and modern technologies. They have sometimes been accused of grafting Western ideas, theories and methodologies onto local soil in a way that produces not meaning but chaos.

Ola Hnatiuk has argued persuasively that there have been attempts to manipulate this cultural discourse into a clash between "modernists" and "nativists" (Hnatiuk 2006). It is instructive in this context to consider the experience of the avant-garde in the years 1910–30. As these essays indicate, the earlier generation of innovators had to deal with similar tensions between the new and traditional, the international and national, the ironic and intuitive. The discourse at that time was also politicized and was subjected to manipulation, as it was in later decades. The experience of the "historic" avant-garde therefore provides useful lessons with regard to current debates. Its ideas, like those of contemporaries, were conditioned by a similar discourse around creative freedom, identity and relations with Europe. The tensions within this discourse proved artistically productive until in the late twenties a rigid censorship was imposed and prescriptive demands were made of all artists.

The earlier conflicts between proponents of the old and new still resonate with contemporaries and provide parallels with today's situation. The need to choose between the local-national and European-international was a challenge faced by the earlier avant-garde, one that it accepted enthusiastically and often solved brilliantly. The dilemmas presented by this choice were central to the great Literary Discussion of the 1920s, the last great open debate before Stalinism effectively prevented many from engaging in a personal dialogue with the non-Soviet world.

Among contemporary researchers there is less controversy attached to some figures. Archipenko and Bohomazov, for example, have been restored to a position of prominence in Ukrainian cultural history, and this has in turn benefitted their reputations abroad.[2] Kavaleridze, Meller, and Boichuk still await definitive studies in Ukraine and recognition abroad, although the first has been the beneficiary of an excellent recent study and collection (in 2017), which, it is to be hoped, will lead to a rediscovery of his films and an in-depth study of his life and art.[3]

Burliuk's legacy has proved to be more problematic. The 1995 exhibition of his work in St. Petersburg in 1995, the publication of Evdaev's work on the artist's life in the United States, and Krusanov's volumes devoted to the early futurists, show little awareness of the Ukrainian context in the artist's work.[4] The artist's case is symptomatic of the gap in understanding among Russia critics concerning many figures from Ukraine.

---

2 See, for example, the two exhibitions *Alexander Archipenko* 2005, held in New York, and *Alexandre Bogomazov* 1991, held in Toulouse.

3 Kozlenko and Menzelevskyi 2017.

4 See *David Burliuk, 1882–1967* 1995, and Evdaev 2002, and Krusanov 1996–2003. For a counter-position, see *Futurism and After: David Burliuk 1882–1967* 2008

The same can be said of Malevich, whose links to Ukraine have been similarly ignored in most exhibitions and publications originating in Russia. The exhibition that traveled to Los Angeles, Washington and New York in 1990–91 was conceived as a contribution to détente and good relations between Russia and the United States. The catalogue contains forewords from George Bush, Mikhail Gorbachev, and Raisa Gorbacheva. Given these circumstances it is hardly surprising that the painter is introduced as a "renowned Russian artist," the "greatest and most original spokesman of the entire Russian avant-garde." This catalogue also omits the first half of Malevich's 1933 autobiography. The translated text only begins from the moment the artist left Ukraine for Russia. Such omissions have contributed to an interpretive bias and a reluctance to consider different evidence. By neglecting the Ukrainian dimension scholars miss an opportunity to refresh and enrich the analysis of Malevich. Recently, Ukrainian scholars have provided previously unknown documentation, which has led to new insights into this artist's life and work.[5]

Some marked biases, of course, also affect the analysis of other important figures. Vertov, too, would benefit, as has been argued here, from a better scholarly understanding in the West of political and cultural realities in the Ukrainian film industry at the time he produced his greatest films. He still awaits this contextualization.

The situation with scholarship on the Jewish avant-garde in Ukraine is more positive. We now have a number of excellent works on the Kultur-Lige and interest in these and other avant-gardists of Jewish origin has continued to grow with publication of articles in Ukrainian journals and increased attention in Western publications.[6] It should be noted, however, that the lives of many individuals are not well known. Even in some cases, awareness of their Jewish origins and connections are lacking. More research is required into both their biographies and art, and into their interaction with other figures—those who remained in Ukraine and those who emigrated from the country.

Discussions concerning the biographies, identities, and works of Ukraine's avant-gardists now involve scholars in Ukraine, Russia and the West. Collections, archives, and documentary materials from around the world continue to yield fresh information. In spite of the conflicting judgements—and, in some cases, a hotly contested history—in the last three decades this avant-garde has gained increasing recognition as a phenomenon with its own internal dynamic and characteristic traits. It now commands attention as a richly rewarding topic of study in its own right.

---

5 See especially Nayden and Horbachov 1993, Horbachov 2006, and Filevska 2010.

6 See especially Kazovsky 2003, 2007, and 2011; Orlianskii 2000; Rybakov 2001.

Bibliography

Alexander Archipenko: Vision and Continuity. 2005. Exhibition catalogue. Curator Jaroslaw Leshko. New York: The Ukrainian Museum.

Alexandre Bogomazov Jampol, 1880—Kiev, 1930. 1991. Exhibition catalogue. Musee d'Art Moderne. Exhibition catalogue. Toulouse: Arpap.

Andersen, Troels ed. 1968. *K. S. Malevich: Essays on Art: 1915–1933*, vol. 2. *1928–1933*. Copenhagen: Borgen.

Antonova, Irina, and Iorn Merkert. 1996. *Moskva-Berlin/Berlin-Moskva, 1900–1950*. Munich-New York: Prestel and Moscow: Galart.

Apollinaire, Guillaume. 1969. "Alexandre Archipenko." *Der Sturm. Siebzehnte Ausstellung: Alexander Archipenko*. March 12, 1914. (English translation in Karshan, 1969, 12–14.)

Apter-Gabriel, Ruth, ed. 1988. *Tradition and Revolution: The Jewish Renaissance in Russian Avant-Garde Art 1912–1928*. Jerusalem: The Israel Museum.

Archipenko, Alexander. 1969. "Polychrone Manifesto." In Karshan, 23–24.

Aronson, B. 1924. *Sovremennaia evreiskaia grafika*. Berlin : Petropolis. (Partial English translation in Apter-Gabriel 235–38.)

Ash, Jared. 2002. "Primitivism in Russian Futurist Book Design 1910–14." In Margit Rowell and Deborah Wye, eds. *The Russian Avant-Garde Book, 1910–1934*, 33–40. New York: The Museum of Modern Art.

Baer, George. 1942. "Brave and Adventurous Painter," *New York Herald Tribune*. December 31.

Baron, Herman. 1944. Introduction to Michael Gold, *David Burliuk, Artist-Scholar: Father of Russian Futurism*, 2. NY: ACA Gallery.

Basner, Elena. 1995. "The Phenomenon of David Burliuk in the History of the Russian Avant-Garde Movement." In *David Burliuk, 1882–1967*, 11–32.

Bazhan, M. 2004. "Pid ukrainskym nebom," *Muzeinyi provulok* 2: 74–77.

Benois, Andre. 1909. "Rech." March 22.

Birnie Danzker, Jo-Anne, Igor Jassenjawsky and Joseph Kiblitsky, eds. 1993. *Avantgarde and Ukraine*. Munich: Klinkhardt and Biermann.

Bowlt, John E. 1986. "David Burliuk, the Father of Russian Futurism." *Canadian-American Slavic Studies* 20.1–2: 25–35.

———. 1988. "From the Pale of Settlement to the Reconstruction of the World?" In Apter-Gariel, 43–60.

———. 1990. "Kazimir Malevich and the Energy of Language," in *Kazimir Malevich*, ed. D'Andrea, 179–86.

Burliuk, David. 1928–29. "Velikii krotkii bolshevik." In his *Tolstoy, Gorkii. Poemy*, 5–21. New York: Izdatelstvo Marii Nikiforovny Burliuk.

———. [1949] *Color and Rhyme* 1: *Burliuk in 1947–48. Eighth exhibition at ACA*. Hampton Bays.

———. 1994. *Fragmenty iz vospominanii futurista. Pisma. Stikhotvoreniia*. St. Petersburg.

———. 2002. "Lestnits moikh let." In Evdaev, 297–304.

Burliuk, Marussia. 1961–62. "Stranitsy zhizni v Amerike. Dnevnik 1930 g." *Color and Rhyme* 48: 16–30.

Burliuk, Nicholas. N.d. "The First Hippie: David Davidovich Burliuk." Mary Holt family archive.

Butler, Christopher. 1994. *Early Modernism: Music and Painting in Europe 1900–1916*. Oxford: Oxford University Press.

Cherevatenko, Leonid. 1987. "'Promovte zhyttia moie – i strymaite slozy' ... Khudozhnyk Oksana Pavlenko zhaluie, rozpovidaie." In *Nauka i kultura. Ukraina. Shchorichnyk.* Vypusk 21: 370–79.

Chipp, Heershcell B. ed., 1971. *Theories of Modern Art: A Source Book by Artists and Critics*. Berkeley: University of California Press.

Crone, Rainer and David Moos. 1991. *Kazimir Malevich: The Climax of Disclosure*. Chicago: University of Chicago Press.

David Burliuk, 1882–1967: Exhibition of Works from the State Russian Museum and Museums and Private Collections of Russia, USA and Germany. 1995. St. Petersburg: Palace Editions.

"Deklaratsiia Vseukrainskoi federatsii revolutsiinykh radianskykh pysmennykiv." 1930. *Molodniak* 1: 124.

Delafield, E. M. 1937. *I Visit the Soviets: The Provincial Lady Looks at Russia*. New York: Harper and Brothers Publishers.

Demosfenova, Galina L., Evgeniia A. Petrova, et al., eds. 1990. *Malevitch: Artiste et théoricien*. Paris, Flammarion.

Domontovych, Viktor. 1928. *Divchynka z vedmedykom: nepravdopodibni istyny*. Kyiv: Siiavo.

———. 1947. *Doktor Serafikus*. Munich: Nakladom Vydavnytstva Ukrainska Trybuna.

———. 1948. *Bez gruntu: Povist*. Regensburg: Vydavnytstvo Mykhaila Boretskoho.

Douglas, Charlotte. 1980. *Swans of Other Worlds: Kazimir Malevich and the Origins of Abstraction in Russia*. Ann Arbor, Michigan: UMI Research Press.

———. 1994. *Kazimir Malevich*. New York: Harry N. Abrams.

Drak, A. 1985. "Maister stsenohrafii Vadym Meller." *Obrazotvorche mystetstvo* 3: 23–24.

———. 1997. "Stsenohrafiia epokhy Kurbasa." *Ukrainskyi teatr* 2: 16.

Dychenko, I. 1984. "Toi nyzhnii vykhor barv (Tvorchyi portret ukr. teatr. khudozhnyka V. Mellera)." *Ukraina* 13: 16–20.

———. 2004. "Arystokrat v avangarde." *Stolichnye novosti*. December 14–20.

Eddy, Sherwood. 1934. *Russia Today: What We Can Learn from It?* New York: Farrar and Rinehart Incorporated.

Efros, A. 1918. 'Lampa Alladina.' *Evreiskii mir: Literaturnye sborniki*. Moscow.

Ellul, Jacques. 1973. *Propaganda: The Formation of Men's Attitudes*. New York: Vintage Books.

Evdaev, Norbert. 2002. *David Burliuk v Amerike: Materialy k biografii*. Moscow: Nauka.

Exter, Alexandra. 1919. "The Artist in the Theater. From an Interview Recorded by Filipp Goziason." *Odesskii listok*, 4. November 26.

———. 1990. "On the Works of Evgeniia Pribilska and Ganna Sobachko." In *Ukrajinska Avangarda, 1910–1930*. Exhibition catalogue, 209–10. Ed. Marijan Suslovski. Zagreb: Galerije grada Zagreba. (Orig. pub. In *Teatralnaia zhizn* Kyiv 9 (1918): 18.)

Filevska, Tetiana, ed. 2016. *Kazymyr Malevych: Kyivskyi period, 1928–1930*. Kyiv: Rodovid.

Fischer, Louis. 1973. *Soviet Journey*. Westport, Connecticut: Greenwood Press. (Orig. pub. New York: Harrison Smith and Robert Hass, 1935.)

Fueloep-Miller, René.1965. *The Mind and Face of Bolshevism: An Examination of Cultural Life in Soviet Russia*. New York: Harper and Row Publishers. (Orig. pub. in German as *Geist und Gesicht des Bolschewismus*, 1926. (First published in English in the United States and England by G. P. Putnam's Sons Ltd. in 1927.)

Futurism and After: David Burliuk 1882–1967. Curated by Myroslav Shkandrij. Winnipeg: Winnipeg Art Gallery, 2008.

Gitelman, Zvi Y. 1972. *Jewish Nationality and Soviet Politics: The Jewish Sections of the CPSU, 1917–1930*. Princeton: Princeton University Press.

Gold, Michael. 1944. *David Burliuk, Artist-Scholar: Father of Russian Futurism*. NY: ACA Gallery.

Goldelman, Solomon. 1921. *Lysty zhydivskoho sotsial-demokrata pro Ukrainu: Materialy do istorii ukrainsko-zhydivskykh vidnosyn za chas revoliutsii*. Vienna: Zhydivske vydavnytstvo "Hamoin" na Ukraini.

———. 1967. *Zhydivska natsionalna avtonomiia v Ukraini 1917–1920. Zapysky Naukovoho Tovarystva im. Shevchenka*, vol. 182. Munich: Dniprova khvylia.

Golding, John. 1991. "Supreme Suprematist." *The New York Review*, January 17.

Gombrich, E. H. 2002. *The Preference for the Primitive: Episodes in the History of Western Taste and Art*. London: Phaidon Press.

Gollerbakh, E. 1930. *Iskusstvo Davida Burliuka*. New York: Izdanie M. N. Burliuk.

Gorbachev, Dmitrii, and Aleksandr Pavlov. 2000. "Evreiskie khudozhniki v Kieve (pervaia tret XX veka)." *Egupets* 6: 290–337.

Gorev, I. 1927. "S Lysoi gory." *Kharkovskii proletarii*. September 13.

Groys, Boris. 1992. *The Total Art of Stalinism: Avant-Garde, Aesthetic Dictatorship, and Beyond*. Princeton: Princeton University Press.

Hicks, Jeremy. 2007. *Dziga Vertov: Defining Documentary Film*. London: I. B. Tauris.

Hill, Edwin C. 1929. "Burliuk Paints What Isn't There." *Sun* (New York City), March 25.

Hirniak, Iosyp. 1982. *Spomyny*. New York: Suchasnist.

Hnatiuk, Ola. 2006. "Nativists vs. Westernizers: Problems of Cultural Identity in Ukrainian Literature of the 1990s." *Slavic and East European Journal* 50.3: 434–51.

Horbachov, Dmytro. 2000. "Oleksandra Ekster u Kyievi i v Paryzhi." *Khronika 2000* 35–36: 499–506.

———. 2006. "*Vin ta ia buly Ukraintsi": Malevych ta Ukraina*. Kyiv: Sim Studiia.

Horbachov, Dmytro, ed. 1996. *Ukrainskyi avanhard 1910–1930 rokiv: Albom*. Kyiv: Mystetstvo.

Hordynskyi, Sviatoslav. 1947. "Na velykykh shliakhakh: Do problem sohochasnoho ukrainskoho obrazotvorchoho mystetstva." *Ukrainske mystetstvo: Almanakh I*, 26–30. Munich: Spilka.

———. 2007."Mysttsi pro mystetstvo." *Artaniia* 8: 13–15.

Humenna, Dolia. 1956. *Khreshchatyi iar (Kyiv 1941–43: Roman-khronika)*. New York: Slovo.

Kapelhorodskyi, N. M., O. R. Synko, H. Ia. Skliarenko, L. I. Baraban, Iu. D. Shlapak. 2007. *Ivan Kavaleridze: zhyttia i tvorchist*. Kyiv: KYI.

Karshan, Donald H. 1969. *Archipenko: International Visionary*. Washington: Smithsonian Institution Press.

Kavaleridze, Ivan. 1978. "Paryzh, Paryzh … Iz spohadiv myttsia." *Vitchyzna* 1: 121–30.

———. 1977. "Ranok krainy." *Vitchyzna* 7, Nicolas, 112–22.

———. 1988. *Sbornik statei i vospominanii*. Kyiv: Mystetstvo.

———. 2017a. "Prokazhennyi Ivan," 81–230. In Kozlenko, Ivan and Stanislav Menzelevskyi, 81–230.

———. 2017b. "Tini." In Kozlenko, Ivan and Stanislav Menzelevskyi, 231–55.

Kazimir Malevich 1878–1935. 1988. Exhibition catalogue. Ed. W. A. L. Beeren and J. M. Joosten. Amsterdam: Stedelijk Museum.

Kazimir Malevich 1878–1935. 1990. Exhibition catalogue. Ed. Jeanne D'Andrea. Los Angeles: The Armand Hammer Museum of Art and Cultural Center.

Kazovsky, Hillel (Gregory). 2003. *The Artists of the Kultur-Lige*. Jerusalem: Gesharim and Moscow: Mosty Kultury.

———. 2011. *The Book Design of Kultur-Lige Artists*. Kyiv: Dukh i Litera.

———., ed. 2007. *Kultur-Lige: Artistic Avant-garde of the 1910s and 1920s*. Kyiv: Dukh i litera.

Khardzhiev, N. 1976. *K istorii russkogo avangarda*. Stockholm: Almqvist and Wiksell Intern.

Khiterer, Viktoria. 1999. *Dokumenty sobrannye Evreiskoi istoriko-arkheograficheskoi komissiei Vseukrainskoi Akademii Nauk*. Kyiv: Institut iudaiki, and Jerusalem: Gesharim.

———. 2002. "Konfiskatsiia evreiskikh dokumentalnykh materialov i evreiskoi sobstvennosti v Ukraine v 1919–1930 gg." In Aronov and Finberh, 10.

Khlebnikov, V. 1964–65. "Burliuk." *Color and Rhyme* 55: 30.

Khmuryi, Vasyl. 1930. "Vadym Meller." *Kultrobitnyk* 3: 35–37.

———. 1948. "Iosyp Hirniak: Etiud." In V. Khmuryi, Iu. Dyvnych and Ie. Blakytnyi, *V maskakh epokhy: Iosyp Hirniak*, 11–46. N.p.; Ukraina. (Orig. pub. Kharkiv: Rukh, 1931.)

Khvylovyi, Mykola. 1926. "Une lettre." *Nove mystetstvo* 26: 10–11.

———. 1960. *Stories from the Ukraine*. New York: Wisdom Library.

———. 1986. *The Cultural Renaissance in Ukraine: Polemical Pamphlets, 1925–1926*. Ed. Myroslav Shkandrij. Edmonton: Canadian Institute of Ukrainian Studies, University of Alberta.

Khrushchev, Nikita Sergeevich. 1970. *Khrushchev Remembers*. Ed. Strobe Talbott. Boston: Little, Brown.

Kleiner, Israel. 2000. *From Nationalism to Universalism: Vladimir (Ze'ev) Jabotinsky and the Ukrainian Question*. Edmonton and Toronto: Canadian Institute of Ukrainian Studies.

Koliazin, Vladimir. 1996. "Gastroli russkikh teatrov 20-kh–30-kh godov v Berline: S Vostoka na Zapad, ot Tairova k Meierkholdu." In Antonova and Merkert, 173–76.

Kopelev, Lev. 1980. *The Education of a True Believer*. New York.

Kotliar, Ie. and V. Susak. 2005. "Ievreiske mystetstvo: tradytsiia i novyi chas." In Leonid Finberh and Volodymyr Liubchenko, eds., *Narysy z istorii ta kultury ievreiv Ukrainy*, 300–29. Kyiv: Dukh i litera.

Kozlenko, Ivan. 2017. "Kavaleridze: Kinokubistychne zhytiie." In Kozlenko and Menzelevskyi, 59–80.

Kozlenko, Ivan and Stanislav Menzelevskyi, eds. 2017. *Ivan Kavaleridze: Memuary, dramaturhiia, publitsystyka*. Kyiv: Natsionalnyi tsentr Oleksandra Dovzhenka.

Krasylnikova, O. V. 2000. "Oleksandra Ekster i Vadym Meller." In *Ukrainske mystetstvo ta arkhitektura kintsia XIX-pochatku XX st.*, 106–19. Ed. P. O. Biletskyi. Kyiv: Naukova dumka.

Krusanov, A. V. 1996. *Russkii avangard: 1907–1932: Istoricheskii obzor*. Vol. 1. Boevoe desiatiletie. St. Petersburg: Novoe literaturnoe obozrenie.

———. 2003. *Futuristicheskaia revoliutsiia 1917–1921: Istoricheskii obzor*. Vol. 2. Books 1 and 2. Moscow: Novoe literaturnoe obozrenie.

Kucherenko, Z. V. 1975. *Vadym Meller*. Kyiv: Mystetstvo.

Kucherenko, Zoia. 1997. "Vadym Meller," *Khronika 2000* 19–20: 325–43.

Ladzhynskyi, V. 1973. "Ukrainski mysttsi v Paryzhi." *Notatky z mystetstva* (Philadelphia) 13: 17–33.

Lahutenko, Olha. 2007. *Graphein Hrafiky: Narysy z istorii ukrainskoi hrafiky XX stolittia*. Kyiv: Hrani-T, 2007.

Lavrentev, Boris. 1959. "Avtobiografiia." *Novyi mir* 4: 56–63.

Lavrinenko, Iurii. 1959. *Rozstriliane vidrodzhennia: Antolohiia 1917–1933. Poeziia—Proza—Drama—Esei*. Munich: Instytut Literacki.

Livshits, Benedikt. 1977. *The One and a Half-Eyed Archer*. Newtonville, Mass.: Oriental Research Partners.

Lubchak, Vadym. 2012. "Anti-imperialistic film by Ivan Kavaleridze." *Den*, May 15. https://day.kyiv.ua/en/article/culture/anti-imperialistic-film-ivan-kavaleridze.

Lysiak-Rudnytskyi, Ivan. 1973. *Mizh istoriieiu i politykoiu: Statti do istorii ta krytyky ukrainskoi, suspilno-politychnoi dumky*. N.p.: Suchasnist.

Makaryk, Irena R. 2004. *Shakespeare in the Undiscovered Bourn: Les Kurbas, Ukrainian Modernism and Early Soviet Cultural Politics.* Toronto : University of Toronto Press.

———. 2010. "On the World Stage: The Berezil in Paris and New York." In Makaryk and Tkacz, 479–513.

Makaryk, Irena R. and Virlana Tkacz, eds. 2010. *Modernism in Kyiv: Jubilant Experimentation.* Toronto: University of Toronto Press.

Malevich, Kazimir [Malevych, Kazymyr]. 2016. "Arkhitektura, stankove maliarstvo ta skulptura," 117–20. In Filevska 2016. (Orig. pub. Avanhard-Almanakh, B (1930): 91–93.)

———. [Malevych, Kazymyr]. 1928. "Sproba novoho vidchuttia prostorony." *Nova generatsiia* 11: 311–22.

———. 1959. *The Non-Objective World.* Chicago: Theobald.

———. 1976. "Glavy iz avtobiografii khudozhnika." In Khardzhiev, K istorii russkogo avangarda, 85–127.

———. 1985. "Chapters from an Artists' Autobiography." Trans. Alan Upchurch. October 34: 25–34.

———. 1990. "From 1/42: Autobiographical Notes, 1923–1925." In Kazimir Malevich, ed. D'Andrea, 169–72.

"Maliarska maisternia prof. V. Mellera." 1923. Chervonyi shliakh 6–7: 221–22.

Margolin, Arnold. 1922. *Ukraina i politika Antany. (Zapiski evreia i grazhdanina).* Berlin: Izdatelstvo S. Efron. (English translation as *Ukraine and Policy of the Entente*, 1976.)

Markov, Vladimir. 1968a. "Predislovie." In V. V. Khlebnikov, Sobranie sochinenii. Vol. 1. Munich: Wilhelm Fink Verlag.

———. 1968b. *Russian Futurism: A History.* Berkeley and Los Angeles: University of California Press.

Menzelevskyi, Stanislav. 2017. "Avto/Bio/Kino." In Kozlenko and Menzelevskyi, 11–18.

Milner, John. 1984. *Vladimir Tatlin and the Russian Avant-Garde.* New Haven: Yale University Press.

Movchan, Raisa. 2008. "Proletarska literature 1920-kh rokiv i modernizm." In T. I. Hundorova, ed., *Modernizm pislia postmodernu*, 203–11. Kyiv: Polihrafichnyi tsentr Foliant.

Mudrak, Myroslava M. 1986. *The New Generation and Artistic Modernism in Ukraine.* Ann Arbor, Michigan: UMI Research Press.

———. 1987. "The Painted Surface in the Ukrainian Avant-garde: from Facture to Construction." *Pantheon* 45: 138–43.

———. 2001. "Rupture or Continuum? Ukraine's 'Avant-Garde' In Search of a System." In *Phenomenon* 2001, 25–29.

Nakov, Andre. 1991. "De l'expression futuriste au formalisme construit." In *Alexandre Bogomazov, Jampol, 1880—Kiev, 1930*, 13–24. Musee d'Art Moderne, Refectoire des Jacobins, Toulouse. N.p.: Editions Arpap.

Naiden, Oleksandr and Dmytro Horbachov. 1993. "Malevych muzhytskyi." *Khronika 2000* 3–4: 210–31. (Reprinted in Horbachov 2006, 199–209.)

Nimenko, A. 1967. *Kavaleridze-skulptor*. Kyiv: Mystetstvo.

Olenska-Petryshyn, Arkadiia. 1997. "Arkhypenko—peredovyi novator skulptury XX viku," *Khronika 2000* 19–20: 486–98.

Orlianskii, V. S. 2000. *Ievrei Ukrainy v 20–30 roky XX storichchia: sotsialno-politychnyi aspect*. Zaporizhzhia: Zaporizkyi derzhavnyi universytet, Zaporizke miske viddilennia tavarystva 'Ukraina-Izrail'.

Papash, Olha. 2017. "Ivan Kavaleridze: Mizh istoriieiu i mopvchanniam." In Kozlenko and Menzelevskyi, 21–32.

Papeta, S. P. 2006. "Nina Henke-Meller: Vid narodnoho suprematyzmu do radianskoho mystetstva." Vistnyk KhDADM 2: 121–27. http://www.nbuv.gov.ua/articles/2006/06pspssa.pdf. Accessed January 15, 2012.

Pavlyshyn, Marko. 1997. "Ukrainska kultura z pohliadu postmodernizmu." In his *Kanon ta ikonostas*, 213–22. Kyiv: Vydavnytstvo Chas.

"Peredmova do katalohu pershoi vystavky 'Kultur-Ligy.'" 2003. In Kazovsky 2007, 78–79. (Orig. Yiddish *Kultur-Lige. Biuliten numer 2*. Kyiv, 1920, 15–20. Partial English translation in Apter-Gabriel, 230.)

Petrovskii, Miron. 1996. "Lev Kvitko v krugu ukrainskikh pisatelei." In Wolf Moskovich, et al., eds., *Jews and Slavs*, vol. 5, 238–54. Jerusalem.

Petrova, Yevgenia. 2001. "Futurism in Russian Fine Art." In *The Russian Avant-Garde: Representation and Interpretation*. Ed. Yevgenia Petrova. St. Petersburg: The State Russian Museum, Palace Editions.

Pevnyi, Bohdan. 1992. "Pid zakhystom Bohorodytsi." Ukraina 15: 11.

Phenomenon of the Ukrainian Avant-Garde, 1910–1935. 2001. Exhibition catalogue. Ed. Myroslav Shkandrij. Winnipeg: Winnipeg Art Gallery.

Plokhy, Serhii. 2005. *Unmaking Imperial Russia. Mykhailo Hrushevsky and the Writing of Ukrainian History*. Toronto: University of Toronto Press.

Popovych, Volodymyr. 1968. "Sofiia Levytska (1874–1937)." *Notatky z mystetstva* (Philadelphia) 7: 33–42.

———. 1977. "Arkhypenko u Frantsii." *Notatky z mystetstva* (Phladelphia) 17: 5–18.

———. 1983. "Mykhailo Andriienko-Nechytailo." *Notatky z mystetstva* (Philadelphia) 23: 15–23.

Postupalskii, Igor. 1932. *Literaturnyi trud Davida D. Burliuka*. New York: Izdanie Marii Burliuk.

Pribilska, Evgeniia Ivanovna. N.d. "Zhizneopisanie." Archive of Brigitta Vadymivna Vetrova.

Propaganda and Slogans: The Political Poster in Soviet Ukraine 1919–1921. 2013. Exhibition catalogue. Curated by Myroslav Shkandrij. New York: The Ukrainian Museum.

Ratanova, Maria. 2010. "The Choreographic Avant-garde in Kyiv, 1916–1921: Bronislava Nijinska and Her Ecole do Mouvement." In Makaryk and Tkacz, 311–20.

Ravich, Meilekh. 2008. "Kratkaia istoriia dinamicheskoi gruppy trekh poetov v Varshave, 1921–1925," 2–15. In Grigorii Kazovskii, "O 'Khaliastre,'" http://members.tripod.com/~barabash/zerkalo/19-20/Kazovsky.htm. Accessed August 31, 2008.

Ravich-Cherkasskii, M. 1923. *Istoriia Kommunisticheskoi Partii (b-ov) Ukrainy.* Kharkiv: Gosudarstvennoe izdatelstvo Ukrainy, 1923.

Revutskyi, Valerian. 1955. *Piat velykykh aktoriv ukrainskoi stseny*. Paris: Vydannia pershoi ukrainskoi drukarni u Frantsii.

———. 1985. "Zustrich z Iaremoiu Aizenshtokom." *Diialohy* 9–10: 164–5.

Ripko, Olena and Nelli Prystalenko. 1991. *Boichuk i boichukisty, boichukizm. Kataloh vystavky*. Lviv: LKG.

Rowell, Margit, and Deborah Wye. 2002. *The Russian Avant-Garde Book, 1910–1934*. New York: The Museum of Modern Art.

Rosenberg, William G. 1990. *Bolshevik Visions: First Phase of the Cultural Revolution in Soviet Russia*. 2nd ed. University of Michigan Press. (Orig. pub. Ardis Publishers, 1984.)

Rybak, Isakhar-Ber and Borys Aronson. 1919. "Di vegn fun der yiddisher moleray. (Rayoynes fun kinstler)." *Ufgang*. Erster zamlbukh. Kyiv.

———. 2007. "Shliaky ievreiskoho mystetstva (Rozdumy myttsia)." In Kazovsky 2007, 64–74. (Original Yiddish in I. Rybak and B. Aronson, "Di vegn fun der yiddisher moleray. (Rayoynes fun kinstler)." *Oyfgang – ershter zamlbukh*. Kyiv: Farlag Kultur-Lige, 1919. Partially translated into English in Apter-Gabriel, 229.)

Rybakov, M. O. 2001. *Pravda istorii: diialnist ievreiskoi kulturno-prosvitnytskoi orhanizatsii 'Kulturna liha' u Kyievi (1918–1925): Zbirnyk dokumentiv i materialiv*. 2nd ed. Kyiv: Kyiv.

Samchuk, Ulas. 1980. Na bilomu koni: spomyny i vrazhennia. 3rd ed. Winnipeg: Volyn.

———. 1990. *Na koni voronomu: spomyny i vrazhennia*. 2nd ed. Winnipeg: Volyn.

Sarabianov, Dmitry. 1991. "Malevich at the Time of the 'Great Break.'" In *Malevich: Artist and Theoretician*, ed. Galina Demosfenova. Paris: Flammarion.

Semenko, Mikhail. 1924. "Mystetstvo iak kult." *Chervonyi shliakh* 3: 222–29.

———. 1927. "Prohrama i otochennia livykh." *Nova generatsiia* 1: 39–43.

———. 1929. "Komu potribne mystetstvo." *Literaturna hazeta*, May 1.

Sherekh, Iurii. [Shevelov]. 1964. "Khvylovyi bez polityky," 53–676. In his *Ne dlia ditei*. N.p.: Prolog. (Originally published in *Novi dni*, 1953.)

———. 1978. "Chetvertyi Kharkiv," 204–20. In his *Druha cherha*. N.p.: Suchasnist, 1978. (Originally published in *Studentskyi vistnyk*, 1948.)

Shkandrij, Myroslav. 1992. *Modernists, Marxists and the Nation: The Ukrainian Literary Discussion of the 1920s*. Edmonton: Canadian Institute of Ukrainian Studies.

———. 1994. "Modernism, the Avant-Garde and Mykhailo Boichuk's Aesthetic." *Journal of Ukrainian Studies* 2: 43–58.

Shklovsky, Viktor. 1972. *Mayakovsky and His Circle*. New York: Dodd, Mead and Company.

Shlegel, Hans-Ioakhim. 2017. "Onovlennia kinematohrafa z dukhu skulptury." In Kozlenko and Menzelevskyi, 19–20.

Shumylovych, Bohdan. 2006. "Do We Really Need Methodology from the West in Ukrainian Art Education?" In Egle Rindzeviciute, ed. *Contemporary Change in Ukraine*. Sodertorns hogskola: Center for Baltic and East European Studies.

Sichynsky, Vol. 1934. *M. Andriienko-Nechytailo*, Lviv.

Sinyavsky, Andrei. 1990. *Soviet Civilization: A Cultural History*. New York: Arcade.

Skuratovskyi, Vadym. 1998. "Do ievreisko-ukrainskykh literaturnykh zviazkiv: Poperedni notatky." *Khronika 2000* 21–22: 44–57.

Smolych, Iurii. 1986. *Tvory u 8 tomakh*. Vol. 8. Kyiv: Dnipro.

———. 1990. "Z 'Zapysiv na skhyli viku'." *Prapor* 9: 160–78.

———. 1977. *Pro teatr: zbirnykstatei, retsenzii, narysiv*. Kyiv: Mystetstvo.

"Stikhi Davida Burliuka." 1964-65. *Color and Rhyme* 55: 5–23.

Stone, Dan and Annalee Greenberg, eds. *Jewish Life and Times: A Collection of Essays*. Vol. 9. Winnipeg: Jewish Heritage Centre of Western Canada, 2009.

Susak, Vita. 2010. *Ukrainian Artists in Paris, 1910–1939*. Kyiv: Rodovid.

Synko, Rostyslav. 2002. *Na zlamakh epokj: I. Kavaleridze i otochennia: Ese, Spohady, rozdumy*. Kyiv: Avdi.

Todorov, Tzvetan. 1987. *Literature and Its Theorists: A Personal View of Twentieth- Century Criticism*. Trans. Catherine Porter. Ithaca: Cornell University Press.

Tsybenko, P. A. 1967. "Teatralne-dekoratyvne mystetstvo." *Istoriia ukrainskoho mystetstva v shesty tomakh*. Vol. 5. *Radianske mystetstvo 1917–1941 rokiv*, 157–65. Kyiv: AN URSR.

Ukrainian Modernism 1910–1930. 2006. Ed. Anatolii Melnyk. Kyiv: Natsionalnyi khudozhnii muzei Ukrainy.

Vadym Meller (1884–1962): Teatralno-dekoratsiine mystetstvo, zhyvopys, hrafika. Exhibition catalogue. 1984. Kyiv: Spilka khudozhnykiv Ukrainy. Kyiv.

Van Norman Baer, Nancy. 1986. *Bronislava Nijinska*. The Fine Arts Museum of San Francisco.

———. 1991. *Theatre in Revolution: Russian Avant-Garde Stage Design, 1913–1935*. Thames and Hudson, The Fine Arts Museum of San Francisco.

Vakar, I. A. 2004. "Posleslovie," 577–621. In Vakar and Mikhnenko.

Vakar, I. A. and T. N. Mikhienko, eds. 2004. *Malevich o sebe: Sovremenniki o Maleviche*. 2 vols. Moscow: RA.

Vynnychenko, Volodymyr. 1920. *Vidrodzhennia natsii*. Vol. 1. Kyiv-Vienna: n.p.

"What is the Kultur-Liga?" 2003. In Kazovsky, 16–40. (Original Yiddish: "Vos iz di Kultur-Lige?" *Kultur-Lige. Biuliten* 2. Kyiv, 1920, 15–20.)

Williams, Raymond. 1973. *The Country and the City*. New York: Oxford University Press.

Wolitz, S. I. 1981. "Di Khalyastre, the Yiddish Modernist Movement in Poland: An Overview," Yiddish 3: 5–19.

———. 1988. "The Jewish National Art Renaissance in Russia." In Apter-Gabriel, *Tradition and Revolution*, 21–42.

———. 1991. "Between Folk and Freedom: The Failure of the Yiddish Modernist Movement in Poland," Yiddish 1: 26–51.

Zhdanova, Larissa A. 1982. *Malevich: Suprematism and Revolution in Russian Art 1910–1930*. London: Thames and Hudson.

Zhyvotko, A. 1943. *Podon (Ukrainska voronizhchyna) v kulturnomu zhytti Ukrainy*. Prague: Vyd-vo Iu. Tyshchenka.

Index

C

G

H

I

J

K

S

Sedliar, Vasyl, 15, 40, 42, 54–55, 63

www.ingramcontent.com/pod-product-compliance
Ingram Content Group UK Ltd.
Pitfield, Milton Keynes, MK11 3LW, UK
UKHW030720200526
471281UK00004B/238

9 781644 696279